"This is an excellent volume on Jewish philosophy that will cover an important array of topics and thinkers. Such a volume will serve a real interest to graduate and undergraduate students as well as general readers with an interest in the history of Jewish thought. The author of the volume is an experienced scholar expert in the field, with her expertise being broad, extending from early medieval philosophy to the early modern period."
—**Steven Nadler,** *Professor, Department Of Philosophy, University Of Wisconsin, Madison, USA*

"Prof. Tamar Rudavsky, a prominent scholar of medieval Jewish philosophy has written an intelligent and engaging introduction to Jewish philosophy organized thematically. This book is a welcome addition to the literature and will be of great benefit to students."
—**Menachem Kellner,** *Wolfson Professor of Jewish Thought Emeritus, University of Haifa, Israel*

"In the grand tradition of Isaac Husik and Julius Guttmann, Tamar Rudavsky has produced a sweeping history and thematic treatment of Jewish philosophy for our time that is both an intellectually rigorous and compelling narrative. Holding that Jewish philosophy emerges from the conflict between philosophical rationalism and Jewish belief, Rudavsky takes her readers through the works both of well-known thinkers such as Maimonides, Spinoza, Buber, and Levinas as well as lesser-appreciated figures such as Ibn Da'ud, Nachman Krochmal, and Vladimir Jankelevich. This book will be a welcome addition for both students and scholars alike."
—**Jeffrey A. Bernstein,** *Professor of Philosophy at College of the Holy Cross, USA*

JEWISH PHILOSOPHY

This book introduces students and interested readers to two thousand years of Jewish philosophy, from its earliest inception to the current era. Fourteen chapters cover major figures in the medieval, modern and contemporary periods, as well as important themes and topics that have been part of Jewish thought for centuries. Questions and topics covered include:

- What is Jewish philosophy?
- At what point does the introduction of secular knowledge dilute, destroy, or strengthen the basic teachings found in Jewish sources?
- Is it possible to harmonize the domains of science and religion?
- How can philosophy be married to a particular religious tradition?

Containing a comprehensive list of authors, as well as suggestions for further reading at the end of each chapter, *Jewish Philosophy: The Basics* offers an excellent starting point for anyone seeking an engaging and accessible introduction to the rich content of Jewish philosophy.

T.M. Rudavsky is Professor of Philosophy (emerita) at The Ohio State University, USA. Recent publications include the *Cambridge History of Jewish Philosophy* (co-edited with S. Nadler, 2009), *Maimonides* (2010), and *Jewish Philosophy in the Middle Ages: Science, Rationalism and Religion* (2018).

THE BASICS

The Basics is a highly successful series of accessible guidebooks which provide an overview of the fundamental principles of a subject area in a jargon-free and undaunting format.

Intended for students approaching a subject for the first time, the books both introduce the essentials of a subject and provide an ideal springboard for further study. With over 50 titles spanning subjects from Artificial Intelligence to Women's Studies, The Basics are an ideal starting point for students seeking to understand a subject area.

Each text comes with recommendations for further study and gradually introduces the complexities and nuances within a subject.

GLOBAL DEVELOPMENT
Daniel Hammett

FOOD ETHICS (SECOND EDITION)
Ronald Sandler

PERCEPTION
Bence Nanay

PHILOSOPHY OF TIME
Graeme Forbes

CAUSATION
Stuart Glennan

PHILOSOPHY OF LANGUAGE
Ethan Nowak

STOIC ETHICS
Christopher Gill and Brittany Polat

POLITICAL PHILOSOPHY
Bas van der Vossen

INTERVIEWING
Mark Holton

PHENOMENOLOGY (SECOND EDITION)
Dan Zahavi

WASTE
Myra J. Hird

JEWISH PHILOSOPHY
T.M. Rudavsky

Other titles in the series can be found at: https://www.routledge.com/The-Basics/book-series/B

JEWISH PHILOSOPHY

THE BASICS

T.M. Rudavsky

NEW YORK AND LONDON

Designed cover image: Getty Images / guter

First published 2026
by Routledge
605 Third Avenue, New York, NY 10158

and by Routledge
4 Park Square, Milton Park, Abingdon, Oxon, OX14 4RN

Routledge is an imprint of the Taylor & Francis Group, an informa business

© 2026 T.M. Rudavsky

The right of T.M. Rudavsky to be identified as author of this work has been asserted in accordance with sections 77 and 78 of the Copyright, Designs and Patents Act 1988.

All rights reserved. No part of this book may be reprinted or reproduced or utilised in any form or by any electronic, mechanical, or other means, now known or hereafter invented, including photocopying and recording, or in any information storage or retrieval system, without permission in writing from the publishers.

Trademark notice: Product or corporate names may be trademarks or registered trademarks, and are used only for identification and explanation without intent to infringe.

ISBN: 978-1-032-82324-9 (hbk)
ISBN: 978-1-032-82325-6 (pbk)
ISBN: 978-1-003-50403-0 (ebk)

DOI: 10.4324/9781003504030

Typeset in Sabon
by codeMantra

CONTENTS

Preface and Acknowledgements ix
List of Authors Mentioned in this Book xi

Introduction 1

Part I
Early Jewish Philosophy: First to Fifteenth Centuries 15

1 The Greek and Rabbinic Heritage 17
2 Searching for Union with God: The Neoplatonic Quest 30
3 Jewish Kalâm and Aristotelianism 43
4 God, Creation and Miracles 60
5 Evil and Divine Omniscience: Why Do the Innocent Suffer? 80
6 Practical Morality: Living a Good Life 96

Part II
Modern Jewish Philosophy: Fifteenth Century to the Present 115

7 Prelude to Modernity 117
8 Is There a Right Way to Read Scripture? 133

9 The Eighteenth-Century Enlightenment	147
10 The Idealist Turn	164
11 Jewish Existentialism	184
12 Philosophy of Dialogue	201
13 Responding to the Holocaust	223
14 Contemporary Issues: Zionism and Gender Equality	244
15 Concluding Postscript	258
Glossary	261
Bibliography	265
Index	281

PREFACE AND ACKNOWLEDGEMENTS

When first approached by Routledge to provide a 75,000-word book on Jewish philosophy, from ancient to contemporary, I was overwhelmed with doubts. How could I possibly cover over 2,000 years of Jewish philosophy and thought in such a short volume? And yet, the proposal was too tantalizing to turn down, and so I have worked diligently to write a work that crystallizes the major figures and themes in an accessible form for students and non-specialists. Jewish philosophy has always, from its inception, engaged with the secular philosophical world, be it the ancient Greek philosophers, the modern philosophers of the sixteenth and seventeenth centuries, the German philosophers Kant, Hegel, Heidegger and others. This delicate attempt to harmonize or reconcile the major tenets of Jewish belief with philosophical teachings is the major theme of this work.

In this work I have provided an account of how Jewish philosophers from the turn of the millennium to the present day have navigated the interplay between faith and reason, between Judaic belief and secular thought. I have chosen to highlight philosophers and themes that to my mind best reflect this harmonization process. Obviously such a short work can provide only a brief introduction to these major figures. Some of the themes pertaining to medieval Jewish philosophy are treated in greater detail in my book *Jewish Philosophy in the Middle Ages: Science, Rationalism and Religion* (Oxford University Press, 2018). Readers who wish to pursue individual philosophers further are advised to consult the online *Encyclopaedia Judaica*, as well as the online *Stanford Encyclopedia of Philosophy*, both of which contain excellent reference and bibliographic materials. In addition, each chapter contains suggestions for further reading.

Let me end with a number of acknowledgements. First to my editor Andy Beck who first proposed this project to me, and helped me think through the parameters of the work. My thanks to the production team who have overseen the laborious technical side of publishing. I would like as well to thank my anonymous readers who made invaluable suggestions that have enhanced the overall manuscript. To my many students over the years, who have helped clarify my thinking on these issues and figures, I offer my gratitude. I am indebted to Nathaniel, who has offered constant support from afar; to Miriam, who assiduously edited and labored over the bibliography; and finally, to Richard, who has faithfully read and edited so many drafts (those drafts kept on coming at him), and who reminded me repeatedly that he was my ideal target audience, this book is dedicated.

AUTHORS MENTIONED IN THIS BOOK

Abner of Burgos (*c.*1270–1340)
Abravanel, Don Isaac (1437–1508)
Abravanel, Judah (*c.*1460–after 1523)
Abraham ibn Daud (*c.*1110–1180)
Abraham ibn Ezra (*c.*1089–1164)
Albalag, Isaac (13th century)
Albo, Joseph (1380–1444)
Arendt, Hannah (1906–1975)
Aristotle (384–322 BC)
Baḥya ibn Paquda (*c.*1150–*c.*1156)
Bayle, Pierre (1647–1706)
Brandeis, Louis (1856–1941)
Buber, Martin (1878–1965)
Cohen, Hermann (1848–1918)
Cranz, August Friedrich (1737–1801)
Crescas, Ḥasdai (*c.*1340–winter 1410)
Delmedigo, Elijah (1458–1493)
Delmedigo, Joseph Solomon (1591–1655)
Derrida, Jacques (1904–1980)
Descartes, René (1596–1650)
Fackenheim, Emil (1916–2003)
Ganz, David (1541–1613)
al-Ghazâlî, Muhammed (1058–1111)
Halevi, Judah (before 1075–1141)
Hegel, Georg Wilhelm Friedrich (1770–1831)

Heidegger, Martin (1885–1973)
Heraclitus (fl. *c.*500 BCE)
Herzl, Theodore (1860–1904)
Hillel of Verona (1220–1295)
Husserl, Edmund (1859–1938)
Isaac Israeli (*c.*855–955 CE)
Jacobi, Friedrich Heinrich (1743–1819)
Jankélévitch, Victor (1905–1985)
Joseph ibn Kaspi (1279–1340)
Judah ha-Cohen (1215)
Kallen, Horace (1882–1974)
Kant, Immanuel (1724–1804)
Kaplan, Mordecai (1881–1983)
Krochmal, Nachman (1785–1840)
Lavater, Johann Caspar (1741–1801)
Leibniz, Wilhelm von (1646–1716)
Lessing, Gotthold Ephraim (1729–1781)
Levi ben Gershom (Gersonides; 1288–1344)
Levinas, Emmanuel (1905–1995)
Lichtenstein, Aharon (1933–2015)
Luria, Isaac "Ha-Ari" (1534–1572)
Maimon, Solomon (1752–1800)
Maimonides, Moses (Moses ben Maimon; 1135–1204)
Mendelssohn, Moses (1729–1786)
Messer Leon, Judah ben Jehiel (*c.*1470–*c.*1526)
Mirandola, Pico della (1463–1494)
Moses ben Shemtob de Leon (d. 1305)
Nahmanides (Moses ben Nahman; 1194–1270)
Narboni (Moses ben Joshua, Ramban; late 13th or early 14th century – before 1362)
Newton, Isaac (1642–1727)
Parmenides (*c.*515 BCE)
Philo of Alexandria (*c.*20 BCE–50 CE)
Plaskow, Judith (1947–present)
Plato (428/7–348 BCE)

Plotinus (204–270 CE)
Pollegar, Isaac (13th century)
Ptolemy (*c.*100–170 CE)
Reines, Yitzhak Yaakov (1839–1915)
Rosenzweig, Franz (1886–1929)
Ross, Tamar (1938–present)
Rubenstein Richard (1924–2021)
Saadiah Gaon (882–942)
Sartre, Jean-Paul (1905–1980)
Schelling, Friedrich Wilhelm Joseph (1775–1854)
Shem Tov ben Joseph Falaquera (1223/8–1295)
Solomon ibn Gabirol (*c.*1021–*c.*1057/8)
Soloveitchik, Joseph (1903–1993)
Spinoza, Baruch (1632–1677)
Teitelbaum, Joel (1887–1979)

INTRODUCTION

WHAT IS JEWISH PHILOSOPHY?

At my first job interview, I was grilled by the dean of the college over how my purported research area even existed: wasn't the very idea of *Jewish* philosophy an oxymoron? Clearly we don't speak of Jewish math or Jewish science; how can philosophy, which is so often framed as an objectively grounded discipline, be married to a particular religious tradition? More specifically, how could I reconcile my philosophical training, which was based on objective criteria and methods, with a Jewish belief system grounded in nothing but faith? My response was apparently sufficiently cogent that I ended up with the job, but the question has haunted me ever since, and most of my publications have wrestled with this issue. Jewish philosophers, as well as Christian philosophers, have struggled throughout the centuries to reconcile their belief statements with their philosophical training. Recent years have seen the emergence of the Society of Christian Philosophy, the Academy for Jewish Philosophy and other groups devoted to reconciling these different ways of thinking.

So what *is* Jewish philosophy? As a preliminary response, let me suggest that Jewish philosophy deals with problems in which there appears to be a conflict between philosophical speculation and acceptance of dogmas of the Judaic faith. By this characterization, Jewish philosophy consists in analytically engaging with and about the Jewish tradition, asking questions about Judaism as well as using Jewish texts and doctrines to engage in general philosophical speculation about classic problems such as freedom of the will, happiness, the nature of time, epistemological problems about prophecy, and so on. The Jewish philosopher is thus constrained to reconcile two distinct bodies of knowledge – the secular, defined by reason, and the religious, defined by faith.

This struggle between Athens and Jerusalem, between rational speculation and Torah-based study, was introduced already by Philo in the first century CE (see Chapter 1) and reappears throughout the history of Jewish thought. And so for generations of Jews the issue has thus been two-fold: first, how to justify taking time from Torah study for any other type of study (including the most mundane level of career-learning); and second, how to reconcile the content of the secular learning with that of religious knowledge.

But to what extent were Jews even aware of the secular world around them? To presume that their authors were completely isolated from their non-Jewish intellectual environment is to misunderstand the underlying tension inherent in these very texts.[1] Especially in the late medieval and early modern period, religious belief was often threatened by the adoption of a scientific cosmology antithetical to religious thought, be it the cosmology of Plato, Aristotle, Ptolemy or Copernicus. And in modern centuries, the works of Kant, Hegel, and contemporary existentialists provided additional challenges. Sometimes, as in the case of Maimonides, we shall see that this wrestling resulted in a mode of discourse which obfuscated the full force of the compromise. At other times, as in the case of Spinoza, the wrestling resulted in expulsion from the

Jewish community altogether. The real issue in Jewish thought can thus be stated succinctly: at what point does the introduction of secular knowledge dilute or destroy the basic teachings found in Jewish sources.

By the ninth century C.E., most Jews were living under Islamic rule. Under the reign of the Abbasid caliph al-Ma'mun (813–833), we find the first phase of a major translation project of Greek philosophical and scientific texts into Arabic, followed by a second phase in the tenth century. The importance of this project to Jewish philosophy cannot be underestimated. Both Jewish and Islamic (and eventually Christian, when these texts were translated into Latin) philosophers were confronted with an existential set of challenges. What we have then is a clash between two opposing world-views – the Jewish world-view, and those of external philosophical systems – reflective of two sources of truth, one rooted in faith and religion, the other reflecting the science and philosophy of the age. The history of Jewish philosophy can be construed as the history of the successive absorptions of secular ideas which were then transformed and analyzed according to specific Jewish points of view.[2]

Is it truly possible, however, to harmonize the domains of science and religion?[3] As we delve in subsequent chapters into the works of major Jewish figures, we shall see many responses to secularism, rational inquiry and science from the perspective of Jewish belief. Each chapter will develop more fully one or more of these attitudes in an attempt to come to terms with the challenges posed to Jewish belief by a scientific/secular view of the world. Nonetheless, it is important to note that many of our Jewish philosophers were also rabbis or rabbinical leaders. The line of demarcation between theologian and philosopher is fuzzy indeed. Consider, for example, Saadiah Gaon who was both a major religious leader and philosophical figure in the ninth century C.E. And of course no philosopher holds a more august position in the rabbinical world than Maimonides, whose *Mishneh Torah* is to this day held to be a canonical work in rabbinic thought. And so the very attempt to distinguish between rabbinical thinkers and philosophers is itself fraught with contention. I will suggest in subsequent chapters that Jewish philosophers are engaged by the same sorts of issues that consumed their non-Jewish philosophical peers, and use the tools and forms of argumentation common to other traditions, sometimes even for the same purposes.

PART I: EARLY JEWISH PHILOSOPHY: FIRST TO FIFTEENTH CENTURIES

Most histories of Jewish philosophy have approached the subject-matter by focusing on individual figures within Jewish thought. Doing so creates a particular narrative, one in which Jewish philosophers build upon one another in a seamless web. This volume proceeds both chronologically and thematically, in a concerted effort to place individual Jewish philosophers in conversation with their secular contemporaries. It contains two parts: Part I presents the early period, ranging from the first to roughly the fifteenth century CE, while Part II introduces the modern period, ranging from the fifteenth century to the present day. Doing so reinforces the dynamic interplay between Judaic belief and reigning philosophical schools.

Chapter 1 explores in greater detail the underpinnings of late antique and early medieval Jewish philosophy. Reinforcing the overall theme of this work that Jewish philosophers were in conversation with their intellectual contemporaries, this chapter lays out the major features of both Greek philosophy and classical rabbinic texts. Philo of Alexandria (*c.*20 BCE–50 CE) is introduced as the first Jewish philosopher to attempt a reconciliation of

Jewish and Greek influences. A Hellenized Jewish thinker, Philo was the first philosopher to attempt a synthesis of religious and rational truth, harmonizing Greek thought with Torah, and seeing himself as the "great reconciler" who would bridge the traditions of Judaism and Greek philosophy.

Turning in Chapter 2 to the enormous influence of late antique Neoplatonism, we explore the contributions of important Jewish Neoplatonists – Isaac Israeli, Solomon ibn Gabirol, Bahya ibn Paquda and Judah Halevi – all of whom incorporated elements of Greek Neoplatonism into their work. Living during the height of the Arabic reign in southern Spain, Solomon ibn Gabirol (*c*.1021–*c*.1057/8) represents the flourishing of Jewish intellectual life in Andalusia under the enlightened reign of the Umayyad caliphate during the eleventh century. Bahya ibn Paquda (*c*.1150–*c*.1156) was an eleventh-century Jewish philosopher and rabbi who lived in Saragossa, Spain; aligned with Neoplatonic mysticism, he may have gravitated toward asceticism. His major work *Sefer Torat Hovot ha-Levvavot* (*Guide to the Duties of the Heart*) is one of the first attempts to present ethical laws and duties espoused by Judaism in a coherent philosophical system. The philosophical interests of Judah Halevi (before 1075–1141) who was born in Tudela, Spain, lay in defending the truth of Judaism and the essential superiority of the Jewish people. His major philosophical work *The Kuzari* [*Kitâb al-Radd wa'l-Dalîl fi'l-Din al-dhalîl*], written originally in Arabic, is presented in the form of a fictional reconstruction of an actual historical event that took place between 786 and 809, during the reign of King Bulan of the Khazars [a Turkik people].

By the twelfth century the works of Aristotle were being translated into Arabic and then into Hebrew. With this translation process, Jewish philosophy entered what can be characterized as the Aristotelian phase. Chapter 3 introduces the major figures writing under the influence of Kalâm, an influential school of Islamic philosophical theology, and Aristotelianism. Saadiah Gaon (882–942) is known as the founder of scientific activity in Judaism, and was one of the first Jewish thinkers to engage critically with Islamic Kalâm. Jewish philosophers writing against the backdrop of Aristotelianism include Abraham ibn Daud, Moses Maimonides, Gersonides, Ḥasdai Crescas and Joseph Albo. Maimonides (Moses ben Maimon; RaMBaM; 1135–1204) is considered by most scholars as the greatest of all Jewish philosophers. As the famous epitaph on Maimonides's gravestone reads, "from Moses [the prophet] to Moses [Maimonides], there was none like unto Moses." In this chapter we will introduce Maimonides' philosophical work *Guide of the Perplexed*, one of the most influential texts in the medieval period, that systematically laid out his views in theology, metaphysics, ethics and hermeneutics.

We will then turn briefly to his immediate successor Gersonides (Levi ben Gerson; 1288–1344) who took up many of Maimonides's claims in his own work *Wars of the Lord* and subjected them to critical scrutiny. Attempting to show that philosophy and Torah, or reason and revelation, are co-extensive, Gersonides believed that reason is fully competent to attain all the important and essential truths in religion. Ḥasdai ben Judah Crescas (c.1340–winter 1410) is the last outstanding Jewish philosopher in the late medieval period, writing before the expulsion of the Jews from Spain in 1492. His major work *Sefer Or Adonai* (*The Book of the Light of the Lord*), finished several months before his death, is a polemic against his two Aristotelian predecessors Maimonides and Gersonides. In this work, Crescas sought to undermine the Aristotelian cosmology and physics that pervaded the works of his predecessors.

Chapters 4–6 are organized thematically around major philosophical themes in the medieval Aristotelian tradition. Chapter 4 is devoted to divine science, broadly construed, and the attempts on the part of Jewish philosophers to delineate the essential nature of God. It ends with two topics, creation and miracles, both of which were examined against the backdrop of Scripture. In these cases, Jews were enormously affected not only by Scripture but by Aristotle's model of an eternally existing world. Aristotle's cosmology thus forced Jewish philosophers to rethink God's relation to the world.

Chapter 5 focuses more broadly on issues in philosophical theology, in particular the issues surrounding divine omniscience, providence, freedom and evil. Concerned with safeguarding the freedom of human action, medieval philosophers worried whether God's foreknowledge of future contingent events entailed the necessary occurrence of these events. How to allow for the possibility of humans to contravene the prior infallible knowledge that God has of their actions carries tremendous implications when we turn to issues of divine providence, human freedom, and the existence of evil.

Many of the themes and issues we have visited in previous chapters reappear in Chapter 6 in the context of how to live the good life. Here too, Jewish philosophers incorporated material from Greek philosophy, from the rabbis, and from their intellectual peers. The formative texts from Aristotle's *Nicomachean Ethics* promoted a view of happiness (or *eudaimonia*) as a human flourishing or psychic well-being. Yet, if happiness (*pace* Aristotle) is predicated on intellectual knowledge, does it follow that not all humans can achieve intellectual perfection? We examine specific moral codes developed by Jewish thinkers, all of whom worked to accommodate biblical and rabbinic views of moral behavior with that of their philosophical peers. The chapter ends with discussion of the prophet who was often introduced as an ideal model for human felicity.

PART II: MODERN JEWISH PHILOSOPHY: FIFTEENTH CENTURY TO THE PRESENT

Part II of the volume turns to what has come to be known as the modern period of Jewish philosophy, ranging from the fifteenth century to the present. Chapters 7 and 8 introduce the early modern period, during which Copernican and Newtonian science replaced the "old order" represented by Aristotelian physics and cosmology. By the early seventeenth century, Jewish thinkers were interacting even more fully with their intellectual peers, and were fully absorbing the scientific advances in astronomy, mechanics, optics, and mathematics. Chapter 7 surveys the rise of modern science and its effects upon Jewish philosophy; it ends with Baruch Spinoza (1632–1677) whose major work *The Ethics* reflects this influence. Chapter 8 focuses on influential themes in Spinoza's *Theological-Political Treatise*. This revolutionary work revisited a number of topics discussed by medieval philosophers, including the rationality of the commandments and hermeneutic understanding of Scripture. In Spinoza's hands these topics took on a radical turn.

Moses Mendelssohn (1729–1786) was one of the key champions of the Jewish *Haskalah* (enlightenment) period that flourished in the eighteenth and early nineteenth centuries, a period that coincided with the secular Enlightenment in western Europe. It was during this time that Jews for the first time were allowed entry from the ghettos into secular society. Mendelssohn benefited from this emancipation period and early on became friends with major philosophers such as Gotthold Lessing, who became one of his closest friends and wrote a play that centered upon Mendelssohn. Mendelssohn's best-known philosophical work *Jerusalem or On Religious Power and Judaism* is one of the first modern Jewish philosophical works written on behalf of a rational conception of Judaism, and in it Mendelssohn provides an extended argument that Judaism is compatible with Enlightenment thought. Chapter 9 explores Mendelssohn's views on Jewish law and ritual in the context of what he viewed as universal religion. We then turn to the eclectic Salomon Maimon (1785–1840), a protegee of both Mendelssohn and Kant, whose critique of Kant and defense of Mendelssohn set the stage for subsequent German and Jewish philosophy.

Moses Mendelssohn introduced the idea that Judaism represented a religion of reason accessible to all. This rationalist strain continued into the nineteenth century against the backdrop of Hegelian and post-Kantian philosophy. In Chapter 10 we discuss two major figures who epitomized the marriage of Hegelianism and Jewish thought. Nachman Krochmal (1785-1840), a major leader of the Jewish emancipation movement (*Haskalah*) in Eastern Europe, was a committed Hegelian and did his best to marry Hegelian idealism with Judaism. Like Krochmal, Hermann Cohen (1848–1918) was influenced by Hegel, but drew most of his inspiration from Kant; inspired by Kant's works, Cohen introduced a neo-Kantian movement in Marburg. This chapter presents both Krochmal and Cohen's attempts to reconcile Hegelian and Kantian idealism with Judaism.

Chapters 11–13 introduce particular challenges faced by contemporary thinkers, many of whom were writing against the backdrop of the Holocaust. Other challenges include the rise of contemporary science, which threatens the integrity of a spiritual-based life, as well as the response to and incorporation of existentialist themes predominating in continental philosophical circles. Existentialism arose in the early twentieth century as an attempt to reposition the primacy of the individual into philosophical thought. Chapter 11 is devoted to the work of Franz Rosenzweig (1886–1929), one of the most original Jewish existentialists of the early twentieth century. His compelling biography included a near-conversion to Christianity followed by a fervent return to Judaism; the composition of his magnum opus *The Star of Redemption* on military postcards sent home from the Balkan front; and his continued engagement with philosophy after succumbing to ALS. Rosenzweig saw his work as an articulation of a new way of thinking about the relationships between God, individuals and the world.

Chapter 12 introduces what I describe as philosophers of dialogue: Martin Buber, Emmanuel Levinas and Joseph Soloveitchik. Both Martin Buber (1878–1965) and Emmanuel Levinas (1905–1995), writing in the mid twentieth century, attempted to delineate the personal relation between the subject and the other. Buber's famous I-Thou and I-It relations are depicted in his work *I and Thou*, which describes the myriad ways to engage with oneself, with others, and with the Eternal Thou. Levinas was very much influenced by Buber's *I and Thou* but he criticized Buber on the grounds that the dialogical relation is not dependent upon the Other's acceptance and recognition of me, but is fundamentally asymmetrical. We will explore both approaches to the "other," as presented by Buber and Levinas. Nowhere are these existentialist themes expressed more explicitly than in the works of Joseph Soloveitchik (1903–1993), an influential rabbi and philosopher who served as a role-model for an entire generation of Jews. In his seminal work "The Lonely Man of Faith," Soloveitchik uses the two accounts of creation in Genesis I and II to introduce the bifurcation between the world of science and that of faith, represented respectively by Adam I and Adam II. Soloveitchik describes modern society as one that is technically minded, self-centered, and self-loving, in opposition to the faith individual who lives by a law "which cannot be tested in the laboratory."[4] We shall examine how Soloveitchik bridges these two worlds.

We then turn in Chapter 13 to responses to the Holocaust. Issues such as forgiveness, culpability, theodicy must be discussed against the background of Nazi atrocities. One of the best known of these philosophers is Emil Fackenheim (1916–2003), a German-born philosopher who struggled with placing the Holocaust in the context of Judaism. In a number of works, he enjoined Jews not to grant Hitler a posthumous victory: his "614th commandment" was to retain belief in God despite the Holocaust, and not reject Judaism. In a similar vein, French philosopher Vladimir Jankélévitch (1905–1985) struggled with how to incorporate the challenges represented by the Holocaust into his moral philosophy. In his work *Le Pardon (Forgiveness)* Jankélévitch described the tension between the human need to forgive, on the one hand, and the recognition that certain inhumane acts are beyond forgiveness. The chapter ends with the works of Hannah Arendt (1906–1975), noted political theorist known in part for her work *Eichmann in Jerusalem: A Report on the Banality of Evil*, written as a response to the trial of Adolf Eichmann in Jerusalem. In this controversial work Arendt suggested that even the most normal individuals can commit the most egregious crimes; theoretically the Holocaust could have happened anywhere (the truth of which is all too apparent today).

Chapter 14 highlights recent work in two areas: Zionism and the role of women in Judaism. With the recent war in Gaza, the very concept of Zionism has been contested. The longing to return to Zion dates back to the destruction of the first Temple (586 BCE) and has been expressed in numerous prayers and psalms. However, by the late nineteenth century, the term Zionism began to be used to refer to the particular movement whose goal was creation of a Jewish state in what Zionists saw as the historical land of Israel. Chapter 14 traces both Zionist and anti-Zionist factions within Jewish thought. The second topic in this chapter is the status of women in Judaism. Jewish feminist thought emerged in the early 1970s as an attempt to protest the subordination of women within *halakhah*. These original feminists agreed on the parameters of women's subordination, as reflected in their exclusion from the minyan, exemption from study, separation of women from men in traditional synagogue services, and women's inability to function as witnesses in a court of law or to initiate divorce proceedings. I address in this chapter a number of issues raised by these concerns, focusing on the feminist critique of central theological tenets within Judaism.

My hope is that this short volume will serve as an introduction to this rich, multi-faceted two-thousand-year-old tradition of Jewish philosophy, and will encourage you to pursue these philosophers in greater detail in their own right.

NOTES

1 See Ravitsky 1996a for a penetrating discussion of the status of Jewish philosophers vis-à-vis their intellectual environment.
2 Guttmann 1964, 3.
3 By suggesting that Jewish philosophical texts represent the tensions inherent between religion and science, I am not simply returning to the adversarial model of the science-religion wars as they have been portrayed by late-nineteenth-century historians of science. For example, in his enormously influential work *History of the Conflict between Religion and Science*, John William Draper argued that the Church became a stumbling block in the intellectual advancement of Europe for more than a thousand years. See Draper 1874.
4 Soloveitchik 1965, 6.

FURTHER READING

Draper, J.W. (1874). *History of the Conflict between Religion and Science.* New York: D. Appleton and Company.

Efron, N. (2007). *Judaism and Science: A Historical Introduction.* Westport, CT: Greenwood Press.

Frank, D. and Leaman, O. (ed.) (1997). *Routledge History of World Philosophies Vol II: History of Jewish Philosophy.* London: Routledge.

Freudenthal, G. (ed.) (2011). *Science in Medieval Jewish Cultures* Cambridge: Cambridge University Press.

Funkenstein, A. (1986). *Theology and the Scientific Imagination from the Middle Ages to the Seventeenth Century.* Princeton, NJ: Princeton University Press.

Guttmann, J. (1964). *Philosophies of Judaism*, trans. D. Silverman. New York: Holt, Rinehart and Winston.

Jospe, R. (2009). *Jewish Philosophy in the Middle Ages.* Boston, MA: Academic Studies Press.

Kajon, I. (2006). *Contemporary Jewish Philosophy: An Introduction.* New York: Routledge.

Katz, C.E. (2014). *An Introduction to Modern Jewish Philosophy.* London: I.B. Taurus.

Nadler, S., and Rudavsky, T.M. (ed.) (2009). *The Cambridge History of Jewish Philosophy: From Antiquity through the Seventeenth Century.* Cambridge: Cambridge University Press.

Rudavsky, T.M. (2018). *Jewish Philosophy in the Middle Ages: Science, Rationalism, and Religion.* Oxford: Oxford University Press.

PART I
EARLY JEWISH PHILOSOPHY
First to Fifteenth Centuries

GREEK AND RABBINIC HERITAGE

INTRODUCTION

My purpose in this chapter is to present some of the formative biblical, rabbinic and ancient Greek philosophy precursors to the medieval Jewish tradition. We will then turn to influential developments within late antique philosophy and Islamic philosophy, keeping in mind (as noted in the introduction to this volume) that Jewish philosophy throughout the centuries has always reflected a conversation with many other schools of thought. I have chosen to focus upon those writers that most clearly exemplify our main theme, namely the tension between reason and faith, between rationalism and Jewish belief.[1]

THE WORLD OF GREEK PHILOSOPHY

Let us start with several motifs in classical Greek thought that reappear in subsequent medieval Jewish discussions. The earliest sustained philosophical discussions that we might associate with "natural philosophy" or the beginnings of ancient Greek science occur in the fragments of the Presocratic philosophers. Both Heraclitus (fl. *c*.500 BCE) and Parmenides (*c*.515 BCE) tried to account for change and motion in the natural world. All we have of Heraclitus are several fragments in which he argued that flux and becoming are alone real, and that permanence and constancy are merely apparent. Every physical object is subject to temporal change, hence Heraclitus's emphasis upon the eternal flux of reality, and his insistence that all is in flux.[2] Heraclitus became known as the "river philosopher," arguing that we can never step into the same river twice. Parmenides, however, disagreed with Heraclitus's emphasis upon flux. He argued in an extended prose-poem (the first substantial text we have from this early period) that only the permanent and enduring are real, and that everything that is subject to flux, motion and change is unreal. In contradistinction to Heraclitus who emphasized the ontological priority of change, Parmenides argued that what we see as a changing reality is an illusion: reality is unchanging and static. By introducing the importance of change in the natural order, Parmenides and Heraclitus set the stage for thinking about natural science among the two "greats" of ancient Greek thought, Plato and Aristotle.

Against the backdrop of his Presocratic predecessors, Plato tried to resolve the paradoxes of change and permanence. Plato's Academy was founded in 387/8 BCE in Athens and lasted close to nine centuries. Of the many doctrines found in Platonism, the most important for our study is Plato's theory of Forms; the implications of this theory reverberate throughout the history of Jewish philosophy. Forms, according to Plato, are what is really real, as opposed to the "appearances" or phenomena of empirical reality. The material world, he argued, is but a reflection, or imitation of what is "really real." This emphasis upon a reality that transcends the empirical world of change and motion led to a version of idealism according to which abstract ideas or forms are more real than physical reality. Forms can never be known empirically, only conceptually. Thus, for example, an abstract concept of a triangle turns out to contain "more reality" or be "more perfect" than any particular, empirically sensed triangle.

The implications of idealism extend to the human being as well. The physical human body is an imperfect, material, corporeal carrier for the incorporeal soul; the soul represents what is "really real" and a perfect representation of the individual. When the physical human body dies, the immaterial, incorporeal soul continues to exist, participating in the quest for truth and knowledge. So for Plato the abstract, conceptual world of forms or ideas was more real than the physical world around us and one of the purposes of philosophy is to lead us to this realization. Jewish philosophers throughout the centuries were very much influenced by the idealist, anti-materialist tenor of Plato's philosophy.

The second most influential figure in the medieval world was Aristotle, Plato's student and most famous critic. Born in Stagira, Chalcidice (Macedonia) in 384 BCE, Aristotle studied in Plato's Academy. He founded the Lykeion (Lyceum) as his own school in Athens in 335BCE, teaching a new generation of students. Most notably for our purposes, Aristotle rejected Plato's theory of forms, replacing it with a metaphysical system rooted in empirical sense perception. According to Aristotle, we can only discover the essences of entities by investigating their causes; these causes are rooted in empirical reality. Unlike his teacher Plato, who claimed that the senses are deceptive and knowledge based on empirical reality is ephemeral, Aristotle established a scientific method of demonstration that started with a grounding in empirical sense perception. This method was elaborated in an extensive number of works that had enormous influence upon medieval Jewish philosophers. We will examine Aristotle's writings in greater detail in Chapter 3, when we introduce the major Jewish philosophers working in the Aristotelian tradition.

We turn now to Ptolemy (c.100–170 CE), a Greco-Egyptian best known for his work in mathematics, astronomy, astrology and geography. Ptolemy wrote two influential works, the *Almagest* a work devoted to astronomy, and *Tetrabiblos,* devoted to astrology. His geocentric cosmology was presented in the *Almagest*, and his astrological treatise the *Tetrabiblos*, was almost universally accepted until the Copernican Revolution. On Ptolemy's model of the celestial spheres, each concentric planetary orb contained at least three partial eccentric and epicyclical spheres. This system of eccentric and epicyclical spheres contravened the concentric spheres of Aristotle, a fact that was not lost upon Ptolemy or his followers. Most medieval astronomers found that Ptolemy's system did a better job of "saving the appearances" of astronomical data. The implications of Ptolemy's astronomy become relevant when we turn to Gersonides in Chapter 3.

The last important Greek philosophical school is Neoplatonism. Neoplatonism was very much influenced by the writings of Plato, Aristotle, Plotinus and Proclus. Founded by the early Greek philosopher Plotinus (204–270 CE), Neoplatonism became the dominant philosophical school from the third to the sixth centuries. Plotinus wrote a work entitled the *Enneads*, in which he developed a theory of emanation ranging from the highest existent, the One, down to the very lowest existent (prime matter) on the great scale of being. Neoplatonists thus embraced a monistic ontology that emphasized a theory of causal emanation.

Not surprisingly, Plotinus's system found a receptive audience in the medieval period: that these traits are all to some extent reflected in Jewish Neoplatonist writings will become evident in subsequent chapters. Plotinus's major work the *Enneads* was transmitted to Jewish thinkers through an Arabic paraphrase called the *Theology of*

Aristotle. For serious Jewish thinkers, the speculations of certain Neoplatonist philosophies provided epistemological and metaphysical notions that were quite compatible with their own attempts to characterize the nature of God and his nature and relation to humans. Scholars have noted, however, that one of the challenges faced by Jewish philosophers attracted to a Neoplatonist ontology was to attempt to bridge this "impersonal, emanationist scheme of Neoplatonist philosophy with the biblical doctrine of creation by a personal God who knows and relates to his creatures in love."[3] Although not all Jewish thinkers were attracted to Neoplatonism, it was extremely influential on the formation of Jewish thought during the late Hellenistic, Roman and medieval periods. We will turn in Chapter 3 to the most influential and important Jewish Neoplatonists.

THE WORLD OF THE RABBIS

We now turn to a succinct overview of canonical works in Jewish thought. These works include not only Scripture itself, but the entire rabbinic tradition contained in the Talmud. The biblical books that were most influential upon medieval Jewish philosophy included the book of Genesis, with its account of creation, the book of Deuteronomy, which recounts the giving of the Law on Mount Sinai, and the book of Job, which introduces the issue of human suffering. Other biblical books contain passing discussions of occasional philosophical topics; for example, the books of Proverbs, Song of Songs and Ecclesiastes, gave rise to a robust philosophical commentary literature. But even the book of Job (to which we return in Chapter 4) does not provide a complete theodicy.

The situation is somewhat different when we consider what is known as the "wisdom literature;" these works represent the initial influence of Greek philosophy upon biblical works. Works such as the book of Ecclesiastes, the *Wisdom of ben Sira* and the *Wisdom of Solomon* all reflect more marked interest in philosophical themes. The *Wisdom of Solomon*, for example, was written in Greek by a Hellenized Jew of Alexandria and emphasized philosophical themes such as immortality of the soul, as well as the search for Wisdom.

The book of Ecclesiastes provides one of the earliest examples of an author grappling with philosophical themes. Ecclesiastes is a work devoted, among other things, to expressing the challenges faced by an ever-changing reality. Chapter 3 of Ecclesiastes raises a number of themes picked up by subsequent Jewish philosophers. Most obvious is the prevalence of God's predetermination of all human events: that "everything has its appointed time and there is a season for every event under the sky"[4] points to the futility of human striving in light of God's predetermining of all events in their appointed time. This predetermination is reinforced in Eccl. 3.11: "Everything He has made proper in its due time." Death too is a constant motif, underscoring the futility of human endeavors. "Again, I saw that beneath the sun the race is not to the swift, nor the battle to the brave, nor is bread won by the wise, nor wealth by the clever, nor favor by the learned, for time (*'et*) and accident overtake them all,"[5] and human beings are "trapped in a time of misfortune, when it befalls upon them suddenly."[6] Time, then, comes to represent not only the predetermined order into which human beings are thrust, but the cruel means by which they are yanked out of this order into nonexistence, notwithstanding all efforts to the contrary. And yet our anonymous author suggests that the predetermination of temporal events brings with it the comfort of cyclicity. In recognizing that "there is a time to be born, a time to die, a time to plant and a time to uproot,"[7] our author underscores the comforting reality that events do not happen randomly, out of sequence. Planting and uprooting, living and dying, mourning and dancing – these all occur and recur with constant regularity, reinforcing the motif of time as recurrence.

Another work written roughly during this early period, the *Sefer Yetzirah* (*Book of Creation*) is the earliest extant book in Jewish mystical esotericism. When it was written is unclear, nor is its author known. The noted scholar of Jewish mysticism Gershom Scholem suggests that the main part of the work was written between the third and sixth centuries in Palestine by a devout Jew with leanings toward mysticism, whose aim was speculative and magical rather than ecstatic…who endeavored to "Judaize" non-Jewish speculations which suited his spirit."[8] The work exists in both a short and longer version and gave rise to an enormous commentary tradition. This mystical tradition culminated in the 1270s with the arrival of *The Zohar* (*The Book of Splendor*). What we now associate with Jewish mysticism or Kabbalah soon became associated with the *Zohar*.

The *Zohar* is devoted to a description of the act of God's creation of the world through different combinations of what the author called the 32 wondrous ways of wisdom. These ways include the ten numbers (or *sefirot*) and the twenty-two letters of the Hebrew alphabet. Chapter 1 deals with the ten *sefirot* and the subsequent five chapters with the function and operations of the twenty-two letters of the alphabet. These 32 paths, introduced in the first chapter as *sefirot* of nothingness (ten *sefirot beli mah*) represent the foundations of all creation. The author described in great detail the mystical character of the *sefirot*, and their causal efficacy in human life. We will not in this work pursue the kabbalistic works formally, since that would take us far afield from our primary focus. However, we shall have several occasions to highlight kabbalistic themes that permeated subsequent philosophical discussions.

Turning now to the world of the rabbis between the first century BCE and sixth century CE, we must again consider whether the rabbis were technically philosophers. The major works of this period consist of extensive commentaries upon Scripture; they include the Mishnah, the Midrash, as well as both the Palestinian and Babylonian Talmuds. The Mishnah records rabbinical conversations and texts from the second century BCE through the first two centuries CE. These conversations are organized into separate "orders" and represent a variety of legal positions. The Midrash is a collection of books that reflect rabbinic interpretations of the Bible. Both the Palestinian and Babylonian Talmuds were edited in the sixth century CE as commentaries on the Mishnah. These super-commentaries include elaborate conversations on a wide variety of texts, biblical words and chapters.[9] In all these works, we see little if any evidence that the rabbis engaged with Greek philosophy, nor can we find an over-arching philosophical unity to the many books of the Talmud. Even if we agree that philosophical questions and concerns occasionally appear in rabbinic texts, nonetheless, the rabbis do not develop a coherent philosophical theory or system as we find in the Greek philosophical tradition.

THE GREEK–JUDAIC SYNTHESIS: PHILO OF ALEXANDRIA (PHILO JUDAEUS)

So far, we have introduced two strands of influences, the one based on Judaic texts, both biblical and Talmudic, and the second grounded in ancient Greek philosophy. These two strands reached fruition in the Hellenistic world by the turn of the millennium, and their intersection gave rise to attempts among Jews to provide a philosophical underpinning to their beliefs. Philo of Alexandria (*c.*20 BCE–50 CE) is renowned as one of the first Jewish thinkers to attempt a reconciliation of Jewish and Greek influences. Born in Alexandria, Egypt, little is known of Philo's travels and life. We do know that Philo was selected by the Alexandrian Jewish community as the primary representative of the embassy sent in 39/40 CE to meet with the Roman emperor, Gaius Caligula. During this time, there was much civil tension between the Alexandrian Jews and the Hellenized Alexandrian community; at least one purpose of the embassy was to confront the emperor about these problems. Philo is reported to have led his community in refusing to recognize the emperor as a god, erect statues in his honor, or build religious venues such as temples or alters to him.

We know a great deal more about Philo's philosophical life. The noted scholar H.A. Wolfson has argued that Philo is the most important western philosopher after Plato and Aristotle. A Hellenized Jewish thinker, Philo was the first philosopher to attempt a synthesis of Greek thought with Torah, and saw himself as the "great reconciler" who could bridge the traditions of Judaism and Greek philosophy. In this attempt, Philo pioneered what Wolfson has called the "double-belief" theory, according to which both revelation and reason yielded truth. Nonetheless, Philo argued that although they are both sources of truth, philosophy is but the "handmaiden" of Judaism. What this means is that philosophy is ultimately subservient to revelation. Philo wrote for two distinct audiences. In treatises addressed to pagans (Greeks; non-Jews), he introduced readers to what he considered to be universal Judaic truths, whereas in treatises directed to Jews he argued that the Greek truths were akin to those found in Judaic sources. In effect, Philo was working both sides of the ideological and theological divide.

Philo's presentation of creation provides us with a perfect example of this attempt to address both audiences. Philo covered a wide variety of issues in his analysis of creation, drawing upon the works of Scripture, Plato and Aristotle, among others. This discussion of creation occurs in several works, but most notably in his treatise *On the Creation of the Cosmos According to Moses*. In this work he tried to show that both Genesis and Plato's cosmogony shared similar philosophical features. Philo depicted Moses as an author who not only had reached "the very summit of philosophy" but had also been instructed "in the many and most essential doctrines of nature by means of oracles."[10] Such a description of Moses would undoubtedly have appealed to his Hellenistic readers. Turning to the issue of why and when God created the cosmos, Philo rejected the view that the cosmos is "ungenerated and eternal" (a thesis attributed to Aristotle) on the grounds that it would not only have imputed idleness to God, but further that it would have eliminated the doctrine of Providence. In other words, presenting the world as uncreated leaves God with nothing to do. These arguments would undoubtedly have been welcomed by his Jewish readers. Philo argued that the cosmos is, according to Moses, generated, in contradistinction to God itself who is unchanging and ungenerated. According to Philo's reading of Genesis, Moses specified that God fashioned the cosmos in six days in order to provide order. But God was not needful of a length of time, since God "surely did everything at the same time."[11] Philo thus adhered to an instantaneous creation of the entire universe, rather than over the six days specified in Genesis. Time itself was created at this instantaneous instant. But what does Philo mean when he claims that time itself began with the ordered cosmos?

Attempting to accord his view with that of Scripture, Philo maintained that Moses did not take the term "beginning" in a temporal sense but rather in a numerical sense. Commenting on Genesis 1, Philo interpreted the verse

"In the beginning God created ..." to refer to a beginning according to number, rather than a temporal beginning. Time cannot be separated from the cosmos itself; it should be understood "numerically," in the sense of orderliness, since there is a close relation between number and order.[12] That time did not exist before the creation of the world is evidenced in a number of passages. Philo thus followed Aristotle's conception of time as connected with motion. Philo suggested that the purpose of the heavenly bodies was to provide us with both temporal measure and quantitative measure: to give the "right times for the annual seasons; and ... for days and months and years, which indeed have come into existence as the measure of time and also have generated the nature of number."[13] In this latter case, Philo claimed that time makes manifest number: "from a single day the number one is derived, from two days two ... and from infinite time the number that is infinite."[14]

Finally, mention must be made of the treatise *Aeternitate Mundi* (*Eternity of the Universe*), in which Philo adduced Greek philosophical considerations to prove the eternity of the cosmos based on the eternity of time. If time is uncreated, he argued, so too must the world be uncreated. Since time is what "measures the movement of the universe ... the world is coeval with time." But time itself has no beginning or end; the very words "was" and "ever" indicate time, and so it is absurd to suggest that there was a time in which time did not exist. Philo concluded the argument by stating that "it is necessary that both [time and the cosmos] should have subsisted from everlasting without having any beginning in which they came into being."[15] Once again, this treatise would have been accepted readily by a Hellenized audience that was familiar with Aristotle's arguments in favor of the eternity of the universe. We return to these arguments, and the problem of creation, in Chapter 5.

CONCLUSION

In this chapter we have summarized the formative texts and philosophical schools that played an enormous influence upon later Jewish philosophers. Both the Greek philosophers and the canonical Judaic texts provided our thinkers with issues and materials pertaining to Jewish doctrine. And yet these texts represented two different ways of thinking about these issues, one based in rational speculation, and the other upon revelation and faith. Philo was one of the first philosophers to attempt a synthesis of "Athens and Jerusalem," in other words reason and faith. His works were later embraced by prominent Christian scholars, some of whom insisted that Philo was, in fact, Christian. In addition to his interpretation of the Bible, Philo extracted from it a theory of number, cosmology, anthropology, and ethics. In addition to his numerology and cosmology, Philo determined an anthropology and from it, an ethics. Despite his attempts to reconcile Greek philosophy with Judaic texts and doctrines, Philo had little impact upon subsequent Jewish philosophers. And yet, as we shall see in subsequent chapters, his efforts to reconcile Greek philosophy with Judaic texts were later reinforced, and occasionally reinvented.

NOTES

1. For a more comprehensive history of medieval Jewish philosophy, see Guttmann 1964; Sirat 1990; Nadler and Rudavsky 2009; Rudavsky 2018. Studies of individual authors will be mentioned in subsequent pages.
2. Heraclitus, Fragment 10.77(30) in McKirahan 2010, 124.
3. Jospe 2009, 79.
4. Ecclesiastes 3.1.
5. Ecclesiastes 9:11
6. Ecclesiastes 9:12.
7. Ecclesiastes 3:2.

8 For an introduction to the mystical literature, see Scholem 1995.
9 For extensive discussion of the history of the Talmud and the entire commentary tradition, see Neusner 1991; Steinsaltz 1976.
10 Philo 2001, 49.
11 Philo 2001, 49.
12 Philo 2001, 156.
13 Philo 2001, 60.
14 Philo 2001, 61.
15 Philo 1960, 52–55:221.

FURTHER READING

Draper, J.W. (1874). *History of the Conflict between Religion and Science*. New York: D. Appleton and Company.

Funkenstein, A. (1986). *Theology and the Scientific Imagination from the Middle Ages to the Seventeenth Century*. Princeton, NJ: Princeton University Press.

Nadler, S. and Rudavsky, T.M. (ed.) (2009). *The Cambridge History of Jewish Philosophy: From Antiquity through the Seventeenth Century*. Cambridge: Cambridge University Press.

Neusner, J. (1991) [1972]. *There We Sat Down: Talmudic Judaism in the Making*. Nashville, TN: Abingdon Press.

Ravitzky, A. (1996a). *History and Faith: Studies in Jewish Philosophy*. Amsterdam: J.C. Gieben.

Rudavsky, T.M. (2018). *Jewish Philosophy in the Middle Ages: Science, Rationalism, and Religion*. Oxford: Oxford University Press.

SEARCHING FOR UNION WITH GOD
The Neoplatonic Quest

INTRODUCTION: NEOPLATONISM DESCRIBED

As noted in Chapter 1, Neoplatonism was very much influenced by the writings of Plato, Aristotle, Plotinus and Proclus, and it provided the philosophical context for the thought of many cultivated Jews of the eleventh and twelfth centuries. Founded by the early Greek philosopher Plotinus (204–270 CE), Neoplatonism became the dominant philosophical school from the third to the sixth centuries. Providing a unique cosmological and ontological system, Neoplatonism incorporated several important doctrines. First, the Neoplatonists posited as the prime reality an existent (the One/Good) that transcends the world of becoming. Further, they argued that all existents other than the One/Good are ultimately identical with this prime existent reality. And finally, Neoplatonists established two lines of causality – the downward emanation of effects from the One down to the world of becoming, and an upward set of causal relations returning back to the One. This "return" of imperfect beings to the One results in a union and full identification with the One.

In short, Neoplatonists embraced a monistic ontology that incorporated a theory of causal emanation. Positing the existence of the One as the basic reality that transcends all existing things, Neoplatonists claimed that the physical world as we know and experience it emanated from the One in a manner similar to the emanation of the rays of the sun. The One in Plotinus's ontology is "beyond being": it lacks nothing, is impersonal, and yet is the source of everything. It is important to note that the process of emanation does not derive from will, but rather reflects a necessary impersonal outpouring from the One. Just as the sun does not "will" to release its rays down to earth, so too the One does not choose or will to emanate a causal chain. At the top of the Neoplatonic cosmology is "the One," from which everything else emanates in successive stages: universal intellect, universal soul, nature and the material world. Plotinus's radical monism thus posited three stages or hypostases from which the lower stages emanated; the universal intellect emanated directly from the One, while the universal soul functioned as the bridge between the intellect and the natural order, both superlunar (the planets) and sublunar (the natural order). The human soul comes into existence from the universal soul.

Against the backdrop of this hierarchical chain of being, Neoplatonists introduced the important motif of "union" or "return," namely that human souls could achieve perfection or salvation with the One through an upward journey back "home" as it were. Plotinus and the majority of Neoplatonists agreed with Plato that the human soul is enslaved, or trapped, within the human body. The more the soul purifies itself and separates itself from bodily desires, the more easily can it ultimately reunite with the One. Plotinus even envisioned the quasi-mystical possibility of a soul's union with the One while still alive (Plotinus supposedly achieved such a union while still alive). The ultimate purpose of human existence lies in freeing one's soul from the constraints of a physical, material, degrading existence, and ultimately uniting with either the universal intellect, or even with the One.

Not surprisingly, Neoplatonism found a receptive audience in the medieval period: clearly the One was identifiable with the Abrahamic God, and the narrative of the soul's return to the Deity was compelling indeed. During the Islamic period Neoplatonism was complemented by elements stemming from both Islamic religious traditions and Aristotelian ideas. Serious Jewish thinkers recognized as well that Neoplatonic epistemological and metaphysical notions were quite compatible with their own attempts to characterize the nature of God and God's relation to humans. The very idea that the One was beyond Being, and represented the goal of human perfection, accorded with theistic conceptions of the Deity. Although not all Jewish thinkers adopted a rigorous version of Neoplatonism, it was extremely influential on the formation of Jewish thought during the late Hellenistic, Roman and medieval periods.

The transmission of late Greek thought through the writings of Islamic philosophers and ultimately to Jewish philosophers is an interesting and complex story in itself. The writings of Plotinus were transmitted in a variety of ways, most notably through paraphrases, and through doxographies, which were collections of sayings of Plotinus that were circulated among religious communities.

The works and thought of Aristotle underwent a transmission process as well. Greek philosophy declined after the closure of the Academy in Athens in 529 CE. But during this period, Syrian Christians began translating Greek works into Syriac, and then into Arabic. These Arabic translations were supported even further by the Abbasid Caliph al-Ma'mun in Baghdad, who established "The House of Wisdom" (*Beit al-Ḥikmah*) in 830 CE as a center for scientific learning and research. Al-Ma'mun's support thus made possible the rapid spread of philosophy in the Islamic, and ultimately the Jewish, world.

By the twelfth century most of the Aristotelian corpus had been translated into Arabic. By the thirteenth century, when Hebrew translations of these works became available, many of the translations actually incorporated the influence, if not the actual theories, of noted Islamic philosophers such as Al-Farabi, ibn-Sina (Avicenna), and ibn Rushd (Averroes). And so, by the thirteenth century, Jewish philosophers were reading the works of Aristotle, Plotinus and others in Arabic and Hebrew translations that reflected the underlying philosophy of the translators. We turn now to several Jewish philosophers who were very much influenced by Greek Neoplatonism –Isaac Israeli, Solomon ibn Gabirol, Judah Halevi and Baḥya ibn Paquda.

JEWISH NEOPLATONIC ROOTS: ISAAC ISRAELI AND SOLOMON IBN GABIROL

Isaac Israeli (*c*.855–955 CE) was born in Egypt and is known as the father of Jewish Neoplatonism. He was the first writer after Philo to attempt an integration of Greek thought with Jewish belief. Moving to Tunisia to study medicine, he was appointed court physician and became known as one of the great physicians of the Middle Ages. His works were widely circulated and translated into Arabic, Latin and Hebrew. Of his surviving works, the *Book of Definitions* and the *Book of Substances* are the main sources of Israeli's Neoplatonic ideas. His cosmology reflected a Neoplatonic universe in which First Matter and First Form arise from God and give rise to Intellect; from Intellect emanate the world of souls, celestial spheres, and finally the sublunar world with the four elements and their compounds. Israeli's cosmology thus combined in interesting ways a doctrine of creation *ex nihilo* alongside of an emanationist scheme. We will see this combination repeated in later Neoplatonist works as well, as philosophers struggled to combine a biblical view of creation with an emanationist model.

Living during the height of the Arabic reign in southern Spain, Solomon ibn Gabirol (c.1021–c.1057/8) was a product of the rich Judeo-Arabic interaction that dominated Spanish intellectual life during the eleventh century. Much of his work was written in Arabic, and many of his ideas and poetic styles reflect Arab intellectual and stylistic components. Of ibn Gabirol's life we know very little. He was likely born in Malaga, Spain, in 1021/2 and spent the majority of his life in Saragossa. From his poetry we can infer that he was orphaned at a young age and relied upon the patronage of others for his support. At the age of sixteen, Gabirol came under the protection of a Jewish dignitary at the court of the king of Saragossa. Gabirol was known for his arrogant, sometimes virulent temper, and upon the death of his patron, he was soon forced out of Saragossa to Granada, and finally to Valencia. It is not clear exactly when ibn Gabirol died: it is likely, however, that he died in 1057/8 in Valencia at the age of 35–38.

Although ibn Gabirol himself boasted of having written over twenty books, only such two works are extant: *Mekor Hayyim (Fountain of Life)* and *Tikkun Middot ha-Nefesh (On the Improvement of the Moral Qualities)*. Gabirol's major contribution to ethical literature is his work *Tikkun Middot ha-Nefesh*. This work was written in 1045 in Saragossa, and is available in the original Arabic, as well as in a Hebrew translation by Judah ibn Tibbon dated 1167. In this work, ibn Gabirol delineated a complete parallel between the microcosm as represented by the human being and the macrocosm that is the universe.

The contrast between the microcosm and the macrocosm found its fullest expression in ibn Gabirol's most comprehensive philosophical work *Mekor Hayyim (Fountain of Life)*. This text has had an interesting and checkered history. The original work was written in

Arabic, and survived in a Latin translation of the twelfth century. Hebrew extracts were compiled in the thirteenth century by the philosopher Shem Tov ben Josef ibn Falaquera, and then subsequently translated into Latin under the author's name of "Avicebrol" or "Avicebron." Although medieval Hebrew authors were familiar with Gabirol's philosophy, Latin Scholastics reading the Latin version *Fons Vitae*, as it had become known by the thirteenth century, did not connect the work to its Spanish Jewish author. In 1857, a French scholar named S. Munk edited and translated the Hebrew extracts once again. It was while comparing various editions that Munk noted that the appellations "Avicebron," "Avencebrol" and "Avicebrol" all referred to the great Jewish poet Solomon ibn Gabirol. Munk thus reintroduced ibn Gabirol to a nineteenth-century audience.[1]

Many scholars have mentioned the lack of ostensibly Jewish content in *Mekor Ḥayyim* : the work contains virtually no references to other Jewish texts, ideas or sources. As noted above, Gabirol's primary influences appeared to reside in several Neoplatonist texts that represented a variation upon standard Plotinian cosmology. The form of *Mekor Ḥayyim*, a dialogue between a teacher and his disciple, reflected a style popular in Arabic philosophical literature of the period. The work comprises five books of unequal length, of which the third is the most comprehensive (over 300 pages in the Latin edition). A succinct summary of the work is given by ibn Gabirol himself in his introduction:

> In as much as we propose to study universal matter and universal form, we must explain that whatsoever is composed of matter and form comprises two elements: composed corporeal substance and simple spiritual substance. The former further subdivides into two: corporeal matter that underlies the form of qualities; and

spiritual matter which underlies corporeal form. ... And so in the first treatise we shall treat universal matter & universal form; in the second we shall treat spiritual matter. This will necessitate subsequent treatises as well. In the third we shall treat the reality of simple substances; in the fourth, the search for knowledge of matter and form of simple substances; and in the fifth universal matter and form in and of themselves.[2]

This passage introduces one of ibn Gabirol's most creative and influential contributions, namely his hylomorphic conception of matter. Hylomorphism is the view that matter and form are mutually interdependent: matter cannot exist without form, nor can form exist without matter. In the case of human beings, that means that soul cannot exist (or continue to exist) without the body, nor can the body exist without soul. Gabirol's hylomorphism was rooted in the belief that all substances in the world, both spiritual and corporeal, are composed of matter and form. Unlike Aristotle who envisioned the existence of spiritual substance totally devoid of matter, ibn Gabirol argued that spiritual substance cannot be fully incorporeal: he postulated the existence of spiritual matter, which underlies incorporeal substances. Types of matter are ordered in a hierarchy that corresponds to a criterion of simplicity: general spiritual matter, general corporeal matter, general celestial matter, general natural matter, and particular natural matter. Each level of matter is more "coarse" and further away from the source (God) than its predecessor. What follows from this ontology is that even intellects, souls, and angels are composed of matter and form.[3]

In addition to his major work *Mekor Ḥayyim*, ibn Gabirol wrote an elaborate religious poem *Keter Malkhut* (*Throne of Glory*) which replicates in many verses the ontology highlighted in *Mekor Ḥayyim*. In canto 24 of *Keter Malkhut*, ibn Gabirol describes the union of the intellectual soul with what he terms the divine Glory, thus intimating that the incorporeal sphere of the Intellect is the realm of the God's sphere. Ibn Gabirol then turns in canto 26 to the Divine Throne (*Kisse ha-Kavod*), which lies at the outermost limits of the supernal world. Canto 29 tells us that the soul is derived from the radiance of the divine *kavod*. In *Meqor Ḥayyim,* ibn Gabirol likewise described the Divine Throne as the realm of "the Mystery and the Foundation" (*ha-sod ve-ha-yesod*).

As in standard Neoplatonic texts, the ultimate purpose of human existence is the return of the soul to its source. Gabirol modified the standard Neoplatonic picture by claiming that when the soul attaches itself to the Divine Will, it returns to the world of Universal Intellect and thus reaches the Source of Life. "Your intellect should distinguish most clearly matter from form, form from will, and will from movement. For if you do this, your soul will be purified, and your intellect will be enlightened and will penetrate to the world of intellect."[4] In order to achieve this level of perfection, humans must distance themselves from sensible things and turn themselves toward God. Only by turning from material existence toward will is spiritual perfection achieved.

But can humans acquire knowledge of the Divine Throne? *Keter Malkhut* suggests that the human intellect can in theory penetrate to the Throne. This reading is reinforced in *Meqor Ḥayyim* 5.35, where ibn Gabirol describes form and matter as "two closed gates," which the intellect finds difficult to enter. ibn Gabirol does allow for the exceptional individual to attain knowledge of both Universal Matter and Form through philosophy. But God, or First Essence cannot be known: the Divine Throne marks the boundary between is knowable and what lies beyond human knowledge.

Like Isaac Israeli, ibn Gabirol posited universal matter and universal form as preceding universal intellect; thus all beings are characterized by both matter and form. But in a sharp contrast to classical Neoplatonism, he also introduced divine will at the top of the hierarchy. Ibn Gabirol's hylomorphism thus provided an ontology in which all entities (even God?) had a material component; in part for this reason, his philosophical masterpiece had a mixed reception among subsequent thinkers. The very idea that God was comprised of both matter and form threatened the standard Neoplatonic picture of God/the One as beyond materiality. Unfortunately, *Mekor Hayyim* was not translated into Hebrew during ibn Gabirol's lifetime, and the original Arabic text was soon lost. Possibly because he did not discuss issues close to the heart of the thirteenth-century Jewish world, such as faith and reason, Jewish philosophers steeped in Aristotelianism had little interest in his work. In contrast, ibn Gabirol's work influenced several generations of Christian philosophers who were intrigued by and adapted aspects of his hylomorphism. A number of important sixteenth-century Jewish and Christian Kabbalists were influenced by the more esoteric conceptions of ibn Gabirol's cosmology.

TWO ECLECTIC THINKERS: BAHYA IBN PAQUDA AND JUDAH HALEVI

We turn now to two eclectic thinkers who incorporated ideas from a variety of sources, including Islamic Sufism (a mystical movement in Islam), Kalâm, Neoplatonism as well as classical Jewish sources. Bahya ibn Paquda (*c*.1150–*c*.1156) was an eleventh-century Jewish philosopher and rabbi who lived in Saragossa, Spain. His texts display knowledge of Arabic, Greek, and Roman science and philosophy as well as a clear grasp of traditional Jewish texts. Bahya is best known for his system of Jewish ethics, which appeared in 1040 in Arabic and later translated into Hebrew by Judah ibn Tibbon. His major work *Sefer Torat Hovot ha-Levvavot* (*Guide to the Duties of the Heart*) is one of the first attempts to present ethical laws and duties espoused by Judaism in a coherent philosophical system. We examine this work, which draws together material from medieval Aristotelians, Neoplatonism, Kalâm thinkers and traditional Jewish thought, in Chapter 6.

Judah Halevi (before 1075–1141) was born in Tudela, Spain, and lived in a number of cities including Córdoba, Lucena, Granada, Christian Toledo, and finally the Land of Israel. Along with ibn Gabirol he is considered one of the most important Hebrew poets of the Middle Ages. While in Granada, Halevi wrote close to 800 poems, including eulogies, poetical letters, secular wine poems and love poems. Halevi had to leave Granada shortly after 1090 due to the arrival of the Almoravides of Africa, who had conquered Muslim Spain. Eventually, Halevi became overwhelmed with an urge to see the land of Israel, for in his (philosophical) view it was the "Gate of Heaven" and the only place where prophecy occurred. He thus embarked on a long and arduous journey (by way of Alexandria and Cairo) to the land of Israel in his old age. Halevi is said to have died shortly after reaching the holy land.

Philosophically, Halevi's interests lay in defending the truth of Judaism and what he considered the essential superiority of the Jewish people. Although he is often included among the Neoplatonist thinkers, Halevi is an interestingly eclectic thinker who was influenced not only by Neoplatonism, but by Kalâm thought and Aristotelianism as well. His major philosophical work *The Kuzari* (*Kitâb al-Radd wa'l-Dalîl fi'l-Din al-dhalîl*), written originally in Arabic, is presented in the form of a fictional reconstruction of an actual historical event that took place between 786 and 809 CE, during the reign of King Bulan of the Khazars (a Turkish people). According to historical accounts, the king of the Khazars was on a quest for the most authentic monotheistic religion, and called together Muslim, Christian and Jewish scholars along with a philosopher. After asking each representative about their beliefs, the king was so impressed by the description of the rabbi that he converted his entire tribe to Judaism. Halevi used this historical event as the basis for his work, reconstructing the hypothetical conversations between the king, the philosopher, and the rabbi, who was described as the *haver* or friend. The rabbi/*haver* clearly represents Halevi's own views on many (but not all) of the topics under discussion.

Like his predecessor Baḥya, Halevi drew upon many sources, including the Kalâm theologians, Neoplatonism, Aristotelianism, as well as the Islamic philosopher al-Ghazâlî. In the context of presenting the views of the other interlocuters, Halevi presented a trenchant critique of the various philosophical schools of the period. The Khazar king was not convinced by either the Christian or the Moslem representatives, nor was he impressed by the views of the philosopher.

The Kuzari reflects Halevi's ambivalence over the status of philosophy as a discipline. Halevi used the king's criticisms to reject both Neoplatonist and Aristotelian views, even though, like Aristotle, he believed that truth (of Jewish doctrine) can and ought to be defended by rational means. And while there does exist a deep Neoplatonic strain in the work, there are many contexts in which Halevi criticized the Neoplatonic emanationist ontology, arguing that it was nonsensical: "these rudiments are as unacceptable to reason as they are extravagant in the face of logic. Neither do two philosophers agree on this point, unless they be disciples of the same teacher."[5] Halevi criticized Aristotelian philosophers on the grounds that they failed to demonstrate their philosophical claims conclusively, claiming that "their philosophy was based on conventional assumptions which they accepted without scientific justification, and is, therefore, a 'closed system'."[6]

Aristotelianism on Halevi's view does not qualify as a true scientific method, for as the rabbi/*haver* pointed out to the king, no two philosophers ever agree: "They are full of doubts, and there is no consensus of opinion between one philosopher and another."[7]

The tension between faith and reason was dissolved in Halevi's view: he was adamant that universal scientific truth (not the error-prone science of Aristotelianism) does not, indeed cannot, ever contradict revelation. In fact, following a line of reasoning we have seen already in Philo (see Chapter 1), Halevi suggested that scientific truth derives ultimately from Jewish sources. On the picture presented by the rabbi/*haver*, philosophy was once native to Jewish-Semitic culture, from which it passed to the Greeks. Greek science and philosophy, according to the rabbi, belong "to the descendants of Japheth ... The Greeks only received it when they became powerful, from Persia. The Persians had it from the Chaldeans. It was only then that the famous [Greek] philosophers arose."[8] Aristotle's philosophy, he claimed, is "not deserving of credence," since "he had no tradition from any reliable source at his disposal."[9] On this alternative history of ideas, Moses was an original philosopher centuries before the Greek philosophers came on the scene. Halevi was thus able to incorporate the truths of reason with those of revelation.

CONCLUSION

This chapter has introduced the earliest Jewish philosophers of the ninth to twelfth centuries, many of whom were engaged in the project of reconciling Jewish beliefs with Greek and Islamic philosophy. Starting with the Islamic Kalâm, we mentioned the work of Saadiah Gaon, who was writing against the backdrop of the Islamic Kalâm theologians. We then introduced major Jewish

Neoplatonist Solomon ibn Gabirol who incorporated Neoplatonic themes into his writings. We ended with two eclectic thinkers Baḥya ibn Pakuda and Judah Halevi. While generally considered Neoplatonic in orientation, both Baḥya and Halevi incorporated elements into their works from a variety of philosophical and theological, including Kalâm, Neoplatonism and Aristotelianism. As we turn now to the twelfth to fourteenth century, we will find Jewish philosophers writing more fully within the scope of Aristotelian thought.

NOTES

1. See Rudavsky 1997; Pessin 2013; Scheindlin 1986.
2. Solomon ibn Gabirol 1987, I.1.
3. Solomon ibn Gabirol 1987, 5.4.
4. Solomon ibn Gabirol, *Meqor Ḥayyim* V.43.
5. Jospe 2009, 248; see Halevi 1947, 4:25, 238–239.
6. Jospe 2009, 238.
7. Halevi 1947, 5:14, 273.
8. Halevi 1947, 1:63, 53.
9. Halevi 1947, 1:65, 53.

FURTHER READING

Frank, D. and Leaman, O. (ed.) (1997). *Routledge History of World Philosophies Vol II: History of Jewish Philosophy*. London: Routledge.

Nadler, S. and Rudavsky, T.M. (ed.) (2009). *The Cambridge History of Jewish Philosophy: From Antiquity through the Seventeenth Century*. Cambridge: Cambridge University Press.

Pessin, S. (2013). *Ibn Gabirol's Theology of Desire: Matter and Method in Jewish Medieval Neoplatonism*. Cambridge: Cambridge University Press.

Rudavsky, T.M. (2018). *Jewish Philosophy in the Middle Ages: Science, Rationalism, and Religion*. Oxford: Oxford University Press.

JEWISH KALÂM AND ARISTOTELIANISM

INTRODUCTION

This chapter focuses upon Islamic Kalâm thought and the impact of Aristotelianism upon Jewish philosophy. By the thirteenth century, the works of Aristotle had more fully permeated both Islamic and Jewish philosophy. With the availability of Aristotle's works by means of translations from Greek into Arabic, and eventually Hebrew, philosophers in Southern Spain incorporated Aristotelian themes into their own systems. Abraham ibn Daud (c.1110–1180) and Maimonides (1135–1204) stand out as key Aristotelian figures, along with the works of Gersonides (1288–1344) and Ḥasdai Crescas (c.1340–winter 1410).

THE ISLAMIC KALÂM SCHOOL

The Kalâm theologians represented a school of Islamic thinkers who presented a strict and rigorous interpretation of the Quran. Followers of Kalâm were called Mutakallimûn, and were divided into two main schools of thought: the Mu'tazilites, a moderate branch of Kalâm that emphasized human freedom, and became known as "the partisans of justice and unity," and the Ash'arites, who emphasized God's unknowability, and God's power over human action. The Mu'tazilite school was founded in 748 CE by Wasil ibn 'Ata in Abassid Baghdad. The major figure in the Kalâm school was al-Ghazâlî, whose presentation of Kalâm atomism in his *Maqāsid al-falasifah* (*Aims of the Philosophers*) was influential upon subsequent Jewish philosophers.

What was so important about Kalâm thought? Most importantly, the Mutakallimûn rejected Aristotle's ontology, one that emphasized the existence of a continuing material substrate that endured through change. Aristotle's ontology was accepted by the majority of philosophers in the eleventh to fourteenth centuries, as evidenced in particular in discussions of theories of creation; we examine these discussions in more detail in Chapter 4. In contradistinction to Aristotle, the Kalâm theologians described the world in terms of occurrences, or events, in space and time. On this Kalâm atomist picture, the world appeared as a set of synchronic time-slices, and movement from one to another state of the world was orchestrated by God, who recreates the world anew at each instant.

More specifically, the main features of Islamic atomism can be summarized as follows: the created world divides up into atoms of matter, qualities, space and time. Every event can be analyzed into discrete moments, completely independent of one another; events are brought together by the will of God. Qualities exist only for a single instant, and substances persist by means of a process of continuous recreation at each instant. On this occasionalist model, as it later came to be known, there is no necessary connection between cause and effect other than what God has ordained, and Aristotelian notions of time, change and motion have been abandoned in favor of a robust theory of divine omnipotence.[1] In short, the atomistic theory of the Kalâm reinforced God's absolute omnipotence, which eschewed any laws of nature or laws of causality independent of God's power: without God's continuous intervention, no object would exist from one instant to the next. In a famous passage in one of Ghazâlî's works, he imagines that a book he left in his library might have been transformed by God into a horse who ran through the library destroying everything. It is God who controls the identity of objects through time, and at every instant, all objects are recreated. The ramifications of this view will be explored in greater detail in Chapters 4 and 5.

By the ninth century, Kalâm occasionalism was as influential as the atomism of ancient Greek philosophers such as Democritus and Epicurus. It should be noted however that while both the Aristotelian and atomist positions were available to Jewish thinkers, the majority sided with Aristotle against the Kalâm ontology. Al-Ghazâlî's own attitude toward the Aristotelian philosophical tradition was one of harsh criticism, and yet he integrated into his thought various aspects of the same philosophical tradition that he outwardly rejected. As we shall see in Chapter 4, his dialectical approach to philosophy can also be found in Judah Halevi's major work *The Kuzari*: like al-Ghazâlî, Halevi excoriated the philosophers (and in particular the atomists) while at the same adopting their rationalist methodology.

SAADIAH GAON AND JEWISH KALÂM

Saadiah Gaon (882–942) is known as the founder of scientific activity in Judaism, and was one of the first Jewish thinkers to engage critically with Kalâm ontology. He was born in Pithom, in the Fayyum district of Egypt. Little is known about his life from 905 to 921. In 928 he was appointed head of the Sura academy, where he made it his personal mission to increase student enrollment and acquire funds to maintain the academy. Saadiah was a strong opponent of Karaism, an anti-rabbinic movement within Judaism. Rabbinic law relies on circuitous arguments that often diverge from a straightforward reading of Scripture. The eighth-century Babylonian sage Anan ben David rejected the rabbinic tradition and advocated a return to the text of the Bible itself. Many Babylonian Jews, surrounded by Muslims who referred to the Quran as the central authoritative Scripture of Islam, were compelled by Anan ben David's arguments to reject the hermeneutic rabbinic tradition and to seek truth in the text of the Bible itself, not in external interpretations. This anti-rabbinic movement came be called Karaism and their followers were known as karaites. In an ongoing effort to reject polemical Karaite claims, Saadiah and other rabbis of his time were devoted to validating the legitimacy of rabbinical Judaism.

Saadiah's major work *Kitâb al-Amânât wa-al-I'tiqadât* (*The Book of Beliefs and Opinions*) was written in Arabic in 933 CE and was translated into Hebrew by the noted translator Judah ibn Tibbon in 1186 under the title *Sefer ha-Emunot ve-ha-De'ot*. In this work Saadiah attempted to establish a rational basis for the dogmas of the Law. Influenced by Islamic Kalâm epistemology and cosmology, Saadiah distinguished between the rational commandments, which in theory are discoverable by means of reason, and the traditional laws, which comprise rituals and ceremonial commandments (such as the dietary laws) that are not rooted in reason. Saadiah is the first Jewish philosopher to frame his discussion of ethical precepts in the context of rational apprehension. We present a detailed examination of Saadiah's epistemology and moral theory in Chapter 8.

THE INFLUENCE OF ARISTOTLE

With his emphasis upon scientific knowledge arising from empirical observation, Aristotle provided Jewish philosophers with new ways of thinking about traditional philosophical issues. Aristotle distinguished between the theoretical sciences that included physics, mathematics and metaphysics, and the practical sciences, which included ethics, economics, and politics. The underlying methodology of all these sciences was logic, a method of demonstration developed in Aristotle's logical works. But as we shall see in Chapter 6, the practical sciences relied on what Aristotle called the "practical syllogism;" this less rigorous form of syllogistic reasoning reflected the subjectivity of the practical sciences, as opposed to what he considered the objectivity of those sciences rooted in empirical knowledge. Aristotle also introduced into his ontology the hylomorphism of matter of form, according to which matter and form are mutually interdependent poles of being, leading to a rejection of Platonic and Neoplatonic dualism. Aristotle's conceptualization of the unmoved mover of the universe as "thought thinking itself" was picked up by Jewish philosophers as a paradigm for their depiction of the Deity. As we turn to the major figures writing within the shadow of Aristotelian science, we shall appreciate both the allure and threat provided by Aristotle.

ABRAHAM IBN DAUD

Abraham ibn Daud (c.1110–1180), the first Jewish Aristotelian, was a Spanish astronomer, historian, and philosopher who published works in all three areas. Born in Cordova, Spain and moving eventually to Toledo, he is best known for his *Sefer ha-Kabbalah*, a history of the Jewish people, and his philosophical work *Ha-Emunah ha-Ramah* (*The Exalted Faith*). The purpose of this latter work was to justify rabbinic tradition rather than simply record historical events. Although he was one of the very first Jewish philosophers to harmonize the works of Aristotle with a religious philosophy of Judaism, his attempts were overshadowed by those of his immediate successor Maimonides, whose work *Guide of the Perplexed* was published thirty years after ibn Daud's own work. Further, since *The Exalted Faith* was translated quite late in the fourteenth century, it had little influence on medieval philosophers who did not read Arabic. We shall return in Chapter 5 to some details in this work.

MOSES MAIMONIDES

We turn now to Maimonides (1135–1204), perhaps the most famous and influential Jewish philosopher. Maimonides provided future generations with ample information about himself in letters and documents; many of these documents have been preserved in part in the Cairo Geniza, a repository of discarded documents discovered over a century ago in the Ben Ezra synagogue of Fustât (Old Cairo) where Maimonides lived. He was known by several names: his original Hebrew name Moses ben Maimon; his Latinized name Maimonides; the Hebrew acronym RaMBaM, standing for Rabbi Moses ben Maimon; and the honorific title "the teacher (*ha-Moreh*)."[2]

Moses ben Maimon was born in Cordova, Spain in 1135 or 1138, and died in Cairo in 1204. During his period in Cordova, he wrote several early books, including his *Treatise on the Art of Logic* and a primer on the calendar (*Ma'amar ha-'ibbur*). When the Almohads invaded Andalusia and occupied Cordova in 1148, the Maimon family left and settled in Fustât (Old Cairo) in 1166, after a brief stay in Morocco and then Alexandria. During this period Maimonides wrote his celebrated *Mishneh Torah*. Shortly after Maimonides's arrival in Egypt (1171–1172), Saladin became sultan over Egypt and founded the Ayyûbid dynasty.

Maimonides had a patron in Fustât, Al-Qâdî al-Fâdil al-Baysani (1135–1200), who was a scholar in his own right. He collected many books in Arabic thought, some of which presumably Maimonides read and studied. Maimonides's major work *Guide of the Perplexed* was written in Fustât between 1185–1190, followed by a number of medical works. Maimonides devoted himself to both the community and his intellectual needs, serving as physician to the sultan as well as to the Jewish community in Cairo and abroad. In a letter of 1199 written to Samuel ibn Tibbon, translator of the *Guide* from Judaeo-Arabic into Hebrew, Maimonides attests to his harried schedule:

> God knows that in order to write this to you, I have escaped to a secluded spot, where people would not think to find me, sometimes leaning for support against the wall, sometimes lying down on account of my excessive weakness, for I have grown old and feeble … I attend to my patients, write prescriptions … I converse and prescribe for them while lying down from sheer fatigue, and when night falls, I am so exhausted that I can scarcely speak.[3]

Maimonides devoted himself seriously to medicine in the later years of his life, after the composition of his theological and philosophical works; these treatises contributed to his fame as a physician. According to his grandson David, Maimonides died on December 13, 1204 and is supposedly buried in Tiberias, although we cannot be sure where his body actually resides.

Maimonides's works fall into three broad categories: rabbinics (*halakhah*), philosophy, and medicine. Little is known about Maimonides's educational situation or teachers. We do know from letters that he did not consider philosophy prior to Aristotle worthy of the title of "genuine philosophy," although it is not clear what his actual sources of Aristotelianism were. A different story emerges when we turn to Islamic philosophers.[4] Maimonides had clear regard for the works of al-Fârâbî, ibn Bâjja, ibn Sina (Avicenna) and ibn Rushd (Averroës), and exhorted his disciples to read their work. How extensive was Maimonides's knowledge of Islamic Kalâm? In the *Commentary on the Mishnah*, composed when he was thirty years old, Maimonides mentions several Kalâm positions briefly and rejects them. By the time he wrote the *Guide*, in his fifties, Maimonides refers to the Kalâm much more extensively.

Maimonides began work on *The Commentary on the Mishnah* around 1161, and presented it in Egypt in 1168. As discussed in Chapter 1, the Mishnah is the basis for legal discussions in both the Babylonian and Jerusalem Talmud. Maimonides's commentary reproduced the entire text of the Mishnah with a commentary written in Judeo-Arabic, and later translated into Hebrew. In this work, he proclaimed his aim, namely to simplify and synthesize the content of the Mishnah. Three major introductions were incorporated into his commentary: a long introduction to the entire Mishnah; an introduction to the tenth chapter of tractate Sanhedrin, known as *Pereq Heleq*, in which he set out the thirteen articles of faith; and a prelude to the tractate Avot (*Pirqe Avot* or *Ethics of the Fathers*) known as *Eight Chapters* (*Shemona Perakim*) in which he set out his views on ethics. We return to these ethical works in Chapter 6.

Maimonides compiled his monumental compendium of Jewish Law, known as the *Mishneh Torah* (*Repetition of the Torah*) during the years 1168–1178 (or 1180). Maimonides chose to write the *Mishneh Torah* in the more colloquial Hebrew of the Mishnah, rather than the Hebrew of the Bible, in order to reach as wide an audience as possible. His organization of the laws in this work was designed to make it easy for the student to learn the laws by memory; Maimonides stated that his main concern in this work was science and the study of nature, the foundation of his restoring Judaism as a "religion of reason and enlightenment."[5]

Maimonides's major philosophical work *The Guide of the Perplexed* was composed between the years of 1185 and 1190. The work is written in Judeo-Arabic, that is, in Arabic using Hebrew letters, which was a common mode of writing for Maimonides's contemporaries. The introduction describes the circumstances surrounding the composition of the work. Maimonides tells us that an individual named Joseph ben Judah ibn Shimon had travelled from Morocco to Egypt, hoping to study philosophy with him. Maimonides accepted Joseph as a student and the two studied together for several years (1182–1184/5), focusing on astronomy, logic and philosophy. When Joseph departed (not having finished his full course of study), Maimonides wrote the *Guide* for him and other similar students. The *Guide* is divided into three parts. The first part deals primarily with issues associated with a philosophical conception of God, while part two introduces arguments for the existence of God, philosophical cosmology and creation, and prophecy. In the final part of the *Guide*, Maimonides addresses the cluster of problems connected with theodicy, divine providence, moral theory, and ultimate felicity. Many of these topics will be discussed in Chapters 4–6.

After the composition of his theological and philosophical works, Maimonides devoted himself more seriously to medicine and composed ten medical treatises between 1190 and 1204. Maimonides's most important and popular medical work was his *Medical Aphorisms* (*Fusûl Mûsâ*), a work whose purpose was to transmit Galen's ideas in summary form. This work was repeatedly reprinted in Hebrew, as well as in Latin translations. It has been characterized as a medical equivalent of the

Mishneh Torah in that it offers a summary and compendium of over ninety of Galen's works.[6]

Less than ten years after the publication of the *Guide*, Maimonides's admirers asked his translator Samuel ibn Tibbon, who lived in Lunel, France, to make a translation of the work from Judaeo-Arabic into Hebrew. On November 30, 1204 (fourteen days before Maimonides's death in Fustât), the translation was completed and disseminated throughout southern France (Provence), northern Spain and Italy. Almost immediately, however, opposition to the work sprung up. Ibn Tibbon himself was denounced, and the work was burnt in Paris and elsewhere by Jewish legal authorities who feared that the views contained in the work would encourage apostasy. But within a century, the *Guide* emerged from the opposition even stronger than before, influencing generations of Jewish philosophers. A Latin translation was undertaken during the thirteenth century and studied by the noted Christian scholastic Thomas Aquinas (d. 1274), among others. Aquinas studied the *Guide* carefully and quoted it regularly in his discussions of creation and divine attributes. To this day the phrase "from Moses unto Moses, there is none like unto Moses" epitomizes the stature attained by Moses Maimonides.

THE MAIMONIDEAN CONTROVERSIES

The complex story of the reception of Maimonides's works in the thirteenth and fourteenth centuries has been traced by many scholars. Let me mention just some of the highlights of what have come to be known as the Maimonidean controversies. Not surprisingly, rabbinic leaders even before Maimonides's death were threatened by what they saw as an attack on Jewish belief. One issue had to do with anthropomorphic descriptions of God found in Scripture. A second issue had to do with resurrection of the dead, a topic that held theological implications for theories of retribution. Yet another issue centered around Maimonides's contention that all the commandments had rational explanations. Controversy swirled around the naturalistic doctrine of prophecy and miracles as well. These controversies mirrored similar controversies in the fourteenth-century scholastic world, during which period the Christian church had to accommodate Church teachings with the new and somewhat threatening philosophies of Aristotle and Averroës.

The controversy over Maimonides's works commenced in the East, with an argument over the legitimacy of traditional Jewish institutions. The publication of the *Mishneh Torah* enabled Jews to consult a systematic compendium of Jewish law themselves, and so not surprisingly, the rabbinic academies were opposed to Maimonides's encroachment upon their authority, an encroachment they saw as undermining the institutional foundations of Judaism. This controversy resulted in the Gaon of Baghdad's challenge that Maimonides did not believe in the resurrection of the dead. After Maimonides pointed out that the doctrine of resurrection was already included in his writings, the controversy died down.

But other controversies arose in its wake. The second stage of controversy arose in Provence and spread to northern France and Spain. Provence had an influx of both Sephardi Jews from Andalusia who brought with them from Spain the rich traditions of Arabic philosophy, and Ashkenazi Jews from Northern France who were more interested in traditional rabbinic learning. The Ashkenazi Jews worried that the essence of Judaism was in danger of being overrun by secular learning, as epitomized by philosophy. This second stage was set off by Rabbi Solomon ben Abraham of Montpellier's ban on the study of Maimonides's philosophical works. A series of counter-bans was then proposed by Maimonides's followers.

The thirteenth-century Jewish philosopher Nahmanides tried to reconcile the two camps, but failed in his attempts. The second stage of the controversy ended violently, with the anti-Maimunists bringing the Christian inquisition into the picture, resulting in the subsequent burning of Maimonides's works by the Church.[7] The third ban occurred around 1288/9, leading to another round of bans and counter-bans. In this third stage only the works of Greek philosophy were banned, not those of Maimonides. In fact, the study of scientific and philosophical works continued throughout this period.

GERSONIDES

Turning now to the fourteenth century, Levi ben Gershom (Gersonides; 1288–1344) has been recognized in recent years as one of the most significant medieval Jewish philosophers. Through the works of Ḥasdai Crescas and others, Gersonides's ideas have influenced such modern philosophers as Leibniz and Spinoza. Emphasizing Gersonides's religious rationalism, one scholar described Gersonides as someone who "has taken seriously the fact that he has reason, who believes that this faculty is God-given, and who attempts to understand God with this instrument."[8] Attempting to show that philosophy and Torah, or reason and revelation, are co-extensive, Gersonides was a philosophical optimist who believed that human reason is fully able to achieve all the essential truths in religion. And yet, at the same time, perhaps no other medieval Jewish philosopher has been so maligned over the centuries. Indeed, Gersonides's major philosophical work *Milhamot ha-Shem* (*Wars of the Lord*) was called "Wars against the Lord" by one of his opponents and was depicted as a radical rejection of traditional Jewish tenets.

Since Gersonides left few letters and did not talk about himself in his writings, what we know of his life is sketchy at best. Gersonides was born in 1288 in Provence (southern France) and lived most of his life in Orange and Avignon. We know that Gersonides spoke the Provençal dialect, and resided for a number of years at the Papal court in Avignon as the court astronomer. His works, all written in Hebrew, covered a variety of fields, including mathematics, astronomy, philosophy, logic, biblical commentaries, and philosophical commentaries on Averroës.

In 1317 Gersonides began an essay on the problem of creation. Dissatisfied with Maimonides's treatment of the problem, Gersonides proposed to reopen the issue. This project was soon laid aside, however, for Gersonides felt that it could not be adequately discussed without proper grounding in the issues of time, motion, and the infinite. By 1328 his manuscript had developed to include discussion not only of creation but also of immortality, divination and prophecy, and divine providence. Books 5 and 6 were completed, by Gersonides's own dating, by 1329, and the final work was entitled *Milhamot ha-Shem*. Gersonides's aim with all these topics was to integrate the teachings of Aristotle, as mediated through Averroës and Maimonides, with those of Judaism. With each issue, Gersonides attempted to reconcile traditional Jewish beliefs with what he felt were the strongest points in Aristotle's philosophy.

Gersonides's major scientific contributions in astronomy are contained primarily in book 5, part 1 of *Milhamot ha-Shem* (see details of this work below) in which he reviewed and criticized astronomical theories of the day, compiled astronomical tables, and introduced one of his astronomical inventions. This instrument, which he named *Megalle 'amuqqot* (Revealer of Profundities) and which was called Bacullus Jacobi (Jacob's staff) by his Christian contemporaries, was used to measure the height of stars above the horizon. The astronomical portions of *Milhamot ha-Shem* were translated into Latin during

Gersonides's lifetime, possibly at the request of the Papal court and one of the craters of the moon, Rabbi Levi, is named after him.

Gersonides's innovative work in logic, *Sefer ha-heqesh ha-yashar* (*Book of the Correct Syllogism*, 1319) examined the problems associated with Aristotle's logic and was translated into Latin at an early date, although Gersonides's name was not attached to it. Finally, Gersonides contributed to the corpus of philosophical biblical commentaries, including commentaries on the books of Job (1325), Song of Songs (1326), Ecclesiastes (1328), Esther (1329), Ruth (1329), Genesis (1329), Exodus (1330), most of Leviticus (1332) and the remaining books of the Torah (completed in 1338). Many of these commentaries incorporated philosophical material from the *Wars*, and are still part of the Jewish canon.

As we shall see in subsequent chapters, Gersonides's philosophical ideas went against the grain of traditional Jewish thought. His philosophical work was rejected, or roundly criticized. Only in recent years has Gersonides received his rightful place in the history of philosophy. As scholars have rediscovered his thought and have made his works available to a modern audience, Gersonides has finally been appreciated as an insightful, ruthlessly consistent philosopher, committed to logical argument even when it forces a reconceptualization of Jewish belief. We shall examine his philosophy in Chapters 4–6.

ḤASDAI CRESCAS

Ḥasdai Crescas (*c*.1340–winter 1410), a Catalonian philosopher, rabbi, statesman and amateur poet, is the last fourteenth-century philosopher in our survey. He was born in Barcelona and served as secretary of the Jewish community in Barcelona. Because he was the local authority on Talmudic law, he was asked by King Peter IV of

Aragon to adjudicate cases concerning Jews. He served as a rabbi of the main royal court at Saragossa in 1389, and by 1390 Crescas was considered the judge of all the Jews of the Kingdom of Aragon. In 1391, responding to riots against the Jews, Crescas wrote a polemical work *Sefer bittul Iqqarei ha-Nozrim* (*The Book of the Refutation of the Principles of the Christians*, 1397–1398) in which he argued that major Christian principles such as original sin, the trinity, and transubstantiation were self-contradictory and philosophically absurd.

Crescas's philosophical interests lay in articulating the fundamental beliefs or religious concepts that follow analytically from his view of the nature of the Torah. His major work *Sefer Or Adonai* (*The Book of the Light of the Lord*) was finished several months before his death in 1410. In this work, Crescas sought to undermine the Aristotelian cosmology and physics that pervaded the works of his predecessors Maimonides and Gersonides. He maintained that the Torah was a product of voluntary action from the Commander (lord), and that certain basic concepts follow from this fact. In an attempt to weaken Aristotle's hold upon Jewish philosophy, Crescas subjected Aristotelian physics and metaphysics to a trenchant critique. As we shall see in Chapter 5, the *Light* contains a theory of physical determinism that results from his analysis of Aristotle. In fact, it has been argued that Crescas's critique of Aristotle helped lay the groundwork for the abandonment of Aristotelian science in subsequent centuries.

JOSEPH ALBO

Moving to the fifteenth century, our final philosopher to wrestle with Aristotelianism is Joseph Albo. Born in the Crown of Aragon, Albo studied as a youth with Ḥasdai Crescas. He moved to Soria and was famed as the representative for Daroca in the famous Jewish–Christian debates at Tortosa and San-Mateo from 1413–1414. These debates pitted Albo against major Christian spokespersons of the period, arguing over the truth of Judaism vis a vis Christianity. Albo's major philosophical treatise *Sefer ha-Ikkarim* (*Book of Principles*) addressed the following religious dogmas: God's existence, divine revelation, and punishment and reward. Albo was critical of both Maimonides and his teacher Crescas, warning his readers that his masterpiece contained deliberate contradictions and that the reader ought to read carefully and responsibly.

CONCLUSION

By the twelfth century, both Jewish and Islamic thinkers were absorbing Aristotelian texts and incorporating them into their own systematic thought. This chapter has introduced the major players writing under the aegis of Aristotelian thought. Abraham ibn Daud, Maimonides, Gersonides, Hasdai Crescas and Joseph Albo had to grapple with Aristotle's logic, metaphysics and ethics and wrestle with ways to incorporate Aristotelian themes into their systems. Having introduced the major players writing against the backdrop of Aristotelian philosophy, we are now ready to examine their views more fully.

NOTES

1 For discussion of the importance of the doctrine of divine omnipotence to Kalâm ontology, see Rudavsky 2018.
2 I am very much indebted to recent biographies of Maimonides by Kraemer 2008, Davidson 2005 and Ivry 2016 for details of Maimonides's life and writings.
3 Twersky 1972, 7.
4 For a detailed discussion of the impact of Islamic philosophy upon Maimonides, see Pines 1963; Pessin 2013.
5 Kraemer 2008, 326.

6 See Langermann 2008.
7 Drews 2004, 127.
8 Feldman's comment is found in Gersonides 1987, 54.

FURTHER READING

Crescas, H. (2018). *Light of the Lord*. trans. and intro by R. Weiss. Oxford: Oxford University Press.

Freudenthal, G. (ed.) (2011). *Science in Medieval Jewish Cultures*. Cambridge: Cambridge University Press.

Glasner, R. (2015), *Gersonides: A Portrait of a Fourteenth-Century Philosopher-Scientist*. Oxford: Oxford University Press.

Ivry, A. (2016). *Maimonides' "Guide of the Perplexed": A Philosophical Guide*. Chicago, IL: University of Chicago Press.

Nadler, S. and Rudavsky, T.M. (ed.) (2009). *The Cambridge History of Jewish Philosophy: From Antiquity through the Seventeenth Century*. Cambridge: Cambridge University Press.

Rudavsky, T.M. (2010). *Maimonides*. London: Wiley-Blackwell.

Rudavsky, T.M. (2018). *Jewish Philosophy in the Middle Ages: Science, Rationalism, and Religion*. Oxford: Oxford University Press.

Sirat, C. (1990). *A History of Jewish Philosophy in the Middle Ages*. Cambridge: Cambridge University Press.

GOD, CREATION AND MIRACLES

INTRODUCTION

Medieval Jewish philosophers were writing in light of Islamic and Jewish traditions that promulgated an anthropomorphic conception of the Deity. Not only was it believed that God had a body, but many Jewish and Islamic works were quite willing to describe in great detail the particulars of this divine body. Both the Quran and Scripture could be read as reinforcing a physical view of God, with its many references to God's actions, speech, location, and emotional life. In clear opposition to this anthropocentric conception of God found in popular and religious texts, the philosophers attempted to provide Jews (and Muslims) with a picture of God that more accurately accorded with rational speculation. They were determined to counteract these entrenched beliefs, and their works tackled the philosophical implications of God's incorporeal nature directly.

In this chapter, we concentrate upon attempts on the part of Jewish philosophers to deconstruct corporeal descriptions and predicates of God in a way that avoids attributing to God physical or material features. One of the most important of God's predicates is of course existence, and so we shall have to consider the classic

DOI: 10.4324/9781003504030-6

arguments that attempt to prove the existence of God. These arguments follow an established tradition of inferring, from certain facts in the created world, the existence of a creator. As we shall see, arguments for the existence of God turn out to be intimately intertwined with arguments for creation of the world. And so we will turn to different accounts of God's relation to the world as creator.

ESTABLISHING THE UNITY AND INCORPOREALITY OF GOD

Anthropomorphic descriptions of God abound in the Bible: God is described as king, judge, father, shepherd, to mention only a few, and philosophers committed to the incorporeality of the Deity had to grapple with these descriptions. The uniqueness of God was emphasized by most philosophers, as evidenced by Saadiah Gaon and Maimonides among others. Saadiah presented his work as an attempt to rescue his readers from confusion, particularly in light of Trinitarian and dualist views of the Christians and Persians respectively. Saadiah stated his two-fold goals in his *Book of Beliefs and Opinions*: to establish the existence of God the creator, and to reinforce the incorporeality and unity of God in light of the many passages in Scripture that suggest God's corporeal nature. Saadiah provided an explanation of the attributes existence, omniscience and omnipotence, claiming that since they are not distinct from God's essence, they do not imply plurality in God.[1] These arguments, he tells us, are couched in the context of what he termed "scientific research" and speculative reasoning.[2]

Like Saadiah, Maimonides emphasized the unity and incorporeality of the Deity as givens. Already in his early halakhic works, Maimonides introduced to his readers a philosophical conception of the Deity that was developed in accordance with a rigorous metaphysical and logical program. He emphasized that everybody must be taught to accept two basic metaphysical truths about the Deity – incorporeality and unity – that form the basis of subsequent discussion in both the *Mishneh Torah* and the *Guide*.

The first book of the *Mishneh Torah*, the *Book of Knowledge* begins with an explicit statement of God's existence. The basic principle of all principles, and the pillar of all the sciences, is that "there is a First Being who brought every existing thing into being."[3] If there were no God, nothing else would exist. But even if nothing else were to exist, according to Maimonides, God would still exist: "their non-existence would not involve His non-existence."[4] In the *Guide*, Maimonides reiterated the point that the following characteristics must be taught to all: that God is unique (one), and there is none like God; that God is not a body; that being incorporeal, God has no likeness to God's creatures in any way; that the difference between God and creatures is not one of degree, but rather "one concerning the species of existence;" and that even the term existence "can only be applied equivocally to His existence and to that of things other than He."[5] We can see that already that the predicate "existence" incorporates notions of God as creator of the universe, and we return to the issue of creation below.

PROOFS FOR GOD'S EXISTENCE

Turning now to the actual proofs for God's existence, we must distinguish two types of proof employed by medieval (and many contemporary) philosophers: *propter quid* and *propter quia* arguments. *Propter quid* demonstrations define God into existence; these arguments are based on reason alone, not sense experience. In other words, they are deductive and do not rely upon premises drawn from empirical reality. Although found in scholastic philosophy, these arguments rarely made their way into Islamic and Jewish philosophy. *Propter quia* arguments, on the other hand, are those based on experience, on our sense perception, and they come in several varieties. We find in medieval literature both cosmological arguments (arguments from the existence of effects to the existence of an ultimate cause) and teleological arguments or arguments from design (arguments that draw an inference from the existence of design in the world to the existence of a designer). Most Jewish thinkers adopted variations or combinations of these arguments. The teleological argument was used primarily by Saadiah Gaon, Baḥya ibn Paquda and Gersonides, while different versions of both the teleological and cosmological argument (often combined) were presented by Saadiah, Baḥya, ibn Daud and Maimonides.

Before turning to details of these arguments, however, we should mention yet another way of proving God's existence, namely fideism. Fideists reject the privileging of rational arguments altogether, claiming that direct experience of God or tradition is a more reliable guide than logical argumentation. Fideism was popularized in Jewish thought by Halevi's protagonist *haver*/rabbi in the *Kuzari,* who distinguished between the philosophical conception of God and the God of tradition. The former, he argued, was incompatible with the God of tradition for two reasons. First, the God of the philosophers was not an agent endowed with will, but rather was a necessary first cause; in addition, the God of the philosophers did not have knowledge of particulars and hence was not able to interact with individual human beings. In response to philosophical attempts to prove the existence by means of rational demonstration, Halevi (through the voice of the rabbi/*haver*) articulated a classic fideistic position in describing to the king of the Khazars the unwavering belief of the Jewish people in God: "I believe in the God of Abraham, Isaac, and Israel, who led the children of Israel out of Egypt with signs and miracles."[6] The rabbi had no need of rational arguments, either teleological, cosmological or ontological, to prove God's existence: he regarded the proof as implicit in the words themselves, "and so evident that it requires no other argument."[7] In response to the king's query as to why he does not espouse belief in the God of the philosophers, the rabbi/*haver* replied that philosophers rarely agree on doctrines, but that his own position was grounded both on personal experience and "uninterrupted tradition, which is equal to the former."[8]

The majority of Jewish philosophers did not embrace fideism, however, and searched for rational arguments for God's existence. Cosmological arguments were the most popular and were adopted by a number of thinkers; these arguments for God's existence were intertwined with the necessity of creation, and the impossibility of an eternal universe. Both Saadiah Gaon and Bahya ibn Paquda presented versions of the cosmological argument for God's existence. More specifically, they used the existence of order and design in the universe to postulate the existence of a designer or creator, arguing for the extreme unlikeliness that the universe would have arisen by chance or accident. Let us take Bahya's version of the argument as an example.

Bahya ibn Paquda offered a cosmological argument in *Duties of the Heart* 1:5, claiming that since the world is composite, it must have been put together at some point in time. Since nothing can make itself, it must have been created, its creator being God. In *Duties* I:4, he claimed that we can only ask *whether* God is, not *what* God is, *how* He is, or *why* He is, since God's essence cannot be defined: "About the Creator, however, one may only ask whether He exists."⁹ Baḥya then posited three premises to support his argument: that a thing does not make itself, that causes are limited in number and so must have a first cause, and that everything that is a compound must have been brought into existence.[10] On the basis of these premises (the validity of which he attempted to demonstrate), Baḥya employed in *Duties* 1.6 a standard version of teleological argument. He based his argument on the claim that the universe manifests order, intention and purpose and that the individual parts of the universe exhibit design. That the design manifest in the universe arose from chance is rejected outright: "There are men who say that the world came into existence by chance ... How could any rational human being, in his right mind, entertain such a notion?"[11] Surely we would not expect that if some ink spills accidentally upon a page, that "it would take the shape of orderly writing and legible lines;" so too must we postulate "the existence of an intelligent Designer who intentionally created the order apparent in the universe."[12]

The final *propter quia* argument includes variations of the teleological argument. For example, Maimonides offered a variant on this argument in his attempt to explain the presence of discrete particulars in the world. In *Guide* 2.19, Maimonides tells us that his purpose is to present arguments that "come close to being a demonstration," for the existence of a "purposer."[13] By "purposer" Maimonides means one who is accountable or responsible for all the contingent (particular) facts of the matter in the world. Assuming, as did Maimonides, that all things in the world are comprised of one common substance, how can we account for the multiplicity of individuals within each species, let alone the many varieties of species in the world? Maimonides argued that the fact that particularization exists is evidence of a particularizer, namely God.[14]

DIVINE PREDICATION: WHAT CAN WE SAY ABOUT GOD?

Once the existence of God is demonstrated, philosophers must next determine how to describe this existent Deity. The problem of divine attributes is straightforward: if God is the only Necessarily Existent being, and qualitatively different from all other entities, how can we begin to ascribe predicates to this entity? Can we make meaningful statements about God? Once again, several traditions prevailed in medieval Jewish texts. We have alluded already to the rich literature in which anthropomorphic characteristics were applied to God: Jewish liturgical works, poetry, mystical texts and even philosophical texts are replete with ornate descriptions of God's actions, emotions and nature, all of which suggest a similarity between God and human beings.

In contradistinction, the doctrine of skeptical theism or apophatic thought rejects the ability of humans to know or say anything about the Deity. The most radical medieval Jewish example of apophatic thought was presented by Maimonides who argued in the *Guide* that we must be careful not to attribute to God any predicates that imply or impute to God anthropomorphic or corporeal features. He analyzed both positive attributes and relational terms, arguing that neither is appropriate to predicate of God. In fact, as we shall see, we can say very little, if anything, either positive *or* negative, about God: *all* attempts to describe God fall short.

Maimonides developed in part I, chapters 51–60 of the *Guide* an elaborate theory of divine predication, the purpose of which was to claim that linguistic utterances are inadequate to say anything about God.[15] Chapters 59 and 60 present Maimonides's celebrated theory of negative predication, according to which the process of negating or eliminating predicates brings the mind closer to an understanding of God: "Know that the description of God, may he be cherished and exalted, by means of negations is the correct description."[16] What Maimonides meant was that eliminating positive ascriptions to the Deity was the only way to approach God's nature. Rather than attributing the positive predicate "good" to God, for example, we should recognize that God is *not the sort of entity* to which either "good" or "not-good" can be applied. Similarly, we can continue this process of recognizing the inappropriateness of predicating anything of God. Achieving proficiency with removing predicates attributed to God becomes for Maimonides a mark of personal excellence and perfection, and Maimonides presented to his astute readers an epistemological taxonomy according to which "with every increase in the negations regarding Him ... you come nearer to that apprehension than he who does not negate with regard to Him that which, according to what has been demonstrated to you, must be negated."[17] In other words, the individual who describes God in glowing, flowery language is more distant from God than the individual who recognizes that God cannot be described at all. Maimonides is explicit on this point: whenever a person affirms of God positive attributes, said person recedes from God's true reality. Ultimately silence is the only appropriate linguistic response to divine predication: "silence with regard to You is praise."[18]

Not surprisingly, Maimonides's theory of negative predication was contested by subsequent philosophers. Both Gersonides and Crescas rejected Maimonides's theory of negative predication, arguing that if God is to be intelligible to human beings, His attributes must be understood as positive predications. Gersonides criticized Maimonides's theory of negative predication in *Wars* III.3. Gersonides believed that positive predicates could be applied to God literally; he argued that their primary meaning was derived from their application to God, while their human meaning was secondary. He thus attempted to salvage the ability of humans to talk meaningfully about God, claiming that divine predicates are to be understood as what he called *pros hen* equivocals. What this means is that, according to Gersonides, predicates applied to God represent the prime instance or meaning of the term, whereas human predicates are derivative or inferior instances. So, for example, knowledge when applied to God is to be understood as the paradigm of perfect knowledge and constitutes the standard for human knowledge, which is less perfect than divine knowledge: "the term 'knowledge' is predicated of God (may he be blessed) *primarily* and of others *secondarily*."[19] Gersonides denied that terms have completely different meanings when predicated of God and of humans; it is only because of an underlying commonality of meaning that we can use language meaningfully at all. Crescas too criticized Maimonides's theory of negative attributes on two respects: first that they preclude one's ability to come to know God; and second that the theory is irreconcilable with tradition.[20] In fact, very few philosophers followed Maimonides in his theory of negative theology. Perhaps the closest analogue occurs in Jewish mystical texts, which we mention briefly in Chapter 6.

GOD AND CREATION

We alluded above to the importance of recognizing God's role as a creator. But the very issue of creation was itself a thorny problem, raising a host of metaphysical concerns. In his dialogue the *Timaeus,* Plato reinforced his distinction between two domains, being and becoming. He emphasized the unchanging nature of the domain of being, in contradistinction to the flux and temporal change of the domain of becoming. Although the domain of becoming was rooted in the flow of time, the domain of being incorporated its own "primordial time." Building upon Plato, Aristotle examined in greater detail the domain of temporal flux and change. Aristotle argued that time is inconceivable without motion, implying as it does the existence of a corporeal object in motion. Eternal beings are incorporeal and hence cannot have time or motion associated with them. Because of this close association to matter and motion, time cannot exist prior to their existence. Aristotle thus concluded that neither time nor the heavens is generated. The main difference, then, is that Plato envisioned an eternal domain of being that existed alongside a created domain of becoming, whereas for Aristotle the world was eternal and uncreated.

In Chapter 1 we noted the ways in which Philo attempted to reconcile Platonic, Aristotelian and Stoic ideas of creation with the Jewish sources available to him in Hellenistic Alexandria. In like manner, Maimonides, Gersonides and Crescas grappled with similar issues and all three presented theories that reflect a clear peripatetic influence, either supportive or critical of Aristotle's views. All three thinkers were writing in the context of Genesis, and so the question for them, as it was for Philo, was how to reconcile Aristotelian and Neoplatonic theories with Scripture. Is it possible to adopt "pieces" of Aristotelian cosmology and ontology without jeopardizing basic Judaic beliefs?

Maimonides's theory of creation is presented in *Guide* II:13–30. In *Guide* II.13 Maimonides described three opinions on creation. The main features of these three views, characterized as the Law of Moses (Scripture), Platonism and Aristotelianism, can be summarized as follows: (1) the view of Scripture, that the universe was brought into existence by God after "having been purely and absolutely nonexistent;"[21] (2) the Platonic view, that inasmuch as even God cannot create matter and form out of absolute nonexistence (since this constitutes an ontological impossibility and so does not impute impotence to God), there "exists a certain matter that is eternal as the deity is eternal ... He is the cause of its existence ... and that He creates in it whatever he wishes;"[22] and (3) the view of Aristotle, namely that since matter cannot be created from absolute nonexistence, the universe is eternal and not created.[23] We have then three distinctly different theories of creation: creation "*ex nihilo*" (out of nothing) by God; creation out of an eternally pre-existing material substrate; and an uncreated, eternally existing universe.

Maimonides specified several observations concerning the relations among these three characterizations. First, contrary to those who "imagine that our opinion and his [Plato's] opinion are identical,"[24] Maimonides was quick to disabuse those who were tempted to posit a connection between the views of Scripture and Plato. The Platonic view, he stated, cannot be substituted for Mosaic doctrine, even though there appear to be superficial similarities – most notably the postulation of a creator – between the two. But other passages in the *Guide* suggest that Maimonides had not totally ruled out either an Aristotelian or a Platonic view of creation. Some recent scholars have argued that ultimately Maimonides upheld a skeptical stance in light of the evidence and did not ascribe to any of the three positions. Inasmuch as Maimonides had clearly questioned the demonstrability of each of these views, they suggest that Maimonides's ultimate position is one of epistemological skepticism: the human intellect is simply unable to resolve the issue. When the evidence is conflicting and unsupported by sound rational demonstration, the only justifiable stance is to withhold one's belief until such time as adequate demonstration becomes possible. Of course, such a reading of the *Guide* implies that at best Maimonides questioned the Scripture account of God's creating the world *ex nihilo*.[25]

Like Maimonides, Gersonides was concerned with whether the creation of the world can be said to have occurred *ex nihilo* and at an instant. Unlike Maimonides, however, Gersonides's discussion included a detailed analysis of both time and matter, as well as the theoretical implications of temporality. Having posited that the world was created at an initial instant of time by a freely willing agent, Gersonides worried whether the world was engendered out of absolute nothing or out of a pre-existent matter. His examination, therefore, focused upon the concept of matter underlying creation. In *Wars of the Lord* VI.1.2, Gersonides tried to refute Aristotle's model of an eternally existing uncreated universe by undermining Aristotle's theory of time and motion. Gersonides presented an ambitious account of the finitude of time, one that attempted to refute Aristotle while at the same retain a sense of "initial instant" that remained true to Aristotle. His critique of Aristotle reinforced his own position, namely that God created the world at an initial instant out of a pre-existent material substrate.[26]

Let us turn now to Gersonides's major critic, namely Ḥasdai Crescas who reflected the fourteenth century backlash against Aristotelian natural philosophy. Crescas sought to demolish the Aristotelian natural philosophy for primarily theological reasons. In the process of upholding the basic dogmas of Judaism, Crescas subjected Aristotle's physics and metaphysics to a trenchant critique. His rejection of Aristotle's theories of place and the infinite was part of an extended attempt to weaken Aristotle's hold upon Jewish philosophy. One important implication of Crescas's rejection of Aristotelian theory had to do with his postulating the existence of the vacuum. Aristotle had already introduced the notion of bodies occupying a place, and defined "place" in relation to the bodies it surrounded. According to Crescas, place is prior to bodies: in contradistinction to Aristotle's conception of place, space for Crescas is the "interval between the limits of that which it surrounds."[27] Space is construed by Crescas as an infinite continuum ready to receive matter. Because this place or extension of bodies is identified with space, there is no contradiction in postulating the existence of space not filled with body, i.e. the vacuum.[28]

The implications of Crescas's theory of space are apparent when we turn briefly to his discussion of creation in *Light* III.1. Without entering into the intricacies of this technical discussion, several important points can be made. Crescas took as his point of departure the doctrine of creation *ex nihilo*. He first summarized the arguments Gersonides gave on behalf of his thesis that the world was created out of a pre-existent matter. In direct response to Gersonides, Crescas was adamant that both the matter and form of the universe derive directly from God.[29] In contradistinction to his predecessors, however, creation *ex nihilo* for Crescas occurs independently of temporal constraints. Crescas tried to show that eternal creation is a plausible doctrine even in the context of creation *ex nihilo* by strengthening the notion of divine omnipotence. Inasmuch as God's power is infinite in the sense that God's acts are not temporally limited, God acts under no constraints, and so, when God creates the world, he is able to create something that is infinite in duration, or eternal. In other words, there does exist an initial instant to creation, but that instant is non-temporal and the eternity thesis remains a viable option. Since for Crescas, eternity does not pertain to temporality but to the never-endingness of time, he was able to claim somewhat paradoxically that the world is both eternal and created.[30]

THE NATURE OF MIRACLES

Both the notions of creation as well as the element of divine will carry with them the possibility of miracles.

Miracles represent the overturning of the natural order, and so miracles raise an important philosophical question: whether it is epistemically and ontologically possible to hold that the natural order of things is preserved while at the same time admitting the possibility of exceptions.

Most Jewish philosophers accepted the veracity of miraculous events as providing evidence for God's intervention in the natural order. For example, neither Saadiah Gaon nor Ḥasdai Crescas, among others, questioned the possibility of miracles. Al-Ghazâlî had already offered an occasionalist explanation of miracles, arguing in effect that all events, insofar as they reflect the continuous recreation of the world, are miracles. It is the philosophers, he claimed, that are at a loss to explain causality; rejecting the Aristotelian theory of cause and effect, he replaced it with God's continuous recreation of the world at every instant. Both Saadiah and Crescas were influenced by the occasionalist model. In Saadiah's discussion of miracles in *Beliefs* III.4–5, he defined miracles as a change in the essence of the elements, and all of his examples are taken directly from the Bible. Based on Kalâm occasionalist principles, Saadiah saw no contradiction in God's being able to change any entity's behavior. While he emphasized that under normal conditions the elements do follow universal laws and possess fixed essences, these essences can be changed intentionally by God. In a similar vein, Crescas's return to an occasionalist ontology provided him with an effective way of explaining miraculous events, claiming that once the "intrinsic order of nature" is denied, miracles turn out to be no different ontically than "natural" events. Inasmuch as for Crescas the world is continually recreated by the divine will, every event in the world turns out to be a perpetual miracle.

But Maimonides and Gersonides both struggled to provide an account of miracles that accorded with an Aristotelian view. Part of Maimonides's struggle had to do with whether God can perform miracles at will. Since creation is perfect, no new volition can arise in God leading Him to introduce something new. And so Maimonides suggested in *Guide* II.29 that miracles have already been integrated into nature at the time of creation. To whether God is able to introduce even small changes in nature, such as lengthening a fly's wing, Maimonides suggested that "Aristotle will say that He would not wish it and that it is impossible for Him to will something different from what is; that it would not add to His perfection but would perhaps from a certain point of view be a deficiency."[31]

The best known, and most-quoted discussion of miracles, occurs in the context of explaining the splitting of the Red Sea. Here too Maimonides explained that the splitting of the Red Sea was already written into the natural order, as it were. What we or Scripture are tempted to describe as miraculous turns out to represent the actualization of a nature that was determined at the beginning of creation. There are no actions that are *contrary* to nature, and hence there are no "supernatural" miracles. Another way for Maimonides to naturalize so-called miracles in Scripture was to claim that the events in question occurred in the agent's mind and not in reality. Take for example, Jacob's wrestling with God, or Balaam's ass speaking. In both these cases, Maimonides reminded us that the event in question happened in a vision of prophecy and not in reality, thus undermining the objective status of the event.[32]

Gersonides's approach to miracles was even more radical than that of Maimonides. He first provided a general description of miracles, arguing that a prophet was involved in each of the miracles recorded in Scripture. But who is the immediate agent of these "exceptions" to the natural order? For Gersonides the agent is not God but rather the Active Intellect, which acted as an intermediary between God and human beings. More specifically,

Gersonides argued that God is incapable of performing miracles, on the grounds that God does not know the order of future contingents and so is unable to "implant specific miracles in the order in response to particular historical situations."[33] He thus concluded that miracles are providential acts performed by the Active Intellect; they result from the divine will only in the attenuated sense that God created the world order.

Consider for example Gersonides's interpretation of the miracle recounted in Scripture, where Joshua and his men are worried that there will not be sufficient time to defeat the five Amorite kings in battle, and so Joshua prays to God to extend the day. The text from Joshua 10 reads as follows:

> Joshua addressed the Lord; he said in the presence of the Israelites: "Stand still, oh sun, at Gibeon, Oh moon, in the Valley of Ajalon!" and the sun stood still and the moon halted, while a nation wreaked judgment on its foes...thus the sun halted in mid-heaven, and did not press on to set, for a whole day.
> (Joshua 10.12–13)

This miracle posed a particular problem for rationalists who found it hard to accept such a collapse of celestial order, and who tried to attribute the arrest of the sun to natural or semi-natural causes. For these philosophers, the underlying question became whether the heavenly bodies could have actually stopped in their tracks, implying a complete suspension of the natural order, or might there not be some natural explanation of the phenomenon. In *Guide* 2.35 Maimonides claimed that the event in question was temporary. Focusing on the words "for a whole day" to mean "the longest day that may happen," he suggested that the event should be construed "*as if* it said that the day of Gibeon was for them *as* the longest of the days of the summer that may occur there."[34] Maimonides thus undercut the supernaturalist interpretation of this event, according to which the sun actually stopped in its tracks and the entire celestial order was abrogated (in which case the entire world would have been witness to the event). Rather does he suggest that *perhaps* the "sun stood still" only in the minds of the soldiers, for whom the day "was for them *as* the longest of days." Gersonides provided a similar but even more radical interpretation of this example. In the case of Joshua, Gersonides argued that the miracle in question was that the Israelites defeated their enemies while the sun *seemed* to maintain the same altitude, adding that miracles do not involve the abrogation of natural law. Subsequent philosophers, including Galileo and Spinoza (whom we will visit in Chapter 7), struggled as well with this case study.

CONCLUSION

In this chapter we have examined several issues that pertain to God's relation to the world. We first looked at *a posteriori* arguments for God's existence. Those arguments led to a number of arguments dealing with the issue of creation. Although early biblical and rabbinic works did not contain an ontology of time or place, the theological assumptions and constraints underlying these works reverberated throughout the medieval Jewish literature. Whereas in some cases these theological constraints were challenged, as reflected in the works of Maimonides and Gersonides, in other cases, these constraints were rejected altogether. From Scripture comes the unambiguous statement of a "Beginning." From the rabbis comes an understanding of the nuances inherent in interpreting the first instant of creation. And both Plato and Aristotle introduced further perplexities into the issue of creation.

Much of Maimonides's effort was aimed at showing that the Scriptural view of creation is inconsistent with an Aristotelian theory, but it is not clear whether he ultimately sided with Scripture, Plato or Aristotle. Gersonides was less willing ostensibly to compromise the temporal beginning of the universe, and so he creatively reinterpreted Aristotle's notion of the instant in such a way as to allow for a temporal beginning to creation out of a pre-existent matter. In contradistinction to Maimonides and Gersonides, both of whom adhered fairly closely to Aristotle's characterization of time as the measure of motion, Crescas deviated from this Aristotelian depiction of time. Employing elements which are implicitly embedded in Aristotle, Crescas emphasized the discontinuity of time and motion. Drawing upon Gersonides, Crescas then claimed the universe was both created and yet eternal. Their respective views on creation influenced how they view the possibility of miracles that interrupted the natural order.

Underlying all these issues is the way in which religious language works to describe God. Apophatic or negative theology would have us agree that in an ontology that emphasizes God's unique otherness, it follows that nothing at all can be said of God: human language simply cannot talk about this unique ontological entity. One implication of negative theology is that because humans cannot understand the ways, motives or essence of God, we cannot even begin to understand why God permits innocents to suffer, or error and sin to exist. And yet, the problems of evil and suffering were paramount to our thinkers; in the next chapter we turn to their ways of accounting for human suffering.

NOTES

1 Saadiah 1948, I:2ff.
2 Saadiah 1948, II, exordium.
3 Maimonides 1972a, 1.1, 34a.

4 Maimonides 1972a, 1.1, 34a
5 Maimonides 1963, 1.35, 80.
6 Halevi 1947, I:11, 44.
7 Halevi 1947, I:11, 45.
8 Halevi 1947, I:11, 47.
9 Baḥya 2004, I.4, 79.
10 Baḥya 2004, I.5, 81.
11 Baḥya 2004, I.6, 91.
12 Baḥya 2004, I.6, 93.
13 Maimonides 1963, 2.19, 303.
14 Maimonides 1963, 2.19, 306.
15 In these earlier chapters, Maimonides examined many of the attributes we are tempted to predicate of God, and dismissed them for a variety of reasons. For detailed analysis of these arguments see Rudavsky 2010.
16 Maimonides 1963, 1.58, 134.
17 Maimonides 1963, 1.59, 138.
18 Maimonides 1963, 1.59, 139.
19 Gersonides 1987, III.3, 107.
20 Crescas 2018, *Light* I. III.3, 101.
21 Maimonides 1963, II.13, 281.
22 Maimonides 1963, II.13, 283.
23 Maimonides 1963, II.13, 284.
24 Maimonides 1963, II.13, 284.
25 For further details on this position, see Rudavsky 2010.
26 For further details of Gersonides's elaborate set of arguments, see Rudavsky 2018.
27 Crescas 2018, *Light* I.1.2, 46.
28 For a detailed analysis of Crescas's conception of space, see Wolfson 1929, 38–69.
29 Crescas 2018, *Light* III.1.5, 271
30 Crescas's arguments are contained in Crescas 2018, *Light* III.1.5, 271–274.
31 Maimonides *Guide* II.22:319.
32 Maimonides *Guide* 2.42.
33 We will examine Gersonides's views on divine omniscience in the next chapter.
34 Maimonides *Guide* 2.35:368 emphasis is mine.

FURTHER READING

Davidson, H. A. (1987) *Proofs for Eternity, Creation, and the Existence of God in Medieval Islamic and Jewish Philosophy.* Oxford: Oxford University Press.

Ivry, Alfred (2016), *Maimonides' "Guide of the Perplexed": A Philosophical Guide.* Chicago, IL: University of Chicago Press.

Kraemer, Joel L. (2008), *Maimonides: The Life and World of one of Civilization's Greatest Minds.* New York: Doubleday Press.

Nadler, S. and Rudavsky, T.M. (ed.) (2009). *The Cambridge History of Jewish Philosophy: From Antiquity through the Seventeenth Century.* Cambridge: Cambridge University Press.

Rudavsky, T.M. (2010). *Maimonides.* London: Wiley-Blackwell.

Rudavsky, T.M. (2018). *Jewish Philosophy in the Middle Ages: Science, Rationalism, and Religion.* Oxford: Oxford University Press.

EVIL AND DIVINE OMNISCIENCE
Why Do the Innocent Suffer?

INTRODUCTION

The book of Job, with its narrative of undeserved suffering, provided medieval philosophers with an opportunity to explain God's role in human suffering. Job's story is well-known: Job is a good person who is tested by God (via Satan), undergoes many physical and emotional trials, and does not give up his belief in God. At the end of the book, God appears to Job out of the whirlwind and chastises him, and the work ends with Job's being rewarded by God for his steadfastness. One of the main questions raised by the book of Job is why God would have inflicted suffering upon an innocent individual in the first place: surely a providential Deity would do everything to protect individuals from harm, and would not have been seduced by Satan's bargain. And so medieval commentaries upon Job tended to interpolate theories of providence alongside their theodicy.

SUFFERING, DIVINE PROVIDENCE AND THE BOOK OF JOB

Saadiah Gaon was the first medieval Jewish philosopher to offer an extended commentary on Job.[1] In Book 5.3 of

Beliefs and Opinions, Saadiah provided several reasons for the suffering of the righteous: first, God may be punishing the righteous as "penalties for slight failings," or second, the suffering may consist of "incipient trials with which God tests them, when He knows that they are able to endure them, only in order to compensate them for these trials later on."[2] Furthermore, these tests presumably served to demonstrate to their fellow human beings their worthiness in having been chosen by God for divine favors.

These points are discussed in greater detail in Saadiah's elaborate linguistic and philosophical commentary on Job, *The Book of Theodicy*, which was most likely written before *Beliefs and Opinions*. In the introduction to his commentary, Saadiah noted additional reasons God might permit an innocent person to suffer: for the sake of character-building – "discipline and instruction;" as a mode of "purgation and punishment;" and for the sake of "trial and testing."[3] Saadiah emphasized that it is not our right to question the ways of God: ultimately God's ways are a mystery. According to Saadiah, what's important is that Job was tested by God, bore the test with fortitude, and "was assured eternal bliss in the hereafter and granted far more than he had hoped for in this life."[4] Presumably we should do the same, and we too will be rewarded in an afterlife.

Maimonides, however, rejected Saadiah's interpretation, claiming that it is not ultimately supported by Scripture. In contradistinction to Saadiah, Maimonides provided a more robust theodicy, one in which divine providence, human suffering, and Job's trial formed an interdependent unit. Maimonides's analysis of Job is couched against an elaborate theory of divine providence influenced by Aristotle. Maimonides starts his discussion in *Guide* 3.17 by summarizing five different theories of divine providence reflecting Greek and

Islamic views.[5] In contradistinction to these philosophers, Maimonides described his own position on providence as follows: "Divine providence watches only over the individuals belonging to the human species ... but regarding all the other animals, and all the more, the plants and other things, my opinion is that of Aristotle."[6] Incorporating elements of both Aristotle and the divine law, Maimonides argued that although providence in the sublunar universe extends to all and only human beings, it does not necessarily reflect divine retribution or reward.

Maimonides further distinguished between general providence, which extends equally to all members of the human species as part of the natural order, and individual providence, which is provided to individuals according to their merit.[7] Maimonides explained that on his view, divine providence is directly dependent upon the level of intellectual perfection achieved by an agent: it is not equal for all individuals, but is "graded as their human perfection is graded."[8] When we are no longer communing with God and have withdrawn our epistemic attention from the Deity, providence ceases to protect us: "those who are near to Him are exceedingly well protected ... whereas those who are far from Him are given over to whatever may happen to befall them."[9] On this complex theory of divine providence, those individuals who seek out the Deity are protected from harm; but when their attention is averted away from God, they are open to harm. Maimonides's critics responded by pointing out what must be obvious to us, namely that often-times righteous people do undergo suffering (think for example of suffering of the righteous in the concentration camps). Maimonides responded to this criticism in *Guide* 3.51, suggesting that when righteous individuals do undergo harm and suffering, it is because they have ceased to attend to the Deity at that very moment.

How then does this elaborate theory of providence apply to Job, who to all appearances suffered needlessly? Maimonides provided in *Guide* 3.22–24 a case study of how his theory of divine providence works in the case of somebody like Job. The story of Job is, in Maimonides's words "extraordinary and marvelous," a "parable intended to set forth the opinions of people concerning providence."[10] The most marvelous and strange part of this story according to Maimonides was that Job is described at the beginning of story not as wise, but only as moral and righteous. To mention a theme to which we shall return in Chapter 7, moral virtues such as righteousness turn out to be necessary but not sufficient for human perfection: intellectual virtue is required as well for human perfection. Had Job been wise, or attained intellectual virtue, then "his situation would not have been obscure for him, as will become clear."[11] Job's recantation at the end of the work, "Wherefore I abhor myself, and repent of dust and ashes," (Job 42.6) reflects his newly acquired status that enables him to both understand and endure his situation with equanimity. This two-fold ability – understanding and perseverance – brings about his ultimate salvation and the salvation of his family. What Job has learned is to transcend his suffering, and not let it affect his inner being. Maimonides thus used the story of Job to reinforce this theory of intellectual perfection and providence.

We turn now to Gersonides's discussion of suffering and providence, presented both in Book Four of *Wars* and in his *Commentary on Job*. Gersonides was concerned with two issues: the extent of God's providential activity, and an explanation of the suffering of the righteous. As we have seen, Maimonides argued that individual divine providence extends only to those human beings who have achieved intellectual and moral perfection. Gersonides, however, maintained that God cannot know particulars *qua* particular, and so Maimonides's solution would not work for him. According to Gersonides, God only knows universals, and so God cannot individuate or pick out individuals for providential care.[12]

In his *Commentary on Job*, which complements book four of *Wars*, Gersonides claimed (as did Maimonides) that each of the characters in the book of Job represents a different theory of divine providence. That instances of evil exist is a fact borne out by sense experience, which shows "many righteous people suffering great evils most of their lives and receiving very few benefits ... moreover we observe that some righteous men suffer many evils despite their attempt to avert evils from coming to them, but they are not protected from these evils."[13] How can we account for the suffering of the righteous? In a move similar to that of Maimonides, Gersonides distinguished between "general providence" that is embedded in nature itself, and what he termed "special providence" that pertains to an individual's spiritual perfection: special providence is enjoyed in direct relation to the level of spiritual perfection attained by an individual. Only very few individuals achieve the "kind of unity and conjunction with God" that provides individual providence.[14] Maimonides and Gersonides are thus in agreement that divine providence is dependent upon the spiritual and intellectual perfection achieved by an individual. We return to this theme of human perfection in the next chapter.

THEOLOGICAL COMPATIBILISM: SAADIAH GAON, JUDAH HALEVI AND MAIMONIDES

We have seen that the problem of human suffering is intertwined with theories of providence as well as theories of human choice. For if divine providence entails a modicum of divine causal agency, then we must consider the extent to which human beings can exercise their own free will in light of these divine inclinations. What does it mean to say that a providential God is omniscient, or all-knowing? Does God know all events, past, present and future? And if God knows future events before they have occurred, does God's knowledge affect the ultimate outcome of those events? If it does, how does God's foreknowledge of human events affect human free will? In other words, does divine omniscience preclude human freedom? The rabbis had already faced the theological problem of reconciling human freedom and God's providential care and concern for humans. Rabbi Akiba, for example, is said to have taught that "everything is predestined, nevertheless will (or power) is given."[15] Recognizing that there exists a tension between these two concepts, Akiba however did not try to reconcile them.

Within the history of philosophical theology, two main solutions to the problem of divine foreknowledge have presented themselves: (theological) incompatibilism and (theological) compatibilism.[16] The *incompatibilists* hold that God's foreknowledge of future events is incompatible with the contingency of these events, while the *compatibilists* maintain that human freedom is compatible with God's omniscience. As we shall see below, the majority of Jewish philosophers claimed that God's foreknowledge of future contingent events in no way impedes human choice. One reason for the popularity of compatibilism is that it allows for a theory of moral responsibility. Maimonides for example argued that if human beings have no ability to choose their own actions freely, then "by what right could God punish the wicked or reward the righteous?"[17] If we have no free will, then the doctrine of reward and punishment is rendered useless; moral responsibility is thus dependent upon freedom of choice.

Both Saadiah Gaon and Judah Halevi struggled with the problem of reconciling divine providence with human freedom. They both posited the existence of "possible" or "contingent" actions, allowing for human freedom of choice. Saadiah accepted as a given that God has granted to humans free will: "It accords with the justice of the Creator and his mercy towards man that he should have granted him the power and ability to do what he commanded him to do, and to refrain from what he forbade him to do."[18] But how to reconcile free will with God's commands? Saadiah claimed that both acting and desisting to act count equally as free actions: "In the same way as when a man's doing a thing constitutes an action, so too his desisting from it constitutes an action."[19] Saadiah's point here is that the term "action" in its full sense implies free choice; even in not choosing, humans are exercising their free will.

Halevi followed Saadiah Gaon in emphasizing that "possibility" exists, claiming that "Only a perverse, heretical person would deny the nature of what is possible. If he believed that what will be will inevitably be, he would simply submit, and not equip himself with weapons against his enemy, or with food against his hunger."[20] But the acceptance of possibility is "not incompatible with a belief in Divine Providence."[21] In order to support the compatibility of possibility with divine omniscience, Halevi distinguished between two chains of causation. The first chain represents the immediate expression of the divine will, whereas the second represents an intermediary chain of causal events that exists between God and natural events.[22] According to Halevi, human actions of will belong to the intermediary chain of causality, meaning that they are not *directly* caused by God.

Having established that humans have free will, both Saadiah and Halevi are ready to turn to the further issue of whether God's knowledge interferes with this human freedom. Saadiah was the first Jewish philosopher to crystallize the dilemma of divine omniscience in the following terms:

> Perhaps someone will ask further: "If God knows that which is going to be before it comes into being, he knows already that a certain person will disobey him; and it is not possible that that person not disobey God, in order that God's foreknowledge prove to be correct."[23]

His solution was straightforward, namely that God's knowledge is not causative. "He who makes this assertion has no proof that the knowledge of the Creator concerning things is the cause of their existence."[24] Saadiah's reason for rejecting the efficacy of God's foreknowledge draws upon the relation between knowledge and causes; if God's knowledge were causative, then according to Saadiah "they (future contingents) would have existed from eternity, since God's knowledge of them is eternal."[25] In a similar vein, Halevi echoed Saadiah's claim, arguing that "the knowledge of a thing is not the cause of its coming into existence."[26] For example, my knowing that the sun will rise tomorrow does not *cause* the rising of the sun; so too, God's knowledge of my future actions does not *cause*, or bring about, those actions. Having established to his satisfaction that human freedom exists, Halevi concludes by stating that "Man finds in himself this power of doing evil or avoiding it in matters which are possible for him."[27]

Compatibilism received its fullest expression by Maimonides. In *Guide* 3.17, Maimonides stated that humans have an "absolute capacity" to act, meaning that they have the choice to do "everything that it is within the capacity of man to do." Like his predecessors Saadiah and Halevi, Maimonides was quick to point out that God's knowledge does not bring about the necessary occurrence of the entity in question: the possible remains possible.

> His knowledge, may he be exalted, that a certain possible thing will come into existence, does not in any way make that possible thing quit the nature of the possible. On the contrary, the nature of the possible remains with it; and knowledge concerning what possible things will be produced, does not entail one of the two possibilities becoming necessary ... His knowledge concerning what will happen does not make this possible thing quit its nature.[28]

In other words, given two unactualized states of affairs, God's knowledge that one of them will become actualized does not affect its possibly not occurring. Hence, like Saadiah and Halevi (and many Christian Scholastic thinkers) Maimonides asserted without argument that God's knowledge of future possibles does not change their nature. By emphasizing the total otherness of the Deity, the incomprehensibility of the divine attributes, and the inability of humans to understand God's knowledge, Maimonides attempted, like Saadiah and Halevi, to reconcile the fact that on the one hand God has ordered our lives, and on the other hand human freedom is a prerequisite for moral and religious accountability.

THEOLOGICAL INCOMPATIBILISM: ABRAHAM IBN DAUD AND GERSONIDES

As noted above, the incompatibilists argued that divine omniscience and human freedom were incompatible: either God does not know the future and is not omniscient, or humans do not have free will. Abraham Ibn Daud and Gersonides were the only Jewish thinkers to rethink limits to God's omniscience. Ibn Daud dedicated his entire philosophical work *'Emunah Ramah* as a response to the problem of free will and omniscience. As he stated in his preface, "(Someone) had asked the author,

Are the actions of man necessary or does he have choice over them? To answer this question the author stated [this treatise] in one Abstract and three books."[29] Ibn Daud answered this quandary with a hitherto unique position, namely that God's omniscience does not extend to future contingents. In Book II.2, ibn Daud pushed for what he called genuine possibility. Distinguishing between two types of possibility, epistemological and genuine, he claimed that only the first, epistemological possibility, leads to ignorance of future events. Ibn Daud adduced the following example: We might wonder whether the king of Babylonia died today or is alive; his being alive (or dead) is a possibility "because we, the men of Spain, do not know this (state of affairs). Rather, both alternatives are equal to us … But since (this) matter in itself is not possible, of necessity one of the alternatives is correct, and God, may he be exalted, knows in (cases) like this that one of the alternatives is necessary as it is in itself."[30] In other words, such cases are termed *possible* in an attenuated sense because human beings do not have sufficient knowledge of the matter at hand.

Ibn Daud then distinguished a second type of possibility; this genuine ontological possibility is one that God himself has created *qua* possible: God "created it as a thing that can bear one or the other of two contrary attributes."[31] Genuine possibility applies to future contingent events, which by their very nature can either happen or not happen. The most God knows is that such a thing or event is possible; even God, however, does not know which of the two possibilities will be actualized. Take for an example a future sea-fight battle (an actual example used by Aristotle in his discussion of future contingents): such a battle may take place tomorrow or it may not, and not even God knows whether it will happen until the future is rendered present. The most God knows is that a sea-fight battle may or may not happen tomorrow. To the "sophist" who argues that this imputes ignorance to God, ibn Daud replies that "this is not ignorance" because technically speaking, there is nothing determinate to be known. Not to know *what is not* does not constitute a deficiency in God's omniscience. And so ibn Daud felt that he has safeguarded future contingency without limiting God's power to know all that is unknowable.

Gersonides fleshed out ibn Daud's position even more radically in *Wars of the Lord*. Since only humans have free will, to ask whether God knows future contingent events is tantamount to asking whether God has foreknowledge of the free actions of humans. Gersonides rejected the theories of his compatibilist predecessors in favor of an incompatibilist position: he argued that God knows *that* certain states of affairs may or may not be actualized. But insofar as they are truly contingent states, he does not know *which* of the two alternatives will in fact be actualized. For if God did know future contingents prior to their actualization, there could be no contingency in the world.[32] Echoing ibn Daud, Gersonides claimed that God's inability to foreknow future contingents is not a defect in God's knowledge:

> The fact that God does not have the knowledge of which possible outcome will be realized does not imply any defect in God. For perfect knowledge of something is the knowledge of what that thing is in reality; when the thing is not apprehended as it is, this is error, not knowledge.[33]

In this fashion, Gersonides concluded, the problem of divine omniscience is resolved. With respect to future contingents, God knows their ordered nature or essence, and God knows *that* they are contingent, but even God does not know which alternative will become actualized until it occurs.[34]

THE DETERMINIST RESPONSE: CRESCAS ON DIVINE KNOWLEDGE

We have now examined both compatibilism and incompatibilist responses to the question of the extent of God's omniscience. In response to these positions, Ḥasdai Crescas returned to a modified determinist view according to which, although human actions, including future acts, are determined by God's knowledge, these actions are not absolutely necessitated. Crescas's stated goal in *Light of the Lord* was to examine philosophical arguments that threatened the following three principles that are necessitated by tradition: "that God's knowledge encompasses the infinite;"[35] "that God's knowledge extends to the non-existent;"[36] and "that God has knowledge concerning possible alternatives without their nature as possible being changed."[37]

Crescas felt that the latter two principles were being threatened by his near predecessor Gersonides. He thus spent much of his work refuting Gersonides's claim that God knows particulars only through their general order. Crescas argued that events known by God, although "possible in themselves," nevertheless are necessary with respect to their causal history. Using the analogy that a person's knowledge does not change the nature of the possibility of the thing known, Crescas argued that so too God's knowledge does not change the nature of the possibility in question. "God's knowledge of which of two possible alternatives will be realized does not change the nature of the possible."[38] In other words, an event may be possible "in its nature" but known definitively by God.

How does this position apply to human choice? In book II, principle 5, chapter 1 of *Light*, Crescas argued that the possible exists in some respects and in other respects not. The possible exists "only in regard to itself." In other words, when regarded from the perspective of the overall causal nexus of the chain of events, the event is not truly possible. What this means is that from the perspective of its causal history, every event is necessary. Only in light of human epistemological weakness (viz. our inability to know and understand this causal history) can an event be said to be possible. Crescas goes on to suggest that what is necessary before its existence is not possible. In other words, if God knows that I will perform a particular action at a future time, then my doing that action is determined from the perspective of God's knowledge. Even though from my own perspective, I may still (think I can) do the opposite, from God's perspective it is not possible for me to perform the opposite action. Hence from "the perspective of God's knowledge" I am not free with respect to my performance of my future actions. Crescas's determinist position was an outlier in subsequent Jewish thought, and criticized by his own student (see below).

CONCLUSION

We have seen that Jewish philosophers grappled with a number of problems loosely surrounding the existence of evil, suffering and human freedom. We started with philosophical responses to the book of Job, in which the challenge of human suffering was laid out. To what extent is God responsible for human actions? And if God is ultimate cause of human action, can we be held responsible for our actions? More generally, how do we explain the existence of evil and human suffering? Both Saadiah Gaon and Judah Halevi laid the groundwork for Maimonides's compatibilism. Maimonides upheld God's omniscience in the face of numerous objections. On the other hand, ibn Daud and Gersonides disagreed with the thesis that God can know future contingents without this knowledge affecting the contingency of the objects known. Arguing that divine foreknowledge coupled with infallibility precluded the contingency of the objects of God's knowledge, they denied that God had knowledge of future contingents.

Hasdai Crescas attempted to salvage what remained of divine omniscience by arguing that God knows in a timeless fashion those events which occur necessarily with respect to their causes, but which appear to be possible to one not familiar with the causes in question. Crescas's own student Joseph Albo criticized his teacher's theory of free will. Summarizing Crescas's position, Albo's reaction was that it is "very close to the view that all things are determined and that the possible does not exist. For since the things are necessary considered in relation to their causes, if God knows the causes, they are actually necessary."[39] Albo's point, which is in agreement with ibn Daud and Gersonides, is that on Crescas's theory, future events cannot come into existence in any other way than in fact they *do* come into existence: "there is no thing that may equally be or not be when considered in relation to its causes."[40] And so the problem of divine omniscience remained, in his mind, as possibly in our own minds, as unresolved.

NOTES

1 See Saadiah 1988 and Saadiah 1948.
2 Saadiah 1948, 213.
3 Saadiah 1988, 125–126.
4 Saadiah 1988, 127.
5 Pines notes that in his delineation of the five theories, Maimonides is very much influenced by the treatise *On Providence* (*De Fato*) by Alexander of Aphrodisias, who is mentioned by name in *Guide* 3.16.
6 Maimonides 1963, 17, 471. Aristotle's position was that providence was general, not individual.

7. See Nadler 2009 for a philosophically astute discussion of Maimonides's theory.
8. Maimonides 1963, 3.18, 475.
9. Maimonides 1963, 3.18, 476.
10. Maimonides 1963, 3.22, 486.
11. Maimonides 1963, 3.22, 487.
12. See Rudavsky 2018 for discussion of Gersonides's novel position on divine omniscience. See also below.
13. Gersonides 1987, 4.3, 171.
14. Gersonides 1987, 4.4, 175.
15. *Avot*, 3.19. For a sustained discussion of Akiba's dictum and its influence upon the rabbis, see Urbach 1975, 255–285.
16. It should be noted that to this very day, philosophers and theologians generally fall into these two camps.
17. Maimonides 1962, 5.4, 87a.
18. Saadiah Gaon in Altmann 2007, 119. Altmann's translation in 2007 is more accurate than that found in Saadiah Gaon 1948, and hence I am using it here.
19. Saadiah Gaon in Altmann 2007, 119.
20. Halevi 1947, 5.20, 315.
21. Halevi 1947, 5.20, 315. It should be noted that Halevi is using providence as a term encompassing divine omniscience.
22. Halevi 1947, 5.20, 316.
23. Saadiah Gaon in Altmann 2007, 122.
24. Saadiah Gaon in Altmann 2007, 122.
25. Saadiah Gaon in Altmann 2007, 122.
26. Halevi 1947, 5.20, 319.
27. Halevi 1947, 5.20, 326.
28. Maimonides 1963, 3.20, 482.
29. Abraham ibn Daud 1986.
30. Abraham ibn Daud 1986.
31. Abraham ibn Daud 1986, 2.6, 96.
32. Gersonides 1987, 3.4. 116.
33. Gersonides 1987, 3.4, 118.
34. Gersonides's position is strikingly similar to that of William of Ockham, writing during the same time period in Avignon France. See Rudavsky 2018 for further discussion.
35. Crescas 2018, *Light* 2.1.1, 121.

36 Crescas 2018, *Light* 2.1.1, 121.
37 Crescas 2018, *Light* 2.1.1, 121.
38 Crescas 2018, *Light* 2.1.4, 137.
39 Albo 1946, 4.1, 7.
40 Albo 1946, 4.1, 8.

FURTHER READING

Jospe, R. (2009). *Jewish Philosophy in the Middle Ages*. Boston, MA: Academic Studies Press.

Nadler, S. (2009). "Theodicy and Providence," in S. Nadler and T.M. Rudavsky (eds), *The Cambridge History of Jewish Philosophy: From Antiquity through the Seventeenth Century*. Cambridge: Cambridge University Press, 619–658.

Rudavsky, T.M. (2018). *Jewish Philosophy in the Middle Ages: Science, Rationalism, and Religion*. Oxford: Oxford University Press.

Saadiah Gaon. (1988). *The Book of Theodicy: Translation and Commentary on the Book of Job*, trans. L. Goodman. New Haven, CT: Yale University Press.

PRACTICAL MORALITY
Living a Good Life

INTRODUCTION

While earlier chapters addressed issues of cosmology, ontology and natural science, we turned in Chapter 5 to the issue of human suffering and divine providence. One topic we have not yet broached is that of practical morality. In constructing a theory of practical morality, Jewish philosophers incorporated material from Greek philosophy, from the rabbis, and from their philosophical contemporaries. Both Aristotelian and Neoplatonic systems of morality influenced their conception of virtue and happiness. The formative passages from Aristotle's *Nicomachean Ethics* promoted a view of psychic happiness (or *eudaimonia*) as a human flourishing or psychic well-being. All human beings desire to be happy, Aristotle told us, but we tend to confuse what we desire materially with what truly leads to happiness. Rather, the ultimate life of virtue is one that fulfills our function or *telos* as rational animals; *eudaimonia* thus results from living in accordance with reason.

Aristotle argued that human happiness is predicated on the capacity to reason and is defined as life in accordance with the rational principle. But scholars have noted a deep tension in Aristotle's works regarding the actualization of human happiness. On the one hand, Aristotle argued that happiness is actualized through moral action, and the happiest person is one who lives a fulfilled life in the moral and political sphere. On the other hand, in the final book of *Nicomachean Ethics* (10.7–8), Aristotle presented theoretical wisdom as the final end or *telos* of human life, claiming that the truly happy person lives a life of solitary contemplation and intellectual perfection, removed from the masses of humanity. Theoretical wisdom, Aristotle argued in this final book of *Nicomachean Ethics*, is superior to all other activities since it perfects the most noble part of us, is self-sufficient, is done for its own sake, over a long period of time, and is the one activity that makes us most godlike.[1] These two ways of life appear to be incompatible: the contemplative life attaches less importance to the moral, and the morally virtuous individual places much less importance on theoretical contemplation.

Jewish philosophers were very much influenced by Aristotle's conception of human perfection and struggled to reconcile the tensions in Aristotle's work. But if, as Maimonides and Gersonides have argued, most individuals are psycho-physically incapable of embarking on such a rigorous and philosophical course of study, does it follow that not all humans can achieve intellectual perfection: is the road the same, and open, to all? And what status do moral and social development play in the quest for felicity? Is there ultimately only one road to achieve ultimate felicity?

Another set of issues pertains to the type of character training requisite to achieve ethical perfection. Both Aristotle and the early rabbis emphasized the importance of character development in the acquisition of a moral compass. Aristotle emphasized the role played by habit, a habitual repetition of morally conducing actions, while the book of Proverbs described the development of character formation as part of moral education. But in Jewish texts, moral behavior was often subsumed under the domain of divine law or *halakha*. The very notion of Jewish ethics can only be understood within the context of the Mosaic commandments. The incorporation of moral ethical commandments into the wider context of divine command raises yet another important question: can there be ethical dictates independent of the commandments? The rabbis already worried whether there might exist a domain of 'right behavior' that exists independently of divine commandment. More specifically, rabbis disagreed over whether *halakhah* is all-inclusive, or whether there exists an independent moral standard to which even *halakhah* (and the giver of *halakhah*, namely God) is beholden. Another way of stating this question is whether there is room for independent natural law in a theology ultimately dependent upon divine command? Generations of Jewish philosophers, both medieval and modern, have struggled with these issues.

In this chapter, we explore the topic of practical morality, starting with specific moral codes developed by ibn Gabirol, Baḥya ibn Paquda, Maimonides and Crescas. We then turn to the question of whether we can locate a moral or ethical theory in medieval Jewish philosophy independent of *halakhah*. We will focus primarily upon the status of law and ethical theory in the works of Moses Maimonides, although discussions of Saadiah Gaon, Baḥya ibn Paquda and Joseph Albo will emerge as well. This focus upon law introduces the role of the prophet, who for many of our thinkers represents the ideal paradigm, as it were, of human perfection. For not only does the prophet act as a conduit or link between God and human beings, but the prophet represents the culmination of both intellectual and practical virtues. Moses is of course the "prophet of prophets" and best personifies the paradigm of moral and intellectual perfection. But not all our thinkers agreed on the necessary and sufficient conditions required to achieve prophecy. These questions return us full circle to the ultimate purpose of existence.

LIVING A MORAL LIFE

Jewish philosophers incorporated both *halakhah* and Aristotle's moral theory into their discussions of human conduct. The practical syllogism, the doctrine of the mean, and Aristotle's intellectualism all played an important role in defining the domain of practical reason. We have introduced in earlier chapters Aristotle's emphasis upon logical argument and demonstration. But in addition to strict logical or rational syllogisms, Aristotle introduced into his ethical works practical syllogisms that differed from more rational arguments both in their premises and conclusions. Aristotle's point was that ethical or practical reasoning differs from strict logical reasoning, and hence a different mode of syllogism is required. Aristotle's virtue morality is couched in terms of his well-known doctrine of the mean, which represents an intermediate between excess and defect.[2] According to Aristotle, moral virtue must aim at the mean between extremes: to feel fear, confidence, appetite, anger, pity and the like "at the right times, with reference to the right objects, towards the right people, with the right motive, and in the right way, is what is both intermediate and best, and this is characteristic of virtue."[3] And, as noted above, Aristotle's intellectualism infused his discussion of the goal or *telos* of human existence.

Elements of Aristotle's ethical theory appeared throughout medieval Jewish texts, as apparent in the works of ibn Gabirol, Bahya, and Maimonides. Let us take as an example ibn Gabirol's major contribution to ethical literature *Tiqqun Middot ha-Nefesh* (*On the Improvement of the Moral Qualities*) written in 1045.

In this work ibn Gabirol developed a system of ethics dependent upon rational argument. Although many of his ideas are supported by Biblical references, he also included quotations from Greek philosophers and Arab poets. Ibn Gabirol introduced an original element into his work, namely the connection between the moral and physiological makeup of the human. For example, ibn Gabirol described the qualities and defects of the soul in the context of the Aristotelian mean. His discussion of the qualities of the soul – pride/humility, modesty/impudence, love/hate, mercy/cruelty, anger/favoritism, joy/grief and generosity/parsimony – were all unpacked against the backdrop of Aristotle's exhortation to avoid excess (and defect) and aim toward a mean.

Baḥya ibn Paquda's ethical system was more ambitious than that of ibn Gabirol and represented one of the first attempts to organize Judaic ethical laws and duties into a coherent philosophical system. Baḥya explained that his motivation for compiling his work *Duties of the Heart* derived from his impression that many Jews either paid little attention to the duties of Jewish law, or paid exclusive attention to duties performed by the body to the detriment of spiritual perfection. Baḥya was underwhelmed by the supposed evidence that people were obeying and cultivating duties of the heart (or internal intentions). Reflecting both Aristotelian and Neoplatonic emphasis upon intellectual perfection, Baḥya argued that ultimate human happiness is dependent upon intellectual excellence. Well-being of the soul depends upon possessing an accurate knowledge of the structure of the world.

In *Duties of the Heart,* Baḥya distinguished between two types of duties: duties of the heart and external duties. The former are purely rational and intellectual, while the latter are practical. The two types of duties are linked. External duties such as moving one's limbs or helping one's neighbor, for example, are impossible without appropriate internal duties – consent of the mind in the former instance, and love or respect of one's neighbor in the second. In the introduction, Baḥya characterized the "inner duties of the heart" as connected to inward intentionality and expressed surprise that nobody had written about these inner duties, which he found to be the "basis of all the commandments! If they were to be undermined, there would be no point to any of the duties of the limbs."[4] The ultimate purpose of these inner duties is what Baḥya termed "whole-heartedness," and is reached when human beings achieve complete accord of both mind and body. When our outer and inner selves are in conflict, when our actions are not matched by our intentions, "if the actions of our limbs are at odds with the convictions of our hearts," we cannot worship God whole-heartedly.[5] Baḥya presented a list of twenty moral qualities, grouped into contrary pairs: (1) joy and grief; (2) fear and hope; (3) courage and timidity; (4) shame and brazenness; (5) anger and contentment; (6) mercy and ruthlessness; (7) pride and humility; (8) love and hate; (9) generosity and parsimony; and (10) diligence and idleness.[6] He claimed to have recorded the qualities as they occurred to him, and in no particular order. Each of the pairs is discussed in brief. Subsequent sections amplifed these qualities in the context of the duties of the heart, and provide a way of achieving closeness to the Deity. Baḥya's innovation was that inner spirituality, or what we would call intentionality, took on greater importance than external behavior. To this day, readers of Baḥya's work emphasize the importance of intention (or *kavvanah*) in ethical and religious behavior.

We turn now to Maimonides who wrote several works devoted to moral theory. In a selection entitled *Eight Chapters*, Maimonides examined various character traits, reserving the terms virtuous and vicious for character traits rather than for actions. Maimonides emphasized the propadeutic or positive nature of moral virtues: "the improvements of moral habits is the same as the cure of the soul and its powers."[7] Reflecting Aristotle, Maimonides distinguished two types of virtue: rational and moral. Rational virtues include wisdom and intelligence,[8] while moral virtues include a number of characteristics like moderation, liberality, justice, gentleness, humility, contentment, and courage. This separation between intellectual and moral virtues raises a concern however about the epistemological status of ethical knowledge.[9] In the *Guide* Maimonides will emphasize that only intellectual knowledge can lead to rational virtue, while imagination represents a lesser faculty of the soul and leads to social perfection.

The very title of a second work – *Character Traits* (*Hilkhot Deot*) – reinforces the importance of developing a proper character. Inculcation of moral virtues requires habitual repetition of "right actions." According to Maimonides:

> A man shall habituate himself in these character traits until they are firmly established in him. Time after time, he shall perform actions in accordance with the character traits that are in the mean. He shall repeat them continually until performing them is easy for him and they are not burdensome and these character traits are firmly established in his soul.[10]

Just as daily piano practice, for example, improves overall piano virtuosity (we can only hope), so too does daily repetition of virtues improve ones overall moral character.

We come now to the heart of Maimonides's discussion of moral virtue, which incorporates Aristotle's doctrine of the mean. In chapter 4 of *Eight Chapters* Maimonides expressed the doctrine of the mean as follows: "good actions are those balanced in the mean between two extremes, both of which are bad: one of them is an excess and the other a deficiency."[11] Maimonides then provided a number of examples: moderation is the mean between lust and insensibility; liberality is the mean between miserliness and extravagance; humility is the mean between haughtiness and abasement; generosity is the mean between prodigality and stinginess. Once again repetition of these virtues over time results in our "becoming accustomed to them."[12]

But is it possible to reconcile Maimonides's theory with the many actions in Jewish law that do not reflect the mean? How do we account, for example, for adherence to the dietary laws, many of which cannot be accounted for in his doctrine of the mean? Imagine someone arguing that between the extremes of never adhering to the law of avoiding shellfish, and always eating shellfish, the mean lies in occasional indulgence in eating shellfish. In a similar vein, how can we understand Maimonides's characterization of the ḥasid or saint, whose extreme ascetic behavior reflects an apparent repudiation of the mean? Aristotle had already acknowledged these sorts of outliers, and argued that certain cases (theft, murder) lay outside the doctrine of mean; in these sorts of cases, the action is always wrong. Recognizing these difficulties, Maimonides provided an exception in the cases of humility and anger, encouraging the saintly individual (ḥasid) to practice utter meekness so as to leave not even a trace of pride in their soul. But even here, Maimonides's treatment of the saint appears to deviate markedly from Aristotle who in *Nicomachean Ethics* presented both proper pride and appropriate anger as virtues to be achieved.

PROPHECY AND HUMAN PERFECTION

Is the best way to live a spiritually fulfilling life that leads to ultimate happiness or felicity? Medieval Jewish philosophers provided readers with a moral paradigm, namely the prophet. The prophet was not only the one responsible for communicating the law to the Jewish people, but he was the individual who best exemplified the pinnacle of spiritual and intellectual perfection available to humans.[13] In the Hebrew Bible, prophecy was presented as a major source of communication from God to the people Israel, the prophet (*navi*) functioning as the bearer of information. Think, for example, of Isaiah's admonitions to Israel, or Ezekiel's prophetic visions. Often the prophet functioned as a moral and civic leader as well, presented as a model for human behavior and striving.

Elements of the biblical account, combined with philosophical ingredients drawn from Plato and Aristotle, were reflected in the medieval texts of Islamic and Jewish philosophers. Plato's description of the philosopher/king in the *Republic* was readily identified by Jews and Moslems as the prophet-lawgiver of the Abrahamic tradition. Saadiah Gaon argued that while the visions seen by the prophet are not directly from God, but rather from a special created entity called the "created Glory" or "Shekhinah," the prophet resided in close proximity to the Deity. He was the first to draw the explicit connection between Plato's philosopher-king and the perfect individual. In the *Kuzari*, Judah Halevi viewed the prophet as exemplifying the consummate perfection of a human being, resulting ultimately in conjunction with the Active Intellect and God.

In addition to the role played by Active Intellect, philosophers worried about the role of the imagination in knowledge acquisition. The process of knowledge acquisition begins with the senses, passes through the imagination, and as a result of interaction of the possible intellect with the Active Intellect, becomes intellectual. The role of the imagination in perception was depicted already by Aristotle in his *De Anima* III.3.429a. According to Aristotle, imagination cannot be a sense, but neither does it fit the general role of a faculty. Imagination is the result of a movement from sensation. Take for example the color red. At some time or other I have seen the color red. This original experience carries with it a sensation. At a later time, I recreate for myself the color red; this second movement results from my imagination. This movement of the imagination serves as a source of error in human knowing. On this account, imagination is like a sense, but not actually a sense; it is a derived movement from sense.

This ambiguity on Aristotle's account allowed for great leeway among his medieval commentators. Islamic philosophers offered for the most part a naturalistic explanation of prophecy. They presented prophets as scientist-philosophers, well versed in the details of the natural universe. Avicenna for example held that the imagination not only receives movement from the senses, but in its most perfect state also receives movement from the intellect. Building upon Aristotle, Al-Fârâbî's emphasis upon the importance of intellectual, rational reflection added a new dimension to the Scriptural view of prophecy, supplementing the supernatural view with a more naturalized conception. In al-Fârâbî's system, the prophet was presented as a combination of Imâm (priest) and philosopher-king, one who combined his religious and philosophical wisdom to rule the virtuous state.

Maimonides as well contended that prophecy ranks as the highest human perfection. In an extended analogy in the introduction to the *Guide*, Maimonides compared prophetic parables to "apples of gold in settings of silver," suggesting that the prophet communicated on many levels to different people, and that the gold nuggets of prophetic wisdom are often hidden amongst the external silver filigree. The exoteric meaning of prophetic statements contains wisdom useful to the masses, whereas their internal meaning "contains wisdom that is useful for beliefs concerned with the truth as it is."[14] Prophecy on this model represents a form of intellectual illumination, one not achievable by the mass of humanity. Only the rare individual is privy to the truths contained in prophecy. In *Guide* 2.36, Maimonides offered a technical and philosophical account of prophecy that reflected Aristotelian influences. He defined prophecy as follows: "the true reality and quiddity of prophecy consists in its being an overflow from God ... through the intermediation of the Active Intellect, toward the rational faculty in the first place and thereafter toward the imaginative faculty. This is the highest degree of man and the ultimate term of perfection that can exist for his species; and this state is the ultimate term of perfection for the imaginative species."[15] This passage emphasizes the point that prophecy originates with God, and passes through the various intellectual levels to the prophet. The importance of the rational faculty of the prophet cannot be overstated.

Maimonides argued further that the physical and intellectual constitution of the prophet must be perfect: "the perfection of the bodily faculties ... is consequent upon the best possible temperament, the best possible size, and the purest possible matter, of the part of the body that is the substratum for the faculty in question."[16] In a description that hearkened back to Aristotle's emphasis upon intellectual perfection, Maimonides argued that only such a perfectly constituted individual can attain to intellectual, imaginative and moral perfection, by dissociating oneself from all "bestial things," and by controlling emotion or passion.[17] The prophet thus represents the ideal knower, one who combines the best of both rational and imaginative knowledge. It is important to note that Maimonides veered away from the Islamic Aristotelians on two counts: first, he claimed that the prophet will not prophesy unless God wills it; and second, Maimonides recognized the status of Moses as representative of a unique type of prophecy. Only

Moses's prophecy resulted in a legislation that, according to Maimonides, remains non-abrogated.[18] On this picture, the prophet epitomized an ascetic lifestyle; eschewing all corporeal pleasures, the prophet lives in solitude and avoids human interaction.

But it's important to note other passages in the *Guide* that emphasize the social obligations of the prophet/philosopher-king. Consider Plato's famous analogy of the cave toward the end of the *Republic*: in this enormously influential analogy, Plato described the philosopher leaving the cave of ignorance and deception in search of knowledge, but then returning out of obligation to the cave to educate those who have remained imprisoned in their ignorance of true reality.[19] So too, several passages in Maimonides's *Guide* reflect the tension between on the one hand pursuing personal intellectual perfection, and on the other hand fulfilling ones moral obligations to society. In *Guide* 2.33, for example, Moses ascended the mountain to achieve union with God, but then descended the mountain, returning to fulfill his role as a moral and political leader. Subsequent philosophers have continued to struggle with the extent to which they have obligations toward society.

Like Maimonides, Gersonides repeatedly emphasized the superiority of intellect in the attainment of ultimate felicity, but this intellectual knowledge was rooted in what we would call natural science. In the *Wars of the Lord*, Gersonides's analysis of prophetic statements occured against the backdrop of his astrological determinism. More specifically, the information transmitted by the prophet is of a general nature and does not pertain to the individual *qua* particular. The active intellect serves as the repository for information communicated by the heavenly bodies. As a result of this movement, the imaginative faculty receives the "pattern inherent in the intellects of the heavenly bodies from the influence deriving from them."[20] Because as the heavenly bodies do not jointly cooperate with one another in this process, it is possible for the communication to be misconstrued. And of equal importance, the events may be circumvented: "our intellect and choice ... have the power to move us contrary to that which is determined by the heavenly bodies."[21] In other words, human choice guided by reason can subvert astral patterns, and so contingency is retained.

In contradistinction to the radical Aristotelian intellectualism (dare we say elitism?) reflected by both Maimonides and Gersonides, Crescas emphasized a non-intellectual form of felicity, focusing on the love and fear of God. Arguing that the ultimate end of human existence requires perfections of both the body and mind, Crescas disagreed with both Maimonides and Gersonides. He rejected the Aristotelian/Maimonidean/Gersonidean claim that the ultimate human goal is rooted in intellectual perfection. Such opinions, he argued, "destroy the principles of the Torah and the tradition," by denying theories of reward and punishment, rejecting the importance of the commandments, and denying theories of resurrection.[22] Citing passages from traditional Jewish sources, Crescas concluded that the doctrine of intellect (in both its Maimonidean and Gersonidean permutations) was untenable: their followers "were seduced and followed them, and they did not seem to sense, nor did it occur to them that in this way they were destroying the wall of the edifice that is Torah and breaching its enclosures even though the position itself is groundless!"[23]

After rejecting the intellectualist picture, Crescas then presented an alternative understanding of ultimate felicity based on observance of the law and commandments. Crescas denied that God is pure intellect, and replaced the intellectual depiction of God with one rooted in passion, will, joy and love. In contradistinction to Maimonides and especially Gersonides, Crescas emphasized that joy and love are essential to God, describing God not as at active *knower*, but as the active *lover*: "God's love expresses God's essence, goodness and benevolence ... God's love not only sustains the world, it also funtions as the perfection of natural things."[24] The eternal happiness of the soul, he avered, is not dependent upon holding the right opinions or upon actions, but rather the eternal happiness of soul is consequent upon the love and fear of God. It is "love for God ... that leads to the eternal life of the individual soul ... reflected not in the contemplation of intelligibles but in the actual performance of the commandments."[25] Seeing God as a "lover" reinforced the importance of the very act of loving for human beings. Crescas then concluded that love and fear of God are the ultimate aim of human existence, and so from this perspective, philosophers and the multitude stand on the same level: diligence in the satisfaction of the commandments, and not intellectual perfection, is what matters for ultimate felicity.

HUMAN FELICITY: INTELLECTUAL VERSUS MORAL PERFECTION

So far we have emphasized the tension between intellectual perfection on the one hand, and a more faith-based belief system on the other hand. Maimonides and Gersonides both claimed that metaphysical knowledge alone leads to human perfection as epitomized by the prophet, whereas Crescas disagreed, emphasizing a more spiritual perfection based on the commandments. But is it even possible for a human intellect, which itself is rooted in matter, to achieve knowledge of the active intellect? And how is knowledge of the active intellect correlated to knowledge of God? Furthermore, inasmuch as the rabbinic sages did not regard ultimate felicity as dependent upon intellectual perfection, how do our philosophers's views accord with those of the rabbis? What role, for example, does Torah study play in achieving ultimate human perfection?

Maimonides attempted to address some of these questions at the very end of the *Guide* in a famous parable: human beings are seen circling a palace endlessly, and only a few chosen are entitled to enter the palace and commune with the king. Intellectual perfection is the only way to reach God, who is represented by the king; those lacking in intellectual perfection (the masses of humanity) never even manage to enter the gates of the palace, let alone achieve an audience with the king. Maimonides described the intellectual contemplation of God as a form of meditative stance. This parable reinforced the view that very few individuals can actualize a purely intellectual self, one that has transcended a material existence.[26] On the one hand, it is the study of nature as a whole (the facts of the matter) that yields knowledge of the divine. On the other hand, Maimonides has argued (as we saw in Chapter 4) that there are limits to what we can know demonstratively about God. The truest dimension of prayer consists in inner and outer silence, a silence that reflects the profound epistemological limits of human beings.

The intellection dimension is reinforced in an additional passage in which Maimonides extolled the intellectual life as one of "solitude and isolation" and suggested that the truly excellent person avoids human interaction and "does not meet anyone unless it is necessary."[27] We find a similar ambivalence in Maimonides's description of the four ways of achieving perfection. Material perfection comprises possession of material goods; bodily perfection comprises bodily health and strength; moral perfection comprises moral virtue and action; and rational or theoretical perfection consists in contemplation of divine matters. Following Aristotle and and philosopher ibn Bâjja, Maimonides regarded these four perfections as arranged hierarchically, from lowest (material) to highest (theoretical).

Maimonides used a quotation from Jeremiah (9.22–23) to support his defense of the intellectual virtues as the most perfect of the four, claiming that the commandments do not compare with intellectual perfection: "all the actions prescribed by the Law – I refer to the various species of worship and also the moral habits that are useful to all people in their mutual dealings – that all this is not to be compared with this ultimate end, and does not equal it, being but preparations made for the sake of this end."[28] In this remarkable passage, Maimonides seemed to be suggesting that the commandments only served an instrumental purpose, enabling people to interact in society. *Guide* 3.54 reinforces the suggestion that moral habits serve no deontological purpose in and of themselves; one who has achieved intellectual perfection, and surpassed corporeality, has transcended the need for the commandments,

Maimonides then adds what some scholars have described as a fifth perfection, which emphasizes the importance of imitating God's actions (*imitatio Dei*): that we should glory in the apprehension of God's attributes and actions, namely loving-kindness, judgment and righteousness.[29] Does this fifth perfection reintroduce a practical component into the highest form of human existence, or does it represent a by-product of the fourth perfection, consisting in the pleasure one experiences as a result of contemplation? Each of these positions reflects a plausible interpretation of Maimonides's text. Perhaps the most we can say is that there exists in Maimonides a tension between two world views: the Platonic model in which the intellectual ultimately fulfills his political obligations and returns to the community; and the model offered by ibn Bâjja and other Aristotelians who emphasized the intellectual perfection requisite for ultimate felicity.

We have seen that Gersonides agreed with Maimonides's privileging the intellectual aspect of human perfection which is impossible without attaining sufficient knowledge of the natural world. Nowhere is this emphasis on intellectual perfection seen more clearly than in Gersonides's commentary to the biblical book *Song of Songs*. Ostensibly the *Song of Songs* describes the love affair and desires of a shepherd for a maiden. Generations of commentators have seen in the work an allegory of the relation between God and Israel. In his introduction to the commentary, Gersonides stated that "man's ultimate felicity resides in cognizing and knowing God to the extent that is possible for him."[30] Such knowledge is achieved through observation of the state of existing things in the natural universe, that is, through the beings that God has created and caused. Knowledge of God, therefore, is predicated on knowedge of the natural order. The prophet for Gersonides represented the paradigmatic natural scientist, one who had complete knowledge of the natural order. Gersonides claimed that the purpose of *Song of Songs* was meant to guide only select individuals to their felicity: "this book ... guides the elite only, to the way of achieving felicity, and thus its external meaning was not made useful to the masses."[31] Most ordinary mortals will not achieve this felicity: "only very few individuals can acquire even a large measure of it."[32] Many obstacles stand in the way of most humans, including their hankering after their physical desires, as well as the misleading nature of imagination and opinion.

CONCLUSION

We have in this chapter focused on practical morality: those ingredients that undergird a moral life and lead to self-fulfillment and happiness, in the Aristotelian sense of *eudaimonia*. The prophet represents the exemplar of human perfection, but the criteria for achieving the level of a true prophet differ. We ended the chapter with differing conceptions of how to achieve what the philosophers called "ultimate felicity." The prophet played an important propadeutic role in this conception, leading to an intellectualist conception of human perfection. But Crescas reminded us that there are other ways to think about the ultimate aims of human existence, ways that do not emphasize intellectual perfection to the detriment of love, passion and joy.

NOTES

1. Aristotle (1984) makes this point in several texts, including *Nicomachean Ethics* 6.7, 1141a20–22; 10.7, 1177a12–18.
2. Aristotle, *Nicomachean Ethics* II.6, 1106a.30.
3. Aristotle, *Nicomachean Ethics* II.6, 1106b.20–22.
4. Baḥya 2004, 11.
5. Baḥya 2004, 37.
6. Baḥya, *Duties*, III.10.341–347.
7. Maimonides 1975a, I, 61.
8. Maimonides 1975a, II, 65.
9. For discussion of this difficulty, see Twersky 1972.
10. Maimonides 1975a, I.7, 30.
11. Maimonides 1975a, IV, 67.
12. Maimonides 1975a, IV, 68.
13. It's important that the majority of prophets were men, although there were a handful of female prophets. We return to this point in Chapter 14.
14. Maimonides 1963, 12.
15. Maimonides 1963, 369.
16. Maimonides 1963, 369.
17. Maimonides 1963, 371–372.
18. Maimonides 1963.
19. Plato, *Republic*, books 6–7 in Plato 1971.
20. Gersonides, *Wars* vol 2 II.6: 64.
21. Gersonides, *Wars* vol 2 II.2: 34.
22. See Crescas 2018, II.6.1, 211.
23. Crescas 2018, II.6.1, 214. See Tirosh-Samuelson 2003, 383: "Crescas concludes that the doctrine of the acquired

intellect is both philosophically unsound and religiously heretical."
24 See Tirosh-Samuelson 2003, 385.
25 Tirosh-Samuelson 2003, 387.
26 See Chapter 9 for a modern version of this parable by Solomon Maimon.
27 Maimonides 1963, 621.
28 Maimonides 1963, 636.
29 Maimonides 1963, 637.
30 Gersonides 1998, 5.
31 Gersonides 1998, 8.
32 Gersonides 1998, 6.

FURTHER READING

Kreisel, H. (2001). *Prophecy: The History of an Idea in Medieval Jewish Philosophy*. Dordrecht: Kluwer Academic Publishers.

Rudavsky, T.M. (2018). *Jewish Philosophy in the Middle Ages: Science, Rationalism, and Religion*. Oxford: Oxford University Press.

Tirosh-Samuelson, H. (2003). *Happiness in Premodern Judaism: Virtue, Knowledge, and Well Being*. Cincinnati, OH: Hebrew Union College.

PART II

MODERN JEWISH PHILOSOPHY
Fifteenth Century to the Present

PRELUDE TO MODERNITY

INTRODUCTION

In this chapter, which spans the late thirteenth to seventeenth centuries, we note a number of scholastic influences upon late medieval Jewish philosophy, while introducing some of the major figures during this formative but often neglected period. We start with the Hebrew encyclopedists who introduced new developments in science and philosophy to an eager audience. By the fourteenth century, Jews were engaging more regularly with their Christian compatriots; philosophical materials often reflect this rich interaction. After the expulsion of the Jews from Spain in 1492, Jews moved to all corners of the globe, bringing with them this rich tradition. The chapter thus focuses not only upon Spanish Jews, but Jews in the Italian Renaissance as well. It ends with the works of Benedict (Baruch) Spinoza, one of the most unique and influential early modern philosophers in the Western secular world.

THE RISE OF SCIENTIFIC ENCYCLOPEDIAS

During the twelfth and thirteenth centuries, both Christian and Jewish philosophers discovered the treasure-trove of scientific knowledge that was being transmitted from Spain. Provencal Jews did not read Arabic, and so relied on translators of Spanish origin to transmit the new science. By the late thirteenth century, translators had transmitted almost the entire body of Greek science from Arabic texts to Hebrew.[1] In an attempt to systematize this vast new body of knowledge, medieval Hebrew encyclopedias of science and philosophy appeared in the twelfth and thirteenth centuries. Hebrew encyclopedists offered a general introduction to the new sciences as well as translations and summaries of the most advanced scientific texts available. Early encyclopedias were written by Abraham bar Ḥiyya in the early 1200s and by Abraham ibn Ezra, among others.

One of the major encyclopedias was that of Judah ha-Cohen (1215). His encyclopedia *Midrash ha-Ḥokhmah* (*Exposition of Science*), written originally in Arabic and translated into Hebrew, is often considered to be the oldest extant Hebrew encyclopedia of science. Another important encyclopedia was written by Shem Tov ben Joseph Falaquera (1223/8–1295) who was born in northern Spain or Provence. Known as one of the most prolific of the philosophical translators, his most important work *The Opinions of the Philosophers* represents one of the earliest and most comprehensive Hebrew encyclopedias of science in the Middle Ages. Confining himself to reporting the words of the philosophers, he did not strive for originality and described his project as follows: "there is not a thing in this entire composition that I say of my own: rather all that I write are the words of Aristotle as explained in the commentaries of the scholar Averroës."[2] In his encyclopedia, ibn Falaquera attempted to provide readers with a complete summary of Aristotelian science, following the overall structure of the Arab commentators. The work includes long passages from Averroës's commentaries on Aristotle, translated literally, with little comment or elucidation, presenting his audience with a detailed account of Aristotelian science and philosophy.

FOURTEENTH AND FIFTEENTH-CENTURY SCHOLASTIC INFLUENCES

Turning to the scholastic influences upon fourteenth- and fifteenth-century Jewish philosophy, we first note several historiographical issues. Post-Thomist scholasticism had a strong impact upon fourteenth- and fifteenth-century Jewish philosophy.[3] First we must be careful to distinguish by geographical area as well as by period. While the major fourteenth-century Jewish philosophers of northern Spain and Provence (e.g. Gersonides, Isaac Pollegar, Joseph ibn Kaspi and Narboni) showed little ostensible signs of scholastic influence or interaction, the Spanish Jewish philosophers of the late fourteenth and fifteenth centuries (Profiat Duran, Crescas, Albo, Bibago, Arama and Abravanel) were involved in Christian polemics; these polemical disputations required an engagement with scholasticism in order to address the challenges posed by Christianity.[4]

But how was this engagement effected? Did Jewish philosophers, for example, know Latin? Although the anti-Christian polemicists certainly had to be familiar with Christian sources, not all had a reading knowledge of Latin. Furthermore, inasmuch as Jewish philosophers during this period rarely mentioned Christian writers by name, it is often difficult to trace individual scholastic influences. Hillel of Verona, for example, used unattributed passages (a not uncommon practice) from the Latin translations of Avicenna and Averroës, interwoven with passages taken directly from Thomas Aquinas in his own work *Retributions of the Soul*, written in 1291.[5]

By the fourteenth century, the scholastic method of disputation was firmly entrenched among Christian thinkers.

The most prominent method used was the *quaestio* (question) method adopted by Thomas Aquinas, Duns Scotus, and the later scholastics. By mid-century, this method appears in Jewish texts as well. Consider, for example, the works of Gersonides, Crescas and Isaac Abravanel, among others, who organized their discourse thematically as a set of disputed questions with the same order of exposition as found in scholastic texts: formulation of the question, citation of supporting arguments, citation of antithetical argument, and resolution of the original question, generally in support of the antithetical arguments.

In part, this facility with scholastic method can be traced to an increased interest in scholastic logic. As recent scholars have noted, the influence of scholastic logic upon Jewish thought was extensive.[6] One reason for its popularity undoubtedly rested in the perception among Jews that logical training would prepare them for the rigors of disputation with Christians; without such training, the Jews saw themselves at a distinct theological disadvantage. Another reason had to do with the perceived importance of logic for a sound medical education. Inasmuch as Jewish physicians were certified before a mixed tribunal of Jews and Christians, knowledge of scholastic logic was presumed to be helpful in their preparation.[7]

Scholastic thought was particularly influential upon Hebrew logic in Italy. Once Jews were permitted admission to the faculties of medicine and philosophy in Italian universities, they were in a position to incorporate Christian teachings and specifically logic.[8] A good example of this university status for Jews is Judah ben Jehiel Messer Leon (*c*.1470–*c*.1526) who devoted most of his works to logic, rhetoric and grammar. Messer Leon studied at the universities of Bologna and Padua in the latter part of the fifteenth century, was awarded a doctorate in philosophy and medicine, and incorporated principles of scholastic logic into his writings.[9]

FOURTEENTH-CENTURY POLEMICS AND DISPUTATIONS

By the thirteenth century, the topic of human freedom became a pressing issue among philosophers constrained to reconcile God's omniscience with human free will. Moses ben Joshua Narboni (late thirteenth or early fourteenth century; before 1362) began to study Maimonides's works at an early age. The author of over twenty books, he is known primarily for his commentary on Maimonides's *Guide of the Perplexed*. He also composed commentaries on works of al-Ghazâli, ibn Tufayl, and Averroës. Steeped in Averroism, Narboni criticized many of Maimonides's Neoplatonic views.

Abner of Burgos (c.1270–1340) was an anti-Jewish polemicist and apostate who converted to Christianity. Many of his works engaged Jewish scholars in dialogue and debate in an attempt to formulate arguments for their conversion from Judaism to Christianity. Much of Abner's writings were written in Hebrew and later translated into Castilian. While in his polemical work *Minhat Kena'ot* (*Offering of Jealousy*) he tried to convince people, including his former student Isaac Pollegar, to convert to Christianity by rational means, Abner also encouraged the isolation of Jews and mob violence to promote conversion. Upon his own conversion to Christianity, he attacked his former co-religionists, arguing for the superiority of Catholicism.

Abner of Burgos was the first Jewish/Christian convert philosopher to present a strict determinist theory. In his *Treatise on Free Will*, Narboni described Burgos as follows: "There was a scholar, an older contemporary of mine, one of the singular men of his time, who composed a treatise on determinism, in which he stated that "the possible" does not exist, but only "the inevitable" since everything is predestined."[10] Defining a voluntary agent as one who can equally perform one of two alternatives, Abner introduced the notion of "complete will" to describe the causal chain which combines the motivating stimulus and the imaginative faculty. Human actions are completely determined in so far as the will flows necessarily from a rigid causal chain.[11] Thus Abner upheld strict astral determinism, arguing that God's eternal knowledge causally necessitated human actions.[12]

Of the three opponents to Abner – Isaac Pollegar, Narboni and ibn Kaspi – Pollegar was the first to respond and did so vociferously in his treatise *Ezer ha-Dat* (*The Support of the Faith*).[13] Of Pollegar himself we know very little, except that he was a close friend of Abner's before the latter's conversion to Christianity. While Abner saw himself as a defender of astral determinism, Pollegar reiterated Maimonides's arguments against astrology, arguing that astrology is both false and harmful to religion.[14] Presenting his arguments as a dialogue between an astrologer and a wise man (*haver*), Pollegar tried to retain both God's foreknowledge and human freedom. Arguing that determinism is incompatible with human agency, he proposed a theory of "pre-established harmony" according to which God's will and human will are in synchrony: "my will is linked to the will of my creator and both unite at the same instant so that my will is part of His, and thus I am drawn by Him; when He wishes and desires to act, then I too wish it."[15]

THE ITALIAN RENAISSANCE

In the fifteenth and centuries, Jews were influenced by the Italian Renaissance, as evidenced by Elijah Delmedigo (1458–1493), a contemporary and friend of the Italian philosopher Pico della Mirandola. Originally from Candia, Crete, Delmedigo moved to Italy, where he was educated in Islamic and Jewish philosophy, as well as classical literature. While in Italy, he provided Christian Latin scholars with translations and commentaries of *Averro.s*, from medieval Hebrew translations into Latin; the target audience of these works included Pico della Mirandola (1463–1494), who had an interest in Jewish commentaries and Kabbalah. In addition to these translations, Delmedigo also composed original works supporting the Averroist interpretations of Aristotle, primarily in the physics and metaphysics. After a long period of travel throughout northern Italy, Delmedigo returned to Crete in roughly 1490 where he was warmly received by the Jewish community. During these last years of his life, Delmedigo wrote his major philosophic work *Behinat ha-Dat (The Examination of Religion)* in Hebrew at the request of one of his students. This work was not particularly original, but presented a synthetic presentation of Jewish and Renaissance ideas. Influenced by Averroës's *Decisive Treatise*, Delmedigo attempted to legitimize the study of philosophy within the framework of Jewish belief.

Two additional figures are Don Isaac Abravanel (1437–1508) and his son Judah Abravanel (*c.*1460–after 1523). Isaac Abravanel is best known for his philosophical work *Mif'alot Elohim* (*Wonders of God*). Despite his participation in the world of Renaissance humanism, Abravanel's conservative philosophical thought remained medieval in conception. Writing at the height of the Renaissance in Italy, his son Judah Abravanel (1465–1521), better known as Leone Ebreo, is best known for his work *Dialoghi d'amore* (*Dialogues of Love*), which was written in Italian possibly in 1511–1512. Both Judah and his father resided in Spain until the Spanish expulsion, when both families fled to Naples, and eventually to Venice. During this upheaval, Judah's son was kidnapped and forcibly converted to Christianity.

The *Dialogues* represent an excellent example of the fusion of Hebraic thought with the Italian Renaissance revival of Greek philosophy. In his philosophical dialogue, Judah Abravanel constructed an allegory between two Jewish courtiers, Philo and Sophia, in order to illustrate the importance of the philosophical love of God. Through the concepts of beauty and love, Abravanel examined a wide variety of philosophical issues. For example, having explained to Sophia the origins of love, he then turns to the more general question of when love was born: was it produced from eternity or was it created in time? Philo immediately connects this question with questions having to do with the origin of the universe, which leads to an extensive examination of the three regnant positions on the creation of the universe – that of Plato, that of Aristotle, and that of Moses. Following its publication, the *Dialogues* were hugely popular among non-Jews, and were translated into many languages. We do know that Baruch Spinoza had a copy of the work in his library.

THE RISE OF MODERN SCIENCE

The emphasis upon philosophy, theology and science found its way into Jewish philosophical texts in the late fifteenth century onward. Citing the works of Moses Isserles of Cracow, the Maharal of Prague, and David Ganz, Isserles's most successful student in the sciences, scholars have noted the extent to which developments in the new astronomy affected their works.[16] David Ganz (1541–1613), for example, appeared to be up to date on contemporary work in astronomy and science; in his work *Nehmad ve-Na'im*, he traced recent developments in astronomy and mentioned Copernicus as the greatest astronomer since Ptolemy. Joseph Solomon Delmedigo (1591–1655) is a further case in point. Having studied under Galileo, he recognized the challenge of the new Copernican astronomy and tried to understand the natural world outside the framework of Aristotelian physics.[17] His major work *Sefer Elim* was published in 1629, just four years before Galileo's trial. The very style of *Elim* is reminiscent of Galileo's dialogues.[18] Delmedigo placed in the mouth of his interlocuter Moshe Metz a thorough critique of the philosophical foundations of the old geocentric astronomy.[19]

In *Elim*, Delmedigo discussed in great detail the scientific theories of Kepler, Tycho Brahe, Copernicus and Galileo, describing the "strange astronomy," noting the dangers inherent in this new astronomy, which challenged the reigning metaphysics.[20] Both Galileo and his Jewish disciple sought to understand the natural world outside the framework of Aristotelian physics, notwithstanding their strong indebtedness to it in shaping their conceptual discourse.[21] In *G'vurot Hashem*, a work appended to *Sefer Elim*, Delmedigo was more enthusiastic in his attitude toward Copernicus, demonstrating his knowledge of the new astronomy:

> Happiness and joy were added to me when I heard that they (the researchers) have begun in our time to think that the entire universe is like a lantern and is called "*lanterna*;" and the candle burning within it is the solar body which stands in the center and whose light spreads out until the sphere of Saturn which is at the outer limit of this universe.[22]

We know that Delmedigo visited Amsterdam in 1626 and was befriended by Spinoza's teacher Manasseh ben Israel who published, among other works, Delmedigo's *Sefer Elim* in 1629. We know as well that Spinoza had a copy of at least one of Delmedigo's works in his library although it is not clear whether Spinoza had access to *Elim*; the only reference is to a rabbinical mathematical work. In short, Delmedigo thus exemplified the tendency of Jewish philosophers to move beyond Aristotelianism, toward developments in science and philosophy in the secular world. These tendencies reached fruition in the work of Baruch Spinoza.

BARUCH SPINOZA AND NATURAL SCIENCE

By the seventeenth century science and philosophy had become more clearly distinguished, and their methods became subject to different tools of investigation. A major catalyst of this change was the heliocentrism of both Copernicus and Galileo that threatened Aristotelian geocentric cosmology. This heliocentric cosmology replaced an Aristotelian world order in which the earth resided at the center of the cosmos; no longer was Earth, and human beings, privileged above the other planets and celestial spheres. Modern philosophy slowly emerged in conjunction with the scientific advances that arose in the seventeenth and eighteenth centuries. René Descartes (1596–1650) was at the forefront of the confrontation between philosophy and natural science; others soon followed in his footsteps.

Contending with Maimonides for the title of best-known Jewish philosophers, Spinoza is also considered one of the most influential early modern philosophers in the secular world. As we shall see, Spinoza lived for the most part outside the mainstream of Jewish philosophy. Baruch Spinoza (1632–1677) was born in Amsterdam and grew up in the Portuguese-Jewish community, attending Jewish schools in Amsterdam up through at least age fourteen. That Spinoza read works in Jewish philosophy, including medieval Jewish commentaries, is undeniable. From the list of books in Spinoza's estate, we know that he owned a number of Jewish philosophical texts, including works of Maimonides, Abravanel and Delmedigo. From this listing, we can assume that Spinoza was at least aware of such works as Maimonides's *Guide for the Perplexed*, Crescas's *Light of the Lord*, Abravanel's *Dialogue of Love*, and works by Delmedigo.

By 1656 Spinoza's life with the Jewish community came to an abrupt end when he was accused of heresy and excommunicated by Amsterdam's Sephardic community for reasons still contested. Was it Spinoza's denial of personal immortality, a doctrine discussed extensively in Jewish thought, that played the key role in his excommunication (in Hebrew *herem*)? Perhaps.[23] Or perhaps it was Spinoza's public repudiation of the fundamentals of rabbinic Judaism that led to the excommunication. In any event, after his excommunication from the Jewish community, Spinoza changed his name from "Baruch" (blessed) to "Benedict" and lived out the remainder of his short life as a lens-grinder in towns near Leiden and the Hague.

Although circulated among friends during his lifetime, Spinoza's major philosophical work *The Ethics* was published posthumously in 1677. We return in Chapter 8 to the *Theological Political Treatise*, one of only two works published during his lifetime. In part because of this treatise, Spinoza was one of the most reviled and yet beloved philosophers of the modern era. Both before and immediately after his death, Spinoza's writings were assailed for espousing noxious and dangerous beliefs. Willem van Blijenbergh, a seventeenth-century Calvinist, described the *Theological Political Treatise* as "a book full of studious abominations and an accumulation of opinions which have been forged in hell."[24] Subsequent centuries bore witness not only to criticism, rejection and excoriation but adoration and praise as well. To cite just a few examples: Spinoza was vilified by the famous and influential biographer Pierre Bayle (1647–1706) as a "hideous atheist," yet praised by the poet Novalis as a "God-intoxicated man," and by Heinrich Heine as a providential thinker whose works presaged the air of the future; he was upheld as a kindred spirit by Nietzsche; he was characterized by the Italian political philosopher Antonio Negri (writing in an Italian prison) as the quintessential spokesperson for Marxist conceptions of power; more recently, he has been presented by neuroscientist Antonio Damassio as a precursor to contemporary neuroscientific theories of personhood, promoted by French philosopher Gille Deleuze as a forerunner of his own political and social thought, and championed by Einstein who famously claimed that he and Spinoza shared the same conception of a pantheistic god.

Spinoza was very much influenced by scientific and mathematical advances in the seventeenth century, reflected by two of his near contemporaries, Isaac Newton (1642–1727) and Wilhelm von Leibniz (1646–1716) who were at the forefront of innovations in physics and mathematics. At the same time Descartes (1596–1650) was concerned to place philosophy upon an absolute certain axiomatic foundation. In his *Meditations on First Philosophy*, Descartes developed a method of doubt that was intended to guarantee absolute certainty, requiring readers to put aside their entrenched opinions, prejudices and irrational beliefs. In the second meditation, Descartes even doubted the existence of his own physical body; claiming famously that "I think, therefore I am," Descartes privileged the primacy of the cognitive ego. Spinoza devoted a fair bit of energy to studying Descartes's method of doubt and in a work published during his lifetime (*Descartes's Principles of Philosophy*), he rejected Descartes's methodology. Inasmuch as Spinoza denied mind-body dualism in favor of a monistic identity of mind and body, he rejected the primacy of the Cartesian ego. For Spinoza, it is simply impossible for the mind to form an idea of the body as non-existing.

In a step more radical than Descartes's doubting process, Spinoza took Euclid's geometrical method as paradigmatic of mathematical and philosophical certainty.

For Spinoza, the proper method of study of human action, including human emotions, is Euclidean geometry. Reflecting this method, the *Ethics* is written in geometrical form: each book of the work contains axioms and definitions, from which propositions and corollaries are deduced and proofs offered for each proposition. In this work, we will discuss those features of the *Ethics* that are most connected to Jewish philosophy.

"Deus sive Natura" (God or Nature) is the motto Spinoza used to characterize monism in his major work *The Ethics*. But what does this motto amount to? Part one of the *Ethics* presents two theses: first, that there exists one and only one substance, which is identified with God; and second, that God is the only "free" agent in the sense that God acts in accordance with the laws of its own nature, resulting in a strict determinist system. For Spinoza, everything that is real can be understood as either substance, or as a mode of substance. By mode Spinoza had in mind the properties of substance. However, unlike earlier substance theorists, Spinoza was a radical monist and rejected Cartesian dualism. Spinoza's monism posited the existence of only one substance – God; everything else in the universe is a modification of that substance. In other words, everything – rocks, trees, human minds, human bodies, a fountain pen – are modifications of God/substance.

The implications of monism are vast. First, by rejecting the dualism of matter/spirit or body/mind that was accepted by centuries of western thinkers, Spinoza suggested that the human mind is no more than the "idea" of the body. Further, the standard theological position that posits a qualitative distinction between God (the creator) and the world (God's creation), was rejected in favor of a position often described as pan-entheism: God just *is* the world. We can no longer speak of God as a creator, nor can we speak of the world, or human beings, as being dependent upon a transcendent Deity. The God of Spinoza is a far cry from the Abrahamic providential Deity who created the world and stands in a special relationship to human beings.

CONCLUSION

This chapter has surveyed the movements and figures in Jewish philosophy between the thirteenth and early seventeenth centuries. The encyclopedists paved the way for developments in the fifteenth-century Jewish, while Isaac Pollegar, Narboni and ibn Kaspi clashed with the determinism of Abner of Burgos. By the late sixteenth century, Jewish philosophers were moving toward recent developments in science and philosophy, culminating in the works of Spinoza. That Spinoza was influenced by his medieval Jewish predecessors is undeniable. While wrestling with the works of Maimonides and ibn Ezra, much of his philosophical program was antithetical to Jewish beliefs. Spinoza's God is not the God of the Bible. This God is not a creator Deity: rather, God and nature are identical. Further, as we shall see in the next chapter, Spinoza denied that God is literally the author of Scripture or that Moses wrote all, or even much, of the Bible. By pushing the views of his medieval predecessors to their logical extreme, Spinoza thus undermined the carefully constructed hermeneutic methodology introduced by his Jewish predecessors. It would now fall to subsequent Jewish thinkers in the eighteenth and nineteenth centuries to reappropriate the task of accommodating the words of Scripture to the domain of natural philosophy.

NOTES

1 Sirat 1990, 213–214.
2 Falaquera *De'ot* quoted in Harvey 2000, 215; quoted also in Jospe 1988, 50–51.

3   See Pines 1977 for elaborate exploration of these influences.
4   Manekin 1997a, 352.
5   Hillel ben Samuel of Verona 1981.
6   See Manekin 1999, 123–147.
7   For further discussion of this point, see Manekin 1997b, 406.
8   For extensive discussion of the development of medicine among Jews, see Ruderman 1995.
9   For further discussion of Messer Leon, see Manekin 1999; Tirosh-Rothschild 1991, 1997.
10 Quoted in Baer 1966, 332.
11 Manekin 1997a, 367; see Baer 1966, 191–192.
12 Baer 1966.
13 Pollegar 1984.
14 See Pollegar 1984, part 3.
15 Pollegar 1984, 119–120.
16 See Ruderman 1995, 68ff.
17 See Ruderman 1995, 134.
18 See Ruderman 1995, who notes the similarity to Galileo's dialogues.
19 Joseph Delmedigo 1864, 48–62, esp. 54ff.
20 Joseph Delmedigo 1864, 301. Delmedigo most admired Tycho Brahe and Kepler; he praises the precision of his instruments (Delmedigo 1864, 317–319, 432). He calls Kepler the "greatest mathematician of our time" (Delmedigo 1864, 300), and draws attention to his studies.
21 Ruderman 1995, 134.
22 Delmedigo 1864, 292.
23 See Nadler 2001.
24 See Nadler 2011.

FURTHER READING

Barzilay, I. 1974. *Yoseph Shlomo Delmedigo (Yashar of Candia): His Life, Works, and Times*. Leiden: E.J. Brill.

Fraenkel, C. 2013. "Considering the Case of Elijah Delmedigo's Averroism and its Impact on Spinoza," in A. Akasoy and G. Giglioni (eds), *Renaissance Averroism and Its Aftermath: Arabic Philosophy in Early Modern Europe*. Dordrecht: Springer, 213–236.

Ivry, A. L. 1983. "Remnants of Jewish Averroism in the Renaissance," in B.D. Cooperman (ed.), *Jewish Thought in the Sixteenth Century*. Cambridge, MA: Harvard University Press, 243–265.

Judah, A. 2009. *Dialogues of Love*, trans. D. Bacich and R. Pescatori. Toronto: University of Toronto Press.

Levine, H. 1983. "Paradise Not Surrendered: Jewish Reactions to Copernicus and the Growth of Modern Science," in R.S. Cohen and M.W. Wartofsky (eds), *Epistemology, Methodology and the Social Sciences*. Dordrecht: D. Reidel.

Nadler, S. 1999. *Spinoza: A Life*. Cambridge: Cambridge University Press.

Nadler, S. 2020. *Think Least of Death: Spinoza on How to Live and How to Die*. Princeton, NJ: Princeton University Press.

Ravven, H.M. and Goodman, L.E. (eds). 2002. *Jewish Themes in Spinoza's Philosophy*. Albany, NY: SUNY Press.

IS THERE A RIGHT WAY TO READ SCRIPTURE?

INTRODUCTION

Philosophical attempts to underscore the inherent universality of Jewish law and commandments comprised arguments for the inherent rationality of the commandments, and more generally for the rationality of Scripture. The process of providing rational reasons for the commandments dates back to rabbinic times, and continued throughout the medieval and modern periods. In a number of passages, for example, the rabbis were suggesting that some commandments are "inherently" or "intuitively" grounded, and not totally dependent upon divine command. Such commandments, discussed in the Talmudic books *Sanhedrin* 56–60 and *Melakhim* 8:10 and 10:12, represented the minimal moral duties enjoined by the Bible upon all human beings and came to be known as the Noahide Laws. Even if God had not included these commandments in revelation, human beings would have intuitively recognized them as binding upon everyone. The Noahide Laws came to be known in later writings as "natural law." Joseph Albo, Saadiah Gaon and Maimonides were particularly interested in upholding the rationality of the commandments and we will see in Chapter 9 that Moses Mendelssohn returned to the issue. Spinoza, on the other hand, dismissed the rationality of Scripture altogether.

HOW TO READ SCRIPTURE: LITERAL VERSUS FIGURATIVE INTERPRETATION

How does a philosopher, one who is steeped in the analytic methods of philosophical demonstration, approach the reading of a text that is often impervious to those methods? We have confronted in previous chapters numerous instances in which philosophical ideas and methods conflict with the views found in Scripture. Take for example, the doctrine of creation: while Genesis portrays God as having created the world in time, Aristotle and Plato both postulate an eternal world in which matter has always existed. Medieval and modern Jewish philosophers struggled with ways to render Scripture amenable to philosophical scrutiny.

Maimonides presented his *Guide of the Perplexed* in part as a way of resolving the tensions between Scripture and philosophy. He spelled out two major purposes of the *Guide:* to explain the meanings of terms in Scripture, and to explain obscure parables occurring in the books of the prophets. Maimonides introduced the second purpose of the *Guide*, namely biblical hermeneutics, as a way to neutralize the sort of perplexity exacerbated by ambiguous passages in Scripture. Maimonides then complicated matters further by suggesting that it is sometimes incumbent upon a philosopher to conceal his own esoteric position behind the veil of exoteric doctrine. He enjoined his own student not to divulge his secret teachings to others. Once we understand the true meaning of difficult biblical parables, or understand at least that they are parables and not to be understood literally, Maimonides assured the reader that philosophical perplexities can be dissolved.

Yet, even this road is not clear of obstacles, and Maimonides cited three reasons for his inability to explain problematic terms and parables fully: first, the subject matter is simply too comprehensive and vast to be covered in such a work; second, some parables are intentionally vague and must not be fully explicated; and finally, most individuals are simply incapable of penetrating the secrets of Scripture fully. One who is fully steeped in both Torah and philosophy can never be fully rid of perplexity. Maimonides thus reinforced the ambiguities existing not only in Scripture, but in his own works as well.

Maimonides's immediate successor Gersonides rejected the policy of obfuscation. In contradistinction to Maimonides, who introduced allegory, metaphor, and imprecise language into his work to convey the ambiguity of the subject-matter, Gersonides saw as his goal the elucidation of philosophical issues as clearly as possible. He contrasted his method with that of Maimonides, whose *Guide* he saw as unnecessarily obscure and esoteric: "Opacity of language or faulty arrangement should not hide the defect and weakness of our intention. For this reason we have not employed rhetorical flourishes or obscure language... there is no need to add obscurity of language and bad organization."[1] Clearly Gersonides had Maimonides's introduction to the *Guide* in mind as an example of what not to do! In his introductory remarks to *Wars of the Lord*, Gersonides upheld the primacy of reason: "we must believe what reason has determined to be true. If the literal sense of the Torah differs from reason, it is necessary to interpret those passages in accordance with the demands of reason."[2] Gersonides thus believed that reason and Torah cannot be in opposition: "if reason causes to affirm doctrines that are incompatible with the literal sense of Scripture, we are not prohibited by the Torah to pronounce the truth on these matters, for reason is not incompatible with the true understanding of the Torah."[3]

ARE THERE NATURAL LAWS IN SCRIPTURE?

Are there elements of Scripture that point to universal truths? Most of our philosophers pointed to the Noahide Laws as reflecting natural laws independent of divine revelation. One of the earliest articulations of the Noahide Laws can be found in the *Tosefta*, a supplementary work to the Mishnah. The text states: "Concerning seven commandments were the sons of Noah admonished: establishing courts of justice, idolatry, cursing the name [of God], illicit intercourse, bloodshed, thievery and consuming a limb from a living beast."[4] These commandments were presumably derived from divine commands addressed to Adam and Noah, and were regarded by the rabbis as universally applicable. In *Yoma* 67b (another text of the Talmud) we have the suggestion that "they would have been made mandatory even had they not been revealed," suggesting that these commandments were universally applicable to all of humanity. How then did the notion of natural law enter into philosophical discussions?

Joseph Albo's *Book of Principles* is one of the first works devoted in part to investigating the foundations of natural and divine law.[5] Noting that humans are political by nature, and that it is almost necessary for them to be members of a city,[6] Albo argued that human societies were in need of what he termed a "natural law." In other words, humans living in a group require a certain modicum of order allowing them to maintain justice; "this order the wise men call natural law, meaning by natural that it is necessary for man by his nature, whether the order emanates from a wise man or a prophet."[7] But natural law must be supplemented by a *nomos* or conventional law that enables political life to unfold.

Albo distinguished further between three kinds of law, natural, conventional, and divine, as follows:

> Natural law is the same among all peoples, at all times, and in all places. Positive or conventional is a law ordered by a wise man or men to suit the place and the time and the nature of the persons who are to be controlled by it ... Divine law is one that is ordered by God through a prophet, like Adam or Noah, or like the custom or law which Abraham taught men ... or one that is ordered by God through a messenger whom He sends and through whom He gives a law, like the law of Moses.[8]

What is interesting for our purposes is Albo's suggestion that natural law applies equally to all humans, times and places. The reader is left with the impression that natural law serves as the foundation for the two other kinds of law, each of which supplements and complements the natural law.

While Albo is the only Jewish philosopher to mention "natural law" explicitly, other Jewish philosophers did broach issues surrounding the universality of the commandments. One way of broaching the question is to ask whether certain commandments are inherently rational, and if so whether they would be applicable to all human beings independent of divine command. Is there, more specifically, independent rational grounding for at least some of the commandments? Saadiah Gaon was one of the first philosophers to approach these questions explicitly. As we mentioned in Chapter 2, Saadiah was a strong opponent of Karaism, whose members threatened the integrity of the rabbis. In an ongoing effort to neutralize polemical Karaite claims, Saadiah and other rabbis of his time were devoted to validating the legitimacy of rabbinical Judaism.

In the introduction to *The Book of Beliefs and Opinions,* Saadiah presented a rudimentary epistemology, distinguishing four sources of reliable knowledge: sensation, reason, logical inference, and reliable tradition. Sense knowledge is based on empirical contingents and is posited as the basis for all other knowledge forms. Reason represents the faculty of immediate, intuitive knowledge by means of which we apprehend self-evident axioms. Reason itself emanates ultimately from God, resulting in an innatist theory according to which ideas are "implanted" in the mind. The word "implanted" connotes a source for knowledge that lies outside the realm of human consciousness. In contradistinction to the first three sources, Saadiah claimed that "reliable tradition" is shared by the "community of monotheists." Saadiah relegates to tradition two roles: first, tradition enables us to determine the particulars necessary for observing the more general rational precepts; and second, tradition also speeds up the rather tedious process of discovering these rational principles. Revelation thus permits us to access truths we could arrive at rationally after a long process.

Based on these epistemological distinctions, Saadiah distinguished between the rational commandments, which in theory are discoverable by means of reason, and the traditional laws, which comprise rituals and ceremonial laws (such as the dietary laws) that are not rooted in reason. In other words, humans have an intuitive grasp of the content of the rational commandments inasmuch as they determine right action. Saadiah further argued that the rational commandments are inherently related to the dictates of reason, and that they represent logical inferences from these dictates.[9] Revelatory commandments, which constitute the second general division of law, are not inherently dependent upon the above-mentioned rational dictates, but rather are imposed by God without regard to their inherent rationality. Hence, the approbation of these laws implies no more than simple submissiveness to God. Although these laws are not grounded in reason, nevertheless they too may be justified by rational argument. Saadiah offered many examples (sanctifying certain times rather than others; the dietary laws, etc.) to explicate the overall social utility of the traditional laws.

Saadiah's system introduced a theory of rational obligation into the rubric of revelatory commandments, thus incorporating an attempted synthesis, or at least an attempted reconciliation between reason and revelation. We can see Saadiah's sustained efforts to articulate the underlying idea that at least some of the commandments are objective, based on human nature, and accessible to human reasoning.

MAIMONIDES AND RATIONALITY OF THE COMMANDMENTS

Maimonides's analysis of the commandments reflected Saadiah's distinction between rational and ritualistic commandments, but in contradistinction to Saadiah, Maimonides claimed that *all* the commandments are rational: both the laws and the statutes have beneficial ends, the only difference being that the former are recognizable to everyone, whereas the latter possess ends that are only manifest to the wise. The laws correspond to Saadiah's rational commandments, while the statutes correspond (in general) to Saadiah's listing of ceremonial laws and rituals.

For Maimonides both laws and statutes have a basis in reason and he was clear that "governance of the Law is absolute and universal."[10] In *Guide* 3.25 Maimonides offered several proofs based on philosophical reasoning for the rationality of law. For example, he argued that to attribute to God non-purposive and non-rational actions, namely laws that are the arbitrary result of God's will, would be blasphemous, for frivolous actions are the most demeaning. Furthermore, he argued that in order to command the respect of the nations of the world, Jewish law must be rational. In an interesting aside, Maimonides claimed that were the law not rational, the peoples of the world would not look up to the Jews, and they would lose their standing among the moral peoples. Reflecting the Platonic dictum in the *Euthyphro* that the gods command pious acts because they are pious, Maimonides suggested that there exists a rational, autonomous nature of what is right: these actions have been commanded *because* they are intrinsically good and right.

Turning specifically to the utility of the commandments, Maimonides distinguished between the generalities and particulars of a commandment. While the generalities were given for utilitarian reasons, the particular details may not have the same utilitarian value. Maimonides castigated those individuals who tried to find causes and reasons for every particular detail in the laws. Such individuals are stricken with "madness" and "are as far from truth as those who imagine that the generalities of a commandment are not designed with a view to some real utility."[11] In fact Maimonides went to great lengths to warn his readers that for some particulars no cause can be found. Why, for example, did the Law prescribe the sacrifice of a ram rather than a lamb? No reason can be given.

But ought these rationally graspable and intelligible reasons for the commandments be divulged to the public? Maimonides clearly states that all the laws were given with a particular utility which applied to both welfare of the soul (achieved by acquisition of true beliefs) and welfare of the body (achieved by practical and moral virtues). Might not the very process of uncovering the reasons for the commandments lead to a sort of philosophical anti-nomianism among the masses, if they were to understand both the causes and goals of particular commandments? More specifically, could not this understanding lead to the seductive conclusion that these prescribed actions are dispensable? Maimonides had no response to this challenge; his successor Spinoza however, fleshed out the radical conclusions to implications of Maimonides's model.

SPINOZA'S RADICAL TURN

How does Spinoza compare with his predecessors with respect to reading Scripture? Spinoza's goals in his revolutionary and incendiary *Theological Political Treatise* were quite clear and can be juxtaposed against those of Maimonides adduced above. In a letter written in 1665, he stated two explicit aims of his work: to enable ordinary humans to engage in philosophical thinking by freeing them from the errors and prejudices of the theologians; and to free philosophy itself from the shackles and authority of religious authorities. In order to achieve his aims, Spinoza saw as his task the development of a biblical hermeneutic that could allow for a new understanding of Scripture, one that did not enslave philosophy or would-be philosophers. He resolved to "examine Scripture afresh, conscientiously and freely, and to admit nothing as its teaching which I did not most clearly derive from it."[12] But the publication of the *Treatise* in 1670 had the effect of a "lightning bolt:" the work was condemned by churches and universities both because of its naturalistic critique of biblical religion, and its rejection of the Bible's divine authorship.

Concerned to free philosophy and the study of nature from what he saw as the shackles of theology, Spinoza held controversial views on how to read and evaluate statements in Scripture. In the *Treatise*, Spinoza postulated the incommensurability of religion and science:

> Now I found nothing expressly taught in Scripture that was not in agreement with the intellect or that

contradicted it, and I also came to see that the prophets taught only very simple doctrines easily comprehensible by all ... So I was completely convinced that Scripture does not in any way inhibit reason and has nothing to do with philosophy, each standing on its own footing ... I show in what way Scripture must be interpreted, and how all our understanding of Scripture and of matters spiritual must be sought from Scripture alone, and not from the sort of knowledge that derives from the natural light of reason.[13]

In other words, Spinoza sharply demarcated the domain of reason and truth from that of theology, which is concerned with piety and obedience.

What elements in the *Treatise* so provoked his critics? Just as in the *Ethics*, Spinoza's adherence to the importance of using scientific method forced him to reject divine authorship of Scripture. But Spinoza's more radical move was to deny that Scripture had any philosophical or scientific veracity at all. According to Spinoza, Scripture cannot be accommodated to the new sciences and cannot be regarded as a source of knowledge; Scripture provides only moral guidance and piety, not even moral truth, and certainly not scientific or mathematical truth.

More specifically, Spinoza dismissed the truth-claims of prophets, claiming that the authority of the prophets carried weight only in matters concerning morality and true virtue. In matters of truth, their beliefs were irrelevant. By removing the domain of theology from that of "truth," and relegating it to mere piety and obedience, Spinoza undermined the cognitive import of theological statements that presumed to offer a metaphysical vision of reality. And with respect to the many miracles adduced in Scripture, Spinoza argued that inasmuch as everything in Scripture must accord with the laws of nature, it follows that whatever in Scripture contravenes nature must be rejected.

Finally, Spinoza denied that God is literally the author of Scripture or that Moses wrote all, or even much, of the Bible In claiming that Scripture had many authors, Spinoza was not unique; medieval Jewish philosophers had already suggested that Moses, for example, could not have written about his own death. But Spinoza emphasized the hermeneutic implications of this claim: if the Bible is but a historical document, and not the product of supernatural authorship, it must be treated like any other work of nature.

As we have seen in previous chapters, medieval Jewish philosophers had long grappled with how to interpret specific passages in Scripture, and Spinoza too was focused upon the literary and grammatical dimensions of Scripture. The foundation for understanding Scripture is, according to Spinoza, knowledge of the character of the Hebrew language. The whole range of possible meanings in each single utterance occurring in Scripture must therefore be defined by knowledge of ordinary usage of Hebrew. Spinoza claimed that as long as exegetes adopted his method, they would be able to uncover the teachings of the Bible. Presaging the nineteenth-century biblical scholars who deconstructed the authorship of the Bible, Spinoza argued that the Pentateuch was a compilation written by several individuals and assembled during the era of the Maccabees.

Spinoza then dismissed what was considered the incorruptibility of the Bible. For Spinoza, truth of fact represented an absolute reality grounded on the laws of philosophy and science. Just as we use the laws of nature to study and understand nature itself, so too, Spinoza argued, must we use the internal history of Scripture to understand the meaning of Scriptural passages. In order to ascertain the meaning of Scripture, the biblical scholar must approach the text much like a scientist approaches nature. Just as the natural scientist collects and orders data, so too must the Bible scholar collect and order the data contained in Scripture and interpret them in light of historical, social, cultural and linguistic contexts taken from Scripture. Based on this methodology, Spinoza proceeded to show that many statements in Scripture were *factually false*.

Miracles came under particular attack in the *Treatise*. Take for example Spinoza's analysis of the miracle recounted in Joshua 10.12–13, one that we have examined already in Chapter 4. Spinoza used his hermeneutic method of Scriptural interpretation not only to bring home his rejection of supernatural miracles, but also as an example of how to approach an account in Scripture in light of scientific knowledge. All the commentators, said Spinoza, tried to demonstrate that the prophets knew everything attainable by human intellect. In fact, however, the Joshua story is good evidence that prophets do *not* always have knowledge of scientific truths. "Do we have to believe that the soldier Joshua was a skilled astronomer, that a miracle could not be revealed to him, or that the sun's light could not remain above the horizon for longer than usual without Joshua's understanding the cause? Both alternatives seem to me ridiculous,"[14] claimed Spinoza, arguing that we cannot expect scientific knowledge on the part of the prophets. According to Spinoza, Joshua was a simple prophet who, confronted with an unusual natural phenomenon, namely "excessive coldness of the atmosphere," attributed to this phenomenon a supernaturalistic explanation. Spinoza had no patience for those who tried to explain away the passage by attributing to Joshua knowledge that he did not have. On Spinoza's reading of Scripture, Joshua was ignorant of the true causes of the lengthened day, and to suggest otherwise is to go beyond the text. In the case of miracles (and the Joshua example in particular), either the biblical text is compatible with our rational conceptions based on a naturalistic understanding of the cosmos, or it is not; and if it is not, the supernatural understanding of Scripture must be abandoned.

By removing the unique, unassailable quality of biblical statements, Spinoza thus paved the way for the independence of philosophical (and scientific) truth on the one hand, and religious belief on the other. The only truths to be found in Scripture, according to Spinoza, are moral verities, which should be distinguished from objective, scientific truths. We return in the next chapter to the implication of these issues in the works of Moses Mendelssohn.

CONCLUSION

The question of whether Judaism recognizes a natural law independent of Jewish law is contentious, and pertains to the role played by revelation in the promulgation of law. While some scholars have argued that the very notion of natural law precludes the doctrine of revelation and its complex set of divinely revealed laws, others have tried to reconcile the essential components of natural law theory with a theory of divine revelation. In part this question reflects, once more, the age-old tension between reason and revelation: are the basic tenets of Judaism rational, or are they founded in revelation alone? In other words, can we somehow accommodate both reason and revelation into the fabric of Jewish law? As we saw, part of this discussion centered around the "Noahide Laws," which were recognized by Maimonides, Gersonides and Albo. Spinoza provided a further embellishment to the distinctions found in previous medieval philosophers, claiming that the authority of Scripture has been reduced to moral pieties. As we see in the next chapter, Mendelssohn's overarching acceptance of a natural law separate from *halakhah*, coupled with Spinoza's rejection of *halakhah* altogether, marked the start of modernity in Jewish thought.

NOTES

1. Gersonides 1984, 1.1:intro: 101.
2. Gersonides 1984, 1.1.intro: 98.
3. Gersonides 1984, 11.intro: 98.
4. Talmud passage in tractate Avod Zar 8:4.
5. Albo's discussion is based on Thomas Aquinas, who wrote an entire treatise on natural law. For further discussion, see Rudavsky 2018.
6. Albo 1946, I.5, 72.
7. Albo 1946, Preface, 27.
8. Albo 1946, I.7, 78.
9. See Saadiah Gaon 1948, II.5:106; III.1:139
10. Maimonides 1963, III.34:534.
11. Maimonides 1963, III.26:509.
12. Spinoza 2001, Preface: 5.
13. Spinoza 2001, Preface 6.
14. Spinoza 2001, 26.

FURTHER READING

Fox, M. (1990), "Maimonides and Aquinas on Natural Law," in M. Fox, *Interpreting Maimonides: Studies in Methodology, Metaphysics, and Moral Philosophy*, Chicago, IL: University of Chicago Press, 124–151.

Fox, M. (1975), "On the Rational Commandments in Saadia's Philosophy: A Reexamination," in M. Fox (ed.), *Modern Jewish Ethics: Theory and Practice*, Columbus, OH: Ohio State University Press, 175–187.

Kasher, H. (1998), "Biblical Miracles and the Universality of Natural Law: Maimonides' Three Methods of Harmonization." *Journal of Jewish Thought and Philosophy*, 8: 25–52.

Nadler, S. (2011), *A Book Forged in Hell: Spinoza's Scandalous Treatise and the Birth of the Secular Age*. Princeton, NJ: Princeton University Press.

Novak, D. (1998), *Natural Law in Judaism*. Cambridge: Cambridge University Press.

Spinoza, B. (2001), *Theological-Political Treatise*, 2nd edn, trans. S. Shirley. Indianapolis, IN: Hackett Publishing.

THE EIGHTEENTH-CENTURY ENLIGHTENMENT

INTRODUCTION

Descartes, Spinoza, Leibnitz and other seventeenth-century philosophers created a modern movement that incorporated the secular-rationalist and scientific revolution of traditional Western thought. This revolution occurred in part because of the influence of scientists like Giordano Bruno, Galileo, Copernicus and Newton. The new science rebelled against, and staked its independence from, the Christian Church. Just as the secular states were throwing off the yoke of the Church and establishing their political independence, so too were the scientists and philosophers emancipating themselves from religious dogma. The eighteenth-century Enlightenment, therefore, originated in the context of the scientific revolutions of the sixteenth and seventeenth centuries. The heliocentric cosmology of Copernicus and Newton's physics undermined the long-established geocentric view of the world, which was aligned with Aristotelian metaphysics and cosmology.

Immanuel Kant (1724–1804) was a key player in the German Enlightenment as well as a major influence upon German Jewish philosophers. Kant's project in the *Critique of Pure Reason* was a critique of reason itself, resulting in what has come to be known as Kant's Copernican

Revolution. His main point is that the world we perceive has the structure it does because of the way our finite minds conceive it: the human mind imposes *a priori* conditions (e.g. space, time and categories of understanding) upon the empirical data given by the world. Without these conditions there can be no knowledge. Kant thus introduced a revolution in epistemology that probed the limits of rational inquiry. He described the Enlightenment as a release from self-incurred immaturity. "*Sapere aude*" (dare to know) was Kant's challenge to an Enlightenment readership – have the courage to use one's own understanding and not rely upon the authority of others.[1] We return to the implications of Kant's epistemology later in this chapter.

KABBALISTIC INFLUENCES

In order to appreciate fully the trajectory of Jewish thinkers in the Enlightenment, it is important as well to recognize the influential role of Jewish mysticism during this formative period. The cosmological exposition of Jewish mystical teachings, with its emphasis upon emanations from the One source, incorporated both Neoplatonism and Aristotelian ingredients. In contradistinction to the philosophers, the mystics introduced a deep religious impulse that was absent in the scientific world-view espoused by Emancipation thinkers. The term *Kabbalah* (= received tradition) refers in general to Judaism's mystical tradition. This tradition can be traced back to the earliest centuries of the common era, and includes such works as the *Sefer Yetzirah* (*Book of Creation*) in the eighth century; *Sefer Bahir* (*Book of Light*) in the eleventh century, and the *Sefer ha-Zohar* (*The Book of Splendor*) in the thirteenth century; subsequent mystical writings appeared in Sefat, Israel (sixteenth century), which became renowned as a major center for kabbalistic thought.

Speculative kabbalah emerged in Southern France and Spain in the thirteenth century. In this period, the Spanish Kabbalist Moses ben Shemtob de Leon (d. 1305) composed the canonical text *Sefer Ha-Zohar*, a work that became the chief source of inspiration for subsequent generations. After the Spanish expulsion, Isaac Luria "Ha-Ari" (the Lion, 1534–1572) became one of the most influential Kabbalists. Although he left no written works, his disciples spread his teachings throughout the western European countries. The Spanish expulsion, combined with a series of Cossack massacres led by Bogdan Khmer'nitskii in Poland (1648–1658), led to a messianic fervor among surviving Jews and Luria's teachings became even more influential. Centers of kabbalistic thought arose in Italy, Turkey and Palestine and then spread to all the centers of Jewish life, in particular in central and Eastern Europe. It penetrated the works of Christian theologians as well, culminating in the works of German philosopher Friedrich Wilhelm Joseph Schelling (1775–1854) who incorporated elements of the kabbalah into his own cosmology.

Against the backdrop of this kabbalistic fervor, Germany became the leading center of Jewish philosophical activity, in part because of the rarified esteem held by philosophy among the German elite. Modern eighteenth century German Jewish philosophers such as Moses Mendelssohn and Salomon Maimon imbibed the quest for independence, reflecting the struggle for emancipation in Germany. In this chapter, we examine Mendelssohn's major work *Jerusalem* and the many challenges he faced from his Christian peers who urged him to convert to Christianity. We then turn to Salomon Maimon, a protegee of both Mendelssohn and Kant, whose critique of Kant and defense of Mendelssohn set the stage for subsequent German and Jewish philosophy.

MENDELSSOHN: BIOGRAPHY AND MAJOR WORKS

Moses Mendelssohn (1729–1786) was one of the key champions of the Jewish Haskalah period that flourished in the eighteenth and early nineteenth centuries. Coinciding with the secular Enlightenment in western Europe, it was during this period that Jews for the first time were allowed entry from the ghettos into secular society. In Mendelssohn's view, Jews could and should be educated and enlightened, become accepted as citizens in the secular state, and at the same time retain their obligations as observant Jews. One of the major purposes of the Haskalah, initiated by Mendelssohn and his followers, was the transformation of Jewish education in an attempt to integrate Jews into the fabric of secular European culture.

Mendelssohn was born in 1729 and as a young child had memorized the entire Bible by heart and taught himself Hebrew grammar. In 1743 the family moved to Berlin, where the young Mendelssohn was exposed to Jewish philosophical texts, as well European literature; he taught himself German, Latin, Greek, French and English and immersed himself in this new world of secular thought. In 1753 Mendelssohn became friends with the philosopher Gotthold Ephraim Lessing (1729–1781) who was overwhelmed by Mendelssohn's erudition; the two studied Spinoza together, and Lessing published Mendelssohn's essay on Spinoza. This publication spurred Mendelssohn in 1763 to submit an essay titled "Treatise on Evidence in the Metaphysical Sciences" to the Berlin Academy. The essay won first place, beating out Immanuel Kant whose essay placed second. This essay was followed by the publication of the treatise *Phaedon* in 1767, a work modelled after Plato's dialogue the *Phaedo*, which was devoted to proving the immortality of the soul. Although the work contained little original thought, *Phaedon* gained Mendelssohn international fame as "the Jewish Plato," and was praised for its literary elegance.

Mendelssohn's fame attracted the attention of Christian clerics and writers and led to a number of intellectual crises in Mendelssohn's life. The first of these is known as the "Lavater Affair." The Swiss deacon Johann Caspar Lavater (1741–1801) was so impressed with Mendelssohn's erudition that he assumed Mendelssohn could not in true conscience be a Jew, but was a Christian at heart. Lavater wrote a preface to a work by the philosopher Charles Bonnet (1720–1793) defending Christianity, in which Lavater challenged Mendelssohn to publicly refute Bonnet's arguments or convert to Christianity. Mendelssohn's response in an open letter (to which we return below) defended his commitment to Judaism.

The second challenge came in 1783, in the form of an anonymous pamphlet (traced to the French satirist August Friedrich Cranz (1737–1801) that again challenged Mendelssohn to explain his reason for remaining a Jew. Cranz's argument was based on the fact that Mendelssohn had published a number of works decrying the use of excommunication by either Christian or Jewish institutions. Cranz argued that inasmuch as coercion and excommunication were both at the heart of Judaism, it followed that if Mendelssohn rejected them, he must be closer to Christianity.

Mendelssohn wrote his best known philosophical work *Jerusalem; or On Religious Power and Judaism* in 1783 as a response to the criticisms of the theologian Christian Wilhelm von Dohm, Johann Lavater and others who claimed that Jews could never become a part of modern Enlightenment society. It is one of the first modern Jewish philosophical works written on behalf of a rational conception of Judaism, and in it Mendelssohn provided an extended argument that Judaism is compatible with secular Enlightenment thought.

The third challenge, known as the Pantheism Controversy, erupted in 1785 with the counter-Enlightenment thinker Friedrich Heinrich Jacobi (1743–1819), who had claimed that, upon his death bed, Lessing confessed that he had become a Spinozist atheist. Jacobi made the confession public, and Mendelssohn was forced, as Lessing's friend, to respond in a work entitled *To Lessing's Friends*, in which he tried to exonerate Lessing of the charge of atheism. Mendelssohn died in January 1786 while delivering this final manuscript to his publisher.

MENDELSSOHN AND NATURAL LAW

As noted above, Mendelssohn wrote *Jerusalem or On Religious Power and Judaism* in 1783 as a response to claims that Jews could never become a part of modern Enlightenment society.[2] The work is in two parts: part one delineates the differences between religious institutions and political structures (the state), while part two is focused more squarely upon Judaism.

The first chapter of *Jerusalem* is couched in terms of universal laws of nature, laws that apply in many ethical situations. After describing many "natural duties," such as the natural duty of parents to provide an education for their children, Mendelssohn argued for the separation of church and state: the state's obligation is to deal with outward behavior, whereas that of religion is to deal primarily with inward conviction. The state functions as a "moral person" and has the power to dispose of the rights that result from natural law. Whereas the state can achieve its aims by outward compulsion, the church does not have this power. Unlike the relationship between the state and the individual, the relationship between God and individuals – reflected in religious institutions – does not impose duties and obligations that contravene reason.[3] Furthermore, Mendelssohn argued that the church cannot enter into contractual relations with its constituents: "The church does not remunerate; religion buys nothing, pays nothing, and allots no wages," he famously proclaimed.[4] Religion is incompatible with coercion, and religious institutions should have no civil authority. So too, should the state have no interest in legislating an individual's religious beliefs, and membership in a religious organization should be irrelevant to the state.

But if religion cannot coerce, what sense do we make of the *halakhah*, which clearly contains commandments regarded as binding upon Jews? In part two of *Jerusalem*, Mendelssohn attempted to respond to his [anonymous] critics who had accused him of rejecting the foundations of Judaism. Mendelssohn's response to this challenge drew upon the distinction between universal rational truths and what he calls "divine legislation": the former are self-evident principles of reason, whereas the latter are revealed supernaturally.[5] For Mendelssohn, Judaism comprised three elements: universal, eternal truths of natural religion (including God's existence); historical records concerning the Jewish people; and divine command as represented by *halakhah*. Universal eternal truths are truths that are taught (by God) through "creation itself and its internal relations, which are legible and comprehensible to all men."[6] Although they are revealed supernaturally, the laws based upon these truths are nonetheless accessible to all humans, and so all humans have a claim to salvation: Judaism has no exclusive claim to the path to salvation.[7]

Although the universal religion of humankind is accessible to all, and was not revealed at Sinai, Mendelssohn claimed that the laws of Moses contain rational truths: "all laws refer to, or are based upon, eternal verities, or remind us of them, and rouse us to ponder them."[8] What then is the purpose of the divine laws that form the bulk of *halakha*? Like his predecessors Saadiah Gaon and Maimonides, and in contradistinction to Spinoza (whom we discussed in Chapter 8), Mendelssohn distinguished between two levels of commandments: those pertaining to behavior and those pertaining to beliefs. The ritualistic commandments apply to external behaviors alone, and not to inner beliefs. In fact, Mendelssohn argued that the content of Jewish belief is compatible with what he calls "the natural religion of right reason." According to Mendelssohn, the purpose of the commandments is rooted in "Bildung": educating and moralizing human beings. It functions as a "living script" that trains individuals to function in a moral way.[9] Mendelssohn claimed that each ceremony and rite has its special meaning and significance, reminding us of the eternal verities: they "guide the seeking mind to divine truths...on which the religion of this people was based."[10] Like Maimonides, he argued that the commandments have a moral purpose, and like Spinoza, he argued that Scripture does not teach speculative truths. Unlike Spinoza, however, Mendelssohn was committed to the view that the ceremonial law has authority and requires observance: "no sophistry of ours can free us from the strict obedience we owe to the law."[11]

Chapter 8 broached the question of whether Judaism recognizes a natural law independent of Jewish law. In part this question reflects, once more, the age-old tension between reason and revelation: are the basic tenets of Judaism rational, or are they founded in revelation alone? In other words, can we somehow accommodate both reason and revelation into the fabric of Jewish law? Mendelssohn was aware of both Maimonides's and Spinoza's position on the Noahide or Natural Laws, and addressed them directly. We have seen that according to Mendelssohn, any individual can achieve salvation independently of Judaism by practicing the tenets of a universal morality that is grounded in universal eternal truths identified with the Noahide laws. In a letter (1769) to the protestant theologian Johann Caspar Lavater, Mendelssohn upheld the view that non-Jews were charged to abide by the seven Noahide laws: "Those who regulate their conduct in accordance with the laws of this religion of nature and reason are called virtuous men of other nations, and they are children of eternal bliss."[12]

In this early letter to Lavater, Mendelssohn glossed over Maimonides's suggestion that righteous gentiles must acknowledge the *divine basis* for Noahide laws. But Mendelssohn was clearly troubled by Maimonides's stance, and in 1793 he wrote a letter to Rabbi Jacob Emden in which he expressed dismay at Maimonides's position: Maimonides's words, he wrote to Rabbi Emden, "are harder to me than flint … are then, all dwellers on earth … except for us, doomed to perdition if they fail to believe in the Torah?"[13] Mendelssohn thus rejected Maimonides's position, arguing that the ethical laws are rational, universal laws that follow from our nature.[14] Thus in both *Jerusalem* and in his letter to Rabbi Emden, Mendelssohn emphasized the universalistic-humanism of Jewish Law by referring to the dictum that assigns to the righteous among the nations a share in the world to come.[15]

It should be noted that this question has continued to vex Jewish philosophers to this very day. Some scholars have offered evidence of, at the very least, a natural morality reflected in both *halakhah* itself, as well as in Jewish texts. Thus the contemporary Orthodox philosopher Aharon Lichtenstein (1933–2015) makes use of the classic rabbinic passage "If the Torah had not been given, we would have learnt modesty from the cat, [aversion to] robbery from the ant, chastity from the dove, and [conjugal] manners from the cock" to suggest that a cluster of logically ante-halakhic virtues exists and can be inferred from natural phenomena.[16] Lichtenstein carefully distinguishes between natural law and natural morality, and mentions numerous biblical passages supporting the thesis that the bulk of revealed Torah could have been naturally and logically discovered. Arguing that at most, the rabbis rejected natural *law*, not natural *morality*, he goes on to maintain that "the traditional acceptance of some form of natural morality seems to me beyond doubt."[17] We have then, many ways of construing the role of law in Jewish thought, ranging from an explicit denial of any law independent of *halakha* to the implicit postulation of natural law theory in Maimonides and other authors.

Immanuel Kant was one of Mendelssohn's admirers, and yet Kant's major philosophical work *Critique of Pure Reason* threatened to undermine the overall impetus of Mendelssohn's endeavors in *Jerusalem*. Kant's influence was enhanced at least in part because his career overlapped with the entry of Jews into German academic and intellectual life. He had several Jewish students whom he encouraged, and when the ban on Jewish professors was formally lifted, Jews such as Hermann Cohen (whom we encounter in Chapter 10) celebrated a Neo-Kantian revival. Furthermore, there existed a genuine affinity between Jewish philosophy and Kant, in part because of their mutual involvement with Platonism.[18]

While Kant and Mendelssohn both shared the Enlightenment ethos, Kant argued in a letter that on Mendelssohn's own descriptions in *Jerusalem*, Judaism did not satisfy the criteria of an established religion. In his work *Religion within the Limits of Reason Alone*, Kant argued that removing reliance upon supernatural knowledge leads to the conclusion that whatever is beyond the purview of pure reason remains beyond it forever. For example, the existence of God and the human soul are both notions that lie beyond the limits of reason. Kant depicted Judaism as comprising a desiccated, outdated set of legal codes, based on blind obedience, and he argued that it was Christianity that raised Judaism from a theocracy to a spiritual institution. In fact, Kant argued that Judaism was rooted in Christianity, and not the other way round and once Christianity is purified of Judaic elements, Mendelssohn and his followers would be able to convert to Christianity. Mendelssohn himself did not offer a response to Kant; he left it to others to rise to the challenge. One of his strongest supporters was Solomon Maimon.

SOLOMON MAIMON'S DEFENSE OF MENDELSSOHN

Mendelssohn's younger contemporary Solomon Maimon (1752–1800), writing under the aegis of both Kant and Mendelssohn, took upon himself the challenge to critique both philosophers. Maimon (his given name was Shlomo ben Yehoshua) was born and raised in an isolated Jewish community in Poland. A Talmudic prodigy, he was introduced to philosophy through reading a copy of Maimonides's *Guide of the Perplexed*, which led to a life-long spiritual/intellectual struggle. He wrote a commentary on Maimonides's work, hoping to update its teachings for a contemporary audience, and took for himself Maimonides's name as his own. He then discovered the works of Christian Wolff, a German Enlightenment thinker, Hume, Locke, Kant and others, and devoted his energies to reconciling Kant with his own philosophy, as well as with the philosophy of Maimonides.

Maimon addressed Judaic and philosophical issues in a wide-ranging and enormously entertaining autobiography. In this work he presented himself, like Spinoza, as a free-thinker born a Jew but unaffiliated with his Judaism. His autobiography is, in the words of its translator:

> a brilliantly vivid, informative, searing and witty, even hilarious account of his life as a Talmudic prodigy ... a preadolescent husband [at age 14], an aspiring kabbalist-magician, an earnest young philosopher, a bedraggled beggar, an urbane Berlin pleasure-seeker,

and eventually the philosopher of whom Kant would write "none of my critics understood me and the main questions so well as Herr Maimon."[19]

Oddly enough, a ten-chapter outline and detailed critique of Maimonides's *Guide* appears at the center of the autobiography. This outline is key to understanding Maimon's own life and thought, and we return to it below. Maimon acknowledged his admiration for Maimonides in this section, noting that his admiration "for this great teacher reached the point that I regarded him as the *ideal* of a perfect human being."[20] Throughout his autobiography, Maimon presented himself as an outsider (which he surely was), rejecting the scientific ideals of both the German and Jewish Enlightenments for a more Maimonidean contemplative ideal. "I left my people, my homeland, and my family to seek the truth," he tells us in this introduction to the Maimonides chapters, emphasizing his estrangement from both conventional philosophy and Judaism in a search for truth rooted in a rationalist ideal.

Maimon abandoned his young family and, after a circuitous journey, he arrived in Berlin in 1779 where he was befriended by Mendelssohn who came to regard him as an intellectual peer. Maimon described in his autobiography his first interactions with Mendelssohn in detail. Maimon had procured a copy of the philosopher Christian Wolff's work (which was being used as wrapping paper by a local butcher!) and wrote a critique of Wolff's arguments for God's existence. On a lark, he sent this critique to Mendelssohn who was impressed with Maimon's acumen and encouraged Maimon to continue his studies. Maimon then sent to Mendelssohn a metaphysical disputation in Hebrew, attacking twelve of the thirteen articles of faith established by Maimonides. Mendelssohn was so impressed by this work that he befriended Maimon for several years: "he [Mendelssohn] assured me that if I continued in this way, I would make great progress in metaphysics."[21] In a chapter of the autobiography devoted to Mendelssohn, Maimon described in detail the many positive attributes Mendelssohn possessed, and emphasized Mendelssohn's obsession with perfection:

> His God was the ideal of complete perfection; the idea of complete perfection was the foundation of his morality. The guiding principle of his aesthetics was sensuous perfection ... [he] regarded the concept of perfection that forms the basis of morality as extending well beyond knowledge of the truth.[22]

Maimon defended Mendelssohn against a variety of charges and accepted Mendelssohn's conception of natural religion as the common denominator of all religions. Maimon went on to emphasize the uniqueness of Judaism: as a political religion, Judaism is fundamentally rational, and should not be compared with Christianity. He also emphasized the high ethical level that Judaism maintained, highlighting the emphasis upon charity and mutual aid in the *halakhah*. Describing Mendelssohn's views in *Jerusalem* about the revealed laws of religion being identified as eternal truths, Maimon agreed with Mendelssohn that the laws of Judaism should function as the basis for a state, and that those who leave the state are no longer obligated to follow those laws. Maimon did, however, point to a contradiction in Mendelssohn's work in its assertion both that the church has no authority in civil matters, and yet upholding the permanence of the Jewish theocratic state.

MAIMON'S CRITIQUE OF KANT'S *CRITIQUE OF PURE REASON*

Maimon learned about Kant's *Critique of Pure Reason* in 1789 and after a careful study that he described as a kind of coalition system – using Kant's philosophy to coalesce with his own philosophical system – Maimon sent a letter to Kant describing what he took to be internal problems for Kant's system. In his autobiography Maimon described his attempt to grapple with Kant: "My *Transcendental Philosophy* takes up the problem that Kant's *Critique* tries to solve ... but in a much broader sense than in Kant's works. My theory leaves room for Humean skepticism in all its force."[23] Kant responded within six weeks, encouraging Maimon's efforts, claiming that "none of my critics have understood me and the main question I try to address as well as the author ... few people possess the intelligence required for such profound investigations to the degree that Herr Maimon does."[24] Kant's positive encouragement provided Maimon with the opportunity to publish in leading German journals. Receiving support from Kant, Maimon published two works: the *Essay on Transcendental Philosophy* (1790), which brought elements of Jewish philosophy to bear on Kant, and *The Hill of the Guide* (1791), a commentary on the first part of Maimonides's *Guide* which used elements of Kant to elucidate Maimonides.[25]

CONCLUSION

Mendelssohn and Maimon were virtually alone in being active participants in both the German and Jewish Enlightenments. They stood on the margins of two cultures and two world views. But to what extent were they able to harmonize the worlds? Scholars have disagreed over whether Mendelssohn was able to achieve a coherent synthesis between his Jewishness and his Germanness, between his commitment to Judaism and to the Enlightenment. Was Mendelssohn able to make the case that Judaism mattered as a religion, despite the fact that the "universal religion of reason" contained the important verities shared by all religions? Many scholars have argued that Mendelssohn failed to achieve a true synthesis, pointing to the fact that his own children converted to Christianity, seeing no reason to remain within the Jewish fold. To these more conservative voices, Mendelssohn represented the disintegration of authentic Jewish life, a path that led to apostasy and assimilation. Mendelssohn's overarching acceptance of a natural law separate from *halakhah*, coupled with Spinoza's rejection of *halakhah* altogether, marked the start of modernity in Jewish thought. Similarly, Maimon, according to these critics, represented the prototype of Jew seduced by the secular learning to the detriment of his Jewish roots.

Others have argued that Mendelssohn did in fact achieve a seamless synthesis between Judaism and the German Enlightenment. On this reading, Mendelssohn saw both Judaism and Enlightenment rationalism as presenting the same world-view.[26] Mendelssohn thus represented the integration of Jews into German life, an equality that opened the door to an enlightened and emancipated way of Jewish life.

Maimon's autobiography ends with an allegory entitled "The Merry Masquerade Ball" which mirrors in interesting ways Maimonides's own allegory at the end of the *Guide* of the King in his Palace. Maimon's allegory represents the history of philosophy, with Madame Metaphysics at the center of the ball, her chambermaid representing Physics, and the various dancers representing other schools and arguments in the history of philosophy. Just as union with the King in Maimonides's allegory symbolizes union with the Active Intellect, so too dancing with Madame Metaphysics is akin to achieving ultimate metaphysical truth, which represents the ultimate purpose or telos of human existence.

Thus Solomon Maimon represented a foot a bit more firmly placed in the secular Enlightenment represented by German society. Unlike Mendelssohn, Maimon flaunted his otherness and distance from the Jewish world of his upbringing; his autobiography mocked his "Jewish" attributes, presenting them as comedic. He lived at the intersection of various worlds: pre-modern and modern, Jewish and German, philosophical and mystical.[27] And yet his trenchant critiques of Kant helped to lay the groundwork for German Idealism. Chapter 10 deals more specifically with the rise of Hegelian idealism and its influence upon Jewish philosophy.

NOTES

1. Kant, "An Answer to the Question: What is Enlightenment," quoted in Socher 2006, 13.
2. Gottlieb 2011, 43.
3. See Mendelssohn 1983, 59.
4. Mendelssohn 1983, 61.
5. Mendelssohn 1983, 90ff.
6. Mendelssohn 1983, 93.
7. Mendelssohn 1983, 94. "All the inhabitants of the earth are destined to felicity."
8. Mendelssohn 1983, 99.
9. See Mendelssohn 1983, 128. The laws, both written and unwritten, "are also, in large part, to be regarded as a kind of script."
10. Mendelssohn 1983, 99.
11. Mendelssohn 1983, 133.
12. Gottlieb 2011, 9.
13. This portion of the letter is quoted in Gottlieb 2011, 209. See also the complete letter in Gottlieb 2011, 32–35.
14. See Gottlieb 2011, 32–35.
15. Altmann 1973, 294–295.
16. Lichtenstein 1975, 62.
17. Lichtenstein 1975, 64.
18. Consider for example, that Platonism, Kant and the Jewish tradition all oppose sensualism and materialism, emphasizing the priority of intellectual perfection. See Franks 2007, 53.

19 Maimon in Melamed and Socher 2018, xvi.
20 Maimon in Melamed and Socher 2018, 128.
21 Maimon in Melamed and Socher 2018, 195.
22 Maimon in Melamed and Socher 2018, 201.
23 Maimon in Melamed and Socher 2018, 231. The reference "Humean" is to David Hume, known for his philosophical skepticism.
24 Maimon in Melamed and Socher 2018, 232.
25 Franks 2007, 61.
26 Gottlieb 2011, xix–xx.
27 Quinn 2021, 51.

FURTHER READING

Altmann, A. (1973). *Moses Mendelssohn: A Biographical Study*. Tuscaloosa, AL: University of Alabama Press.

Melamed, Y. and A.P. Socher. (2018). *The Autobiography of Solomon Maimon: The Complete Translation*, trans. Paul Reitter. Princeton, NJ: Princeton University Press.

Mendelssohn, M. (1983). *Jerusalem or on Religious Power and Judaism*, trans. Allan Arkush, intro and commentary Alexander Altmann. Hanover, NH: University Press of New England.

Gottlieb, M. ed. (2011). *Moses Mendelssohn: Writings on Judaism, Christianity & The Bible*. Waltham, MA: Brandeis University Press.

10

THE IDEALIST TURN

INTRODUCTION: THE HEGELIAN WORLD

Moses Mendelssohn had introduced the conviction that Judaism represented a universal religion of reason. This rationalist strain continued into the nineteenth century against the backdrop of Hegelian and post-Kantian philosophy. Georg Wilhelm Friedrich Hegel (1770–1831) was one of the most influential philosophers of the nineteenth century, promoting a comprehensive and systematic philosophy based on a dialectical logic. Hegel's major work *Phenomenology of Spirit,* published in 1807, intensified Kant's system by examining further the limits of reason. Hegel argued that because consciousness always includes self-consciousness, there are no "given" objects of perception that are not mediated by thought. Hegel's theory of knowledge was thus even more extreme than that of Kant in that the conscious ego was involved in every act of perception. Hegel introduced what he called absolute spirit (*Geist*) as the ultimate reality we can come to know; he used the term *Geist* in many different contexts but often as isomorphic with God.[1]

Hegel introduced the dialectic method to investigate the historical trajectory of *Geist*. Hegel's dialectic describes a movement of thought from an affirmation (thesis) to a contrary affirmation (antithesis), over and over until a synthesis is achieved that resolves the initial contradictions. There is continual movement back and forth between thesis and antithesis; this process is repeated as the new affirmation (synthesis) functions as a thesis in combination with yet another antithesis that yields a new synthesis. Hegel described the dialectical method as an "overcoming" of the negative antithesis, leading to a linear evolution from less sophisticated to more sophisticated views, culminating ultimately in absolute truth. Each new thesis thus reflected progress beyond past theses. Dialectic was used by Hegel to explain practically everything in his system, including history, religion, science and philosophy. In the final chapters of his *Phenomenology*, Hegel described the progression of religion as moving from early paganism (thesis) to Judaism (antithesis), culminating in Christianity (synthesis) which leads ultimately to absolute spirit. Hegel presented Judaism as a religion of division, setting the finite human being against an all-powerful, infinite God: on Hegel's analysis, the human sphere in Judaism is degraded to the point of nothingness.[2] This dismissal of Judaism led to an opposition between Hegel's philosophy of spirit/*Geist* and Jewish thought.

NAHMAN KROCHMAL AND THE HEGELIAN TURN

Despite Hegel's denigration of Judaism, Nachman Krochmal (1785–1840) was a committed Hegelian. As a major leader of the Jewish emancipation movement (*Haskalah*) in Eastern Europe, Krochmal did his best to marry Hegelian idealism with Judaism. Krochmal was born in the town of Brody in Galicia (Poland/Ukraine). While the Western Haskalah had not yet penetrated much of Galicia, Brody was one of the centers of the emerging movement. In 1803 Krochmal taught himself German by reading newspapers, and soon learned French, Latin, Arabic and Syriac; he then embarked on reading the works of Mendelssohn, Lessing, Maimon, Kant, Fichte, Schelling and Hegel.[3] In addition, Krochmal was drawn to the Jewish Neoplatonism of ibn Ezra as well as to Kabbalah. He spent the last years of his life in Brody after his wife's death, working to finish his magnum opus *Guide of the Perplexed of our Time* (*Moreh Nevukhei ha-Zeman*) which was published posthumously in 1851.[4]

Krochman used the Hegelian method of dialectical logic to argue for the national spirit of the Jewish people. Undeterred by Hegel's negative assessment of Judaism, Krochmal's *Guide* utilized Hegelian dialectic in his analysis of Jewish culture and history. The *Guide* is divided into four sections: chapters 1–7 focus on issues in philosophy of religion, chapters 8–11 provide a summary of Jewish history; chapters 12–15 are an analysis of Hebrew texts; and chapters 16–17 offer a preliminary introduction (unfinished) to his own philosophical views. Krochmal saw no opposition between Hegelian idealistic philosophy and Judaism, insisting that the doctrines of modern philosophy were in complete agreement with Judaism.[5] Like Maimonides, he sought to examine Judaism in light of his contemporary philosophy and eliminate perplexities encountered by this new modern thought. In line with Hegel, Krochmal defined reality as the absolute Spirit (*ha-Ruhani ha-Muhlat*) which corresponded in his system to the concept of God.

The preface of the *Guide* lays out the religious doubts encountered by his contemporaries, rooted in two extremes which Krochmal portrayed as idolatry and religious denial. The first he identified with the Hasidim who were enamored of mysticism and what Krochmal considered holy madness, while the latter were (in his description) mindless Orthodox Jews that emphasized magical powers, rituals and amulets. Both these extremes distorted the essence of Judaism and led to what Krochmal considered "horrifying religious decadence."[6] The *Guide* was written for those perplexed Jews who found the religious decadence represented by these extremes repugnant and yearned for a middle ground.

But who exactly were these perplexed Jews? In the world of Maimonides, the perplexed were individuals confronted with Aristotelian science and Jewish beliefs, which they attempted to reconcile. Krochmal's perplexed Jews, on the other hand, were primarily Eastern Galician Jews who were aware of the new historical scholarship and the denigration of rabbinic texts, and who were familiar as well with the works of Spinoza, Kant, Schelling and Hegel.[7] The conflict thus presented itself as between the rabbinic way to eternal truths rooted in authoritative texts, and the critical scholar's way, based on empirical demonstration. Krochmal's goal was to show that there is no conflict between Judaism and modern thought.[8] While Krochmal clearly saw Maimonides's work as a model for his own book, he argued that since the Aristotelianism of the Middle Ages was now obsolete, a new guide was necessary for "our time."

While the introductory chapters lay out in detail the causes of perplexity, chapters 5–7 of the *Guide* focus on metaphysical themes in Judaism that were challenged by the works of Spinoza, Kant and Hegel. Consider, for example, the teleological argument for God's existence that argues from effects in nature to a final cause responsible for all efficient causes; we have seen medieval versions of this argument in the medieval texts (see Chapter 4, this volume). Krochmal tried to respond to criticisms of this argument, most notably those of Spinoza who rejected all mention of teleology as spurious.

This attempt to revive the teleological argument led to a more general discussion of God's nature, which had been critically deconstructed by Hegel. As noted above, Hegel regarded Judaism as a mere stepping-stone to a more sophisticated Christian theology. On the basis of Hegel's dialectical logic, Judaism's God was totally transcendent, resulting in an "enormous gulf between God and the world, and the removal of divinity from nature and the natural world."[9] Krochmal responded to these criticisms with an elaborate analysis of the role played by God in Jewish Neoplatonism. Using a Neoplatonist emanationist ontology, he countered Hegel's critique by arguing that the Jewish God was indeed not alienated from the world. Krochmal argued further that Hegel's conception of God as absolute spirit or *Geist* was already adumbrated in Jewish sources.[10]

In chapters 8–11 of the *Guide*, Krochmal adopted Hegel's dialectical methodology and applied it to Jewish history. As did Hegel, Krochmal identified absolute spirit/*Geist* with absolute truth, and argued that the goal of human existence is the unification of the human spirit with the divine spirit. But in contradistinction to Hegel who rejected Judaism as an avenue to truth, Krochmal argued that while each nation had its own spiritual essence, the Jewish nation was unique and eternal. Like his predecessor Judah Halevi (see Chapter 2, this volume), Krochmal took into consideration the entirety of Jewish life, arguing that only the nation of Israel had faith in the absolute spirit. Judaism's spirit "flows from the very source of the Absolute Spirit itself," elevating the Jewish people above all other nations."[11] Krochmal's analysis laid the groundwork for a Zionist philosophy of history that emphasized the eventual renewal of the nation spirit. We return to the topic of Zionism in Chapter 14.

HERMANN COHEN: BRIEF BIOGRAPHY

Krochmal was the first modern Jewish philosopher to make not only the Jewish religion but also the Jewish people, a subject for philosophical investigation.[12] His influence was felt in the latter part of the nineteenth century, culminating in the work of Hermann Cohen (1848–1918). Like Krochmal, Cohen was a devotee of Hegel, but he drew most of his inspiration from Kant, creating a neo-Kantian school in Marburg. Hermann Cohen was born in Cowsig, Germany, the son of a cantor. He originally intended to receive ordination at the rabbinical seminary, but decided instead to enroll first at the university in Breslau and then University of Berlin. At the suggestion of his professor who was very much impressed with Cohen's work, Cohen was appointed professor of philosophy at the University of Marburg in 1875, one of the only Jews to achieve such a position in Germany.

Cohen's early works (1871–1889) were devoted to a critical evaluation of idealism as found in the works of Plato and Kant; they included *Kant's Theory of Experience*, *Kant's Foundation of Ethics* and *Kant's Foundations of Aesthetics*. These works contributed to a new interpretation of Kant, leading to the creation of the Marburg school of neo-Kantian philosophy, which flourished from 1876, the date of Cohen's appointment as a full professor, until 1912, the date of his retirement. Cohen then published several works of his own system, which he described as "critical idealism:" *Logic of Pure Knowledge*, *Ethics of Pure Will* and *Aesthetics of Pure Feeling*. These works were followed by *The Concept of Religion within the System of Philosophy*, a work published posthumously. We return to this latter work below.

In addition to his neo-Kantian works, Cohen became increasingly involved in issues pertaining to Judaism. In 1880 Cohen was called upon to defend Judaism in light of "the Jewish question" that resulted when the historian Treitschke attacked German Jews and Judaism as a "national religion of an alien race." Cohen responded with an essay in which he argued that German Protestantism and liberal Judaism were essentially alike, and that liberal Jews were totally integrated into German society, with no double loyalty. After a successful career, Cohen left Marburg in 1912 and spent the remaining years of his life in Berlin, where he taught at the *Academy for the Scientific Study of Judaism*, a Jewish university devoted to the reform of Judaism by promoting the liberal teachings of the Jewish Haskalah. Several of his "Jewish" essays have been included in a volume entitled *Reason and Hope*. These Jewish writings are central to understanding not only Cohen's Jewish faith but also his philosophical principles. In *Reason and Hope*, Cohen emphasized what he sees as the congruence between Kant's philosophy and Judaism, arguing that both rely upon reason for their ethical systems: "The inner affinities between Kant's philosophy and Judaism are evident in the substantive similarity between the ethics of the Kantian system and the basic ideas of Judaism."[13]

In his later work, Cohen's writings turned more specifically to an understanding of the role played by religion in a rational philosophical system. He emphasized the interdependence of religion and ethics, both of which emphasized the status of the autonomous individual. In his final work *Religion of Reason Out of the Sources of Judaism*, drawn in part from lectures given at the *Academy*, Cohen turned specifically to Judaism as the source of a religion of reason. Drawing inspiration from Scripture, the rabbinic sources, Maimonides and Kant, Cohen presented a new approach to religion with an emphasis upon religious love. He introduced the notion of "correlation" to describe the dynamic relations between God and human beings, on the one hand, and human–human relations on the other.

THE MARBURG SCHOOL: CRITIQUE OF KANT AND CRITICAL IDEALISM

Before turning to Cohen's Jewish writings, which embody his attempt to synthesize Judaism with Kant, to marry rationalism with the demands of Judaism, a few words about Cohen's critique of Kant's critical idealism are appropriate. As noted in Chapter 9, Kant understood the world as the sum total of everything that has reality. The transcendental level of reality is mind-independent and includes Kantian things in themselves, while the empirical level comprises the domain of mind-dependent appearances. Idealism is the view that things in themselves (*noumena*) are totally mind-independent, beyond our human knowledge of them, while realism holds that appearances (*phenomena*) are fully mind-dependent; the two levels of reality do not overlap in any way.

More specifically, what this means is that empirical objects themselves are not mind-independent, whereas things in themselves are. But why even think that there are "things in themselves;" and furthermore why argue that empirical reality is mind-dependent? Kant argued that accepting the mind-independence of appearances leads to skepticism, a view that questions how we can even demonstrate the existence of mind-independent empirical objects. Kant claimed that once we recognize that empirical objects are mind-dependent insofar as they exist in space and time (which themselves owe their existence to the mind), then skepticism about their existence is defeated.[14] Kant's critical idealism thus posits both realism and idealism as ways of coming to know reality: on this view, the objects of human experience are not things in themselves but *appearances* of those entities.

Post-Kantians have interpreted his critical idealism in many different ways. Proponents of anti-metaphysical interpretations read Kant as having demolished metaphysics once and for all. On the other hand, proponents of metaphysical interpretations read Kant as the founder of a new way of doing metaphysics, one that differed markedly from more traditional metaphysics.[15] As founder of the neo-Kantian movement, Cohen was one of the foremost proponents of the anti-metaphysical group. Although Cohen subjected Kant's system to trenchant critique, he nonetheless remained very much under the influence of Kant's epistemology. As we have seen in Chapter 9, Kant had argued in many of his works that reason is inherently limited: it cannot demonstrate that the will is free, that the soul is immortal, or that God exists. Cohen agreed in theory with Kant's conception of reason but felt that Kant had not gone far enough in delineating the parameters and limits of reason; he insisted that critical idealism furnished the epistemological foundations not only of the natural world in general, but natural science in particular. More specifically, Cohen claimed that while Kant's Copernican revolution provided the material for justifying scientific laws as necessarily true claims about the world as we know it, he modified Kant's views, arguing that the acquisition of knowledge must be limited to what humans can know, and not to things beyond the purview of human knowledge.[16] Cohen thus provided a corrective to Kant's revolutionary system. But while reason for Cohen was paramount, his anti-metaphysical interpretation of Kant positioned Cohen dangerously close to radical idealism, a position that threatened the existence of an independent reality apart from our perception of it.

GERMANISM AND JUDAISM

Cohen's philosophy of religion represents one of the last attempts in the rationalist Jewish tradition to marry Judaism and modern philosophy, emphasizing the synthesis of Judaism and what he termed Germanism in several essays. In a 1910 essay entitled "The Inner Relations of Kant's Philosophy to Judaism," Cohen attempted to demonstrate the total harmony between Kant's critical reason and Judaism. He noted several affinities between Kant's philosophy and Judaism: Both Kantian and Judaic ethics (using Saadiah Gaon and Maimonides as exemplars) are rooted in reason; both reject a eudaimonistic ethic (drawn from Aristotle) that emphasizes the importance of achieving happiness and well-being, both physical and intellectual; and both distinguish between practical reason, moral reasoning, and theoretical reason. Cohen was emphatic that Jewish philosophy "unequivocally rejects the principle of happiness."[17] And the sharp divide between practical and theoretical reason reinforced Cohen's view that "morality and its principles are neither the equivalent of science and logic nor their equal."[18] Finally, Cohen noted that the ethos of Kant's categorical imperative is reflected in Jewish values: "this concept suggests that every individual represents [such] an end and must therefore never be used merely as a means. And this most profound and clear meaning of the categorical imperative is deeply ingrained in the Jew."[19]

The similarity between Kantian idealism and Judaism was reinforced further in the 1915 essay "Germanism and Judaism,"[20] a work that emphasized the importance of cultural Germanism to Judaism in general. Cohen argued that "Greekness" (as reflected in the works of Plato) is a source of philosophical idealism and can be found both in German philosophy and culture as well as in Judaism. Totally committed to the ideal of German Jews entering the mainstream of German society, Cohen rejected Zionism as undermining this ideal. He could not envision the importance of establishing an independent Jewish state: "The Jew saw his Messianic idea revitalized in and through the German spirit...in these epoch-making times, so fateful for all nations, we as Jews are proud to be Germans."[21] These words were written in 1915; reading them in light of the rise of National Socialism and the Holocaust is particularly ironic and tragic. It is worth nothing that Cohen's own wife perished in the concentration camps at the age of 82.

COHEN'S RELIGION OF REASON: RECOGNIZING THE "THOU"

In an earlier work entitled *Kant's Foundations of Ethics* (1877), Cohen criticized Kant on the grounds that Kant could not provide a transcendental deduction for the categorical imperative, a major principle underlying his moral system. In a second work (*Ethics of Pure Will*, 1904) Cohen returned to this issue and presented a modified version of his own ethical system. In this work he argued that the subject matter of ethics is humanity in general. But this work raised additional problems. The first problem was how to reconcile the universality of moral law with the wills of individual moral agents. But there was an even deeper problem: if ethics pertains to all of humanity and offers a complete account of the relation between God and humanity, what role does religion have to play? Either Cohen's previous ethical system was incomplete, or religion had nothing distinctive to offer to philosophy.

Cohen tackled these problems in his final two works *Concept of Religion Within the System of Philosophy* (1915) and his posthumously published work *Religion of Reason out of the Sources of Judaism* (1919). While Cohen presented his philosophical work as a justification for Judaism, he still had not established a distinctive role for religion independent of ethics. How to move from ethics to religion? In these final works, Cohen argued that the ethical principle, while universally applicable, does not account for the suffering and guilt felt by the individual. Ethics alone cannot provide moral redemption. Cohen assigned to religion a special task as distinguished from ethics, namely to supply a foundation for individual human autonomy. Whereas ethics is concerned with universal precepts, religion provides individual human beings access to God as the source of forgiveness.

Cohen's *Religion of Reason* starts with an elaborate analysis of the meaning of a "religion of reason." Reason is the "rock out of which the concept (of religion) originates and out of which it has to originate for the sake of systematic investigation."[22] The religion of reason is the joint product of rational humanity, not the product of any one people or culture: "insofar as reason is the beginning of human consciousness, all peoples indeed participate in the religion of reason."[23] What role, then, does Judaism play in establishing principles of religion? Cohen argued that Judaism is the "primordial source" or fountainhead of this religion of reason; other religions turn out to be derivative upon Judaism.

How are ethics and religion related – "should ethics have to share its labor with religion?"[24] Cohen suggested that while in traditional ethics "the I of man becomes the I of humanity," religion provides an additional dimension to ethics in its emphasis upon what Cohen called the "fellowman." More specifically, Cohen argued that systematic ethics deals with individuals only *qua* members of humanity as a whole. But religion recognizes individuals in a more personal way, allowing room for the moral failings of moral agents, transforming them from an impersonal "he" to a "Thou." Herein lies the turning point from which religion emerges from ethics: "the observation of another man's suffering is not an inert affect to which I surrender myself ... in suffering, a dazzling light suddenly makes me see the dark spots in the sun of life ... we touch here upon the borderline at which religion arises, and at which it illuminates the human horizon with suffering."[25]

Religion, suffering and sin are thus intertwined: "the discovery of man through sin is the source from which every religious development flows."[26] The most important person to recognize as a "Thou" is oneself: "In myself,

I have to study sin, and through sin I must learn to know myself."[27] The process of recognizing ones own failings, and improving them, is a religious activity that transcends ethical laws. "The discovery of humanity through sin is the source from which every religious development flows."[28] This discovery leads the individual to God who alone can provide forgiveness and absolution, and to the Jewish prophets who alone recognized the suffering of the poor within the state: "the poor became for them [the prophets] the symbol of human suffering ... their God becomes the God of the poor."[29] Having established the religion of reason as the underpinning of ethics, and the Jewish prophets as champions of the poor, Cohen devoted much of the work to concepts in Judaism that supported this system.

"CORRELATION" BETWEEN GOD AND HUMANS

We have seen that Cohen understood the critique of reason in terms of absolute idealism, excluding from it any notion of a transcendent reality. By this Cohen meant that there is no reality beyond experienced objects – there is no metaphysical thing-in-itself. What then, can we make of religious representations, and in particular a Deity? In contradistinction to Kant who found room for the idea of God in his metaphysical system, Cohen argued more radically that God exists not as a metaphysical *reality* but as an epistemological *idea*; its function as an idea is to connect the natural and ethical worlds.

For Cohen, monotheism emphasizes both the uniqueness and transcendence of the Deity: "it is God's uniqueness, rather than his oneness, that we posit as the essential content of monotheism."[30] By transcendence Cohen meant that mode of being that is "beyond an existence verifiable by natural science."[31] Neither time nor space are limitations upon God. In emphasizing God's transcendence, Cohen eliminated personal characteristics to God, rejecting all attempts at anthropomorphizing God: "This is the simple, profound, true meaning of God's transcendence. God is in truth "beyond me," for He is the Holy One, the archetype of all human morality."[32] This unique Deity is the source of the world, nature, and human beings. God is thus both Creator and Revealer. By creation Cohen had in mind not a single instant as described in Genesis, but rather a process of continuous creation and renewal of the world. In revelation, God enters into a relation with human beings. Like creation, revelation is continuous.

In *Religion of Reason*, Cohen returned to a principle he had introduced in earlier works, namely the "principle of origins," to explain the special relation that occurs between God and human beings. "Correlation" is introduced as a religio-philosophical term that denotes the special relationship between God and humans as well as between God and nature. Standing outside both nature and ethics, God is the principle of correlation between human beings, nature and God. Cohen emphasized that "our philosophical language calls it correlation, which is the term for all concepts of reciprocal relation."[33]

It is important to note that the concept of correlation is methodological and should not be understood as a process of dialogical thinking between two personal individuals. God is an idea, not a personal Thou. Cohen once again emphasizes the concept of correlation as generating the concept of God as redeemer of sin. "Through sin, man is to become an individual, and indeed an I conscious of itself … without finding one's way through all of human frailty, man cannot find his way to God. And without the correlation with God, the final act of atonement cannot be accomplished."[34] The correlation of humans to God thus brings about atonement and reconciliation. Let us not forget, however, that God for Cohen is an idea, not a reality, and so the love for God is the "love for an ethical ideal." How is it possible to love an idea, Cohen asks? His answer is clear: "how is it possible to love anything but an idea? Does one not love, even in the case of sensual love, only the idealized person, the idea of the person?"[35] Pure love is directed toward models: "this idealistic meaning is the clear, exact sense of the love for God."[36] Similarly, God's love of humans is an archetype: "the love of man for God is the love of the moral idea."[37]

We might be tempted to conclude that this principle of correlation negated Cohen's previous statements about God and reality. In his 1924 introduction to Cohen's writings, Cohen's successor Franz Rosenzweig (see Chapter 11) argued that the idea of correlation destroyed the idealism of Cohen's previous works. According to Rosenzweig, the last great heir of idealism was the "one who breached its boundaries."[38] Others however disagreed and provided a detailed analysis of correlation according to which correlation expresses a relationship between the *concepts* of God and the human being; it is therefore a principle of logic. On this reading, Cohen applied this idealistic principle in all his works and his position remained consistent throughout his life; it "does not go beyond the realm of thought understood as the generation of concepts."[39]

"THOU," "I" AND SIN

Let us return to the point that for Cohen, God remains an idea: "the love of God is understood as love for a moral ideal, and the concept of the love of God for man is only an archetype upon which the pure moral deed can model itself."[40] Only God can provide forgiveness and redemption, and the religious element of love between God and humans is bound up with the love of one's neighbors.

Cohen argued that by introducing the idea of fellowship (what he called fellow man *Mitmensch*), religion supersedes ethics. I recognize the other, the stranger, as an individual by recognizing their suffering. Through that recognition of the other person as a Thou, I then see myself as an individual I. This discovery of both the Thou and the I leads to a new understanding of God.

In a chapter of *Religion of Reason* entitled "The Discovery of Man as Fellowman," Cohen set out to explore the underlying rationality that underlies ethical relations. For Cohen, religion incorporates the problem of the other, the "fellowman": "If the correlation between God and man is the fundamental equation of religion, then man in this correlation must first of all be thought of as fellowman."[41] The correlation of a human being to God presupposes the recognition of the fellowman. But do ethical relations extend to foreigners (non-Jews)? Cohen used the Noahide commandments to extend ethical obligations to all human beings: "every man is already the brother of every other."[42] The Noahide commandments require of us two things: that we view the stranger as a fellowman, and that the fellowman must abide by the fundamental moral code that applies to all humanity.

In his more Jewish-directed works, Cohen emphasized the role of the Jewish prophets who were devoted to the elimination of human suffering. For Cohen the prophets created the most important ethical concepts – humanity, messianism and God. Cohen addressed the problem of social inequity and poverty in the context of indifference: how ought we to account for the fact that the righteous often suffer and the wicked prosper? Indifference to suffering is unacceptable. Rather, Cohen adverted to the role of the prophet whose function is to rail against injustice: "prophetic thought puts aside [these] questions of life and afterlife in the face of the life whose meaning is in question because of the evil which is represented by poverty. Poverty becomes the main representation of human misfortune."[43] The true riddle of human life is not death, said Cohen, but poverty. Ultimately it is our obligation to alleviate the suffering not only of ourselves but of others; the role of the prophet is to "make pity the primeval feeling of man; he must, as it were, discover in pity man as fellowman and man in general."[44] The prophet thus becomes the practical moralist whose end-goal is the elimination of suffering.

CONCLUSION

Both Krochmal and Cohen were heirs to major Kantian and Hegelian schools of thought. While Krochmal adopted Hegel's absolute idealism, marrying it to an idiosyncratic history of Judaism, Cohen became one of the most influential expositors of Kantian critical idealism. In the area of Kant scholarship, Cohen spearheaded a revolutionary interpretation of Kant's own Copernican revolution, according to which its central problem is the logical justification of, rather than psychological explanation for, synthetic a priori judgments.[45] Under Cohen's leadership, Marburg became known worldwide as one of the best universities to study Kant's philosophy. Students came from all over the world to study under Cohen, among them Boris Pasternak from Russia, José Ortega y Gasset from Spain, Paul Natorp and Ernst Cassirer.[46]

In his "Introduction" to Cohen's Jewish writings, Cohen's successor Franz Rosenzweig popularized the importance of Cohen's having returned to Judaism in 1880, after many years of abandonment. On Rosenzweig's account, Cohen's long return to Judaism started with his response to Treitschke's anti-Jewish comments, and continued throughout his life, culminating with his return to Berlin. But others have challenged Rosenzweig's depiction of Cohen, claiming that it reflected Rosenzweig's own trajectory back to Judaism and not that of

Cohen. Cohen's purpose, as articulated in so many of his works, was to integrate critical idealism and Judaism, arguing that universal humanist culture had its roots in Jewish monotheism and messianism.

And yet, Cohen's stature in both Jewish and European thought diminished in subsequent decades. Three events conspired to marginalize Cohen's work: the rise of existentialism, a philosophical movement that eclipsed neo-Kantianism; the rise of Nazism that shattered the very German-Jewish synthesis that Cohen embraced so passionately; and the success of Zionism that negated Cohen's anti-Zionist stance.[47] Rosenzweig suggested that the neo-Kantian system collapsed of itself to give rise to the Jewish existentialism that he himself advocated.[48] In the following chapters, we turn to Jewish existentialist writers, writing both before and after the Holocaust.

NOTES

1 Scholarly interpretations of Hegel are notoriously complex. For an overview of different ways of understanding *Geist*, see Redding 2020.
2 See Gordon 2005, 95.
3 Harris 1991, 8.
4 This work exists only in the original Hebrew, and has not yet been translated. Most scholars, myself included, use the 1961 edition by Simon Rawidowicz. I will also refer to Harris 1991.
5 Guttmann 1964, 367.
6 Harris 1991, 18.
7 Harris 1991, 22.
8 Harris 1991, 25.
9 Harris 1991, 55.
10 See Chapter 2 for discussion of Neoplatonic emanation.
11 Guttmann 1964, 385.
12 Guttmann 1964, 384.
13 Cohen 1993, 77.

14 I am relying upon Jauernig 2021 for this summary of Kant's critical idealism.
15 See Jauernig 2021 for elucidation of these competing camps.
16 See Schine and Moyn 2021.
17 Cohen 1993, 80.
18 Cohen 1993, 84. Presumably Cohen has Spinoza in mind, who modelled his ethics upon mathematical and logical reasoning.
19 Cohen 1993, 87.
20 Cohen 1993, 176–184.
21 Cohen 1993, 183. We return to his critique of Zionism in Chapter 14.
22 Cohen 1995, 5.
23 Cohen 1995, 7.
24 Cohen 1995, 12.
25 Cohen 1995, 19.
26 Cohen 1995, 20.
27 Cohen 1995, 22.
28 Cohen 1995, 20.
29 Cohen 1995, 23.
30 Cohen 1995, 35.
31 Cohen 1993, 58.
32 Cohen 1993, 58.
33 Cohen 1995, 86.
34 Cohen 1995, 201.
35 Cohen 1995, 160.
36 Cohen 1995, 162.
37 Cohen 1995, 161.
38 Rosenzweig 2021, 225.
39 Altmann 2021, 247.
40 Guttmann 1964, 416.
41 Cohen 1995, 114.
42 Cohen 1995, 118.
43 Cohen 1995, 134.
44 Cohen 1995, 143.
45 Beiser 2018, 1.
46 Beiser 2018, 1.

47 Schine and Moyn 2021, xi.
48 Schine and Moyn 2021, xx.

FURTHER READING

Cohen, H. 1971. *Reason and Hope: Selections from the Jewish Writings of Hermann Cohen*, translated by Eva Jospe, New York: W.W. Norton.

Harris, J.M. (1991). *Nachman Krochmal: Guiding the Perplexed of the Modern Age*. New York and London: New York University Press.

Poma, A. (2007). "Hermann Cohen: Judaism and Critical Idealism," in M.L. Morgan and P.E. Gordon (eds), *The Cambridge Companion to Modern Jewish Philosophy:* Cambridge: Cambridge University Press, 80–101.

Rawidowicz, S. (1961). Nachman Krochmals Werke (Kitvei Rabbi Nachman Krochmal). London: Ararat Publ Society.

JEWISH EXISTENTIALISM

INTRODUCTION: WHAT IS EXISTENTIALISM

Starting with Kierkegaard and reflected in the works of Nietzsche, Heidegger, Sartre and others, the status and importance of the individual received heightened attention, in part as a reaction against Hegelian idealism. Existentialism arose in the early twentieth century as an attempt to reposition the primacy of the individual into philosophical thought. This chapter serves to introduce the challenges faced by contemporary Jewish thinkers in response to and incorporation of existentialist themes predominating in continental philosophical circles. In Chapter 9 we laid out the main features of Hegelianism, and the extent to which Hegelian idealism was embraced by Hermann Cohen among others. This chapter focuses upon the rejection of Hegelianism in Jewish philosophy, both with respect to its content and to its rootedness in a dialectical methodology.

Existentialist philosophers reacted against the heightened influence of scientific thinking, which often marginalized the human experience and the uniqueness of individuals. In the nineteenth century, Kierkegaard, Dostoevsky and Nietzsche already excoriated the undue value placed upon "rational, objective" discourse; they railed against Hegel and everything his system represented. Nietzsche had introduced nihilistic themes that were couched in what has come to be known as the "death of God" philosophy. Nihilism emphasized the loss of a transcendent moral framework in the context of an increasingly secular world view that carried with it feelings of anxiety, alienation and meaninglessness as humans are thrown adrift into a world without absolute values. In light of this nihilist sentiment, existentialists focus upon human freedom and authenticity.

The Hegelian rejection was heightened by both Martin Heidegger (1885–1973) and Jean-Paul Sartre (1905–1980), two of the best-known existentialists in the English-speaking world. Heidegger and Sartre were influenced by Edmund Husserl (1859–1938), known as the father of phenomenology. In contradistinction to Hegelian idealism, phenomenology focused upon the structures of consciousness as experienced from the first-person point of view. Heidegger, Sartre and others followed Husserl's lead in rejecting Hegelian notions of universality, the Absolute, and the System; in contrast they emphasized authenticity, despair, alienation and freedom experienced by the individual subject. Heidegger's major work *Being and Time* (published in 1927) focuses on such themes as human existence, which he terms *Dasein*, anxiety, death and inauthenticity. As we shall see below, Franz Rosenzweig, writing several years before Heidegger, shared many of the same themes and even some of the same terms with Heidegger.

Jean-Paul Sartre was highly influenced by Heidegger; his work *Being and Nothingness* was published in 1943 and introduced many of Heidegger's ideas to a French-speaking audience. In 1944 Sartre wrote an essay entitled "Anti-Semite and Jew: Reflections on the Jewish Question," published after the liberation of Paris from the Nazis. In this work he applied his ontology of self and other to analyze the relation between Jews and those who portrayed them as "the other." Using his notion of "bad faith," he portrayed the anti-Semite as someone who has fled from his own responsibility and adopted a cowardly stance toward the world. In the final portion of this work, he characterized the Jew as someone that others look at and consider to be a Jew; on this portrayal, Jewishness exists only in the eyes of those who regard the Jew as a Jew. Were there no objective observers, Sartre suggested, the very notion of Jewishness would vanish.

Sartre highlighted the main tenets of existentialism in a more popular essay, "Existentialism is a Humanism," published in 1946. In accord with Heidegger, he used the phrase "existence precedes essence" to characterize the main tenet of existentialism. By this phrase, both Heidegger and Sartre mean that we create our own essence by the choices we make freely. In contradistinction to the majority of the western tradition that, starting with Aristotle, emphasized the priority of an essential human nature or essence, the existentialists claimed that we are not born with a pre-existent essence. Our choices inform our values – we are the sum total of our actions. Both Sartre and Heidegger emphasized the importance of authentic behavior in our own self-definition and in relation to others. Again, we shall see Rosenzweig embracing the same rejection of "human essence" in his own work.[1]

Existentialism has stretched far beyond the philosophical world, influencing the arts, literature, film, psychology and politics. Think of the existentialist themes in films of Ingmar Bergman, Jean-Luc Godard and Akira Kurosawa; the paintings of Edvard Munch, Pablo Picasso and Edward Hopper; the writings of F. Scott Fitzgerald, Franz Kafka, R.M. Rilke, Malcolm X and W.E.B. DuBois; the existentialist psychology developed by R.D. Laing, Rollo May and Viktor Frankl. All of these works emphasize the uniqueness of the individual, the ascendancy of anxiety and despair in human life, the pre-eminence of freedom and authentic living in a world devoid of meaning and objective value.

Although many of the existentialists, following in the footsteps of Nietzsche who declared the "death of God," were in fact atheists, a tradition of theistic existentialism arose among both Jewish and Christian thinkers. Franz Rosenzweig, Martin Buber, Emmanuel Levinas and Joseph Soloveitchik are rarely mentioned in general histories of existentialism; nonetheless, they all articulated existentialist themes within the context of Jewish life and thought. Franz Rosenzweig (1886–1929) was one of the most original Jewish existentialists of the early twentieth century. His compelling biography included near-conversion to Christianity followed by a fervent return to Judaism; composition of his magnum opus *The Star of Redemption* on military postcards sent home from the Balkan front; and his continued engagement with philosophy after succumbing to ALS.[2]

Both Martin Buber (1878–1965) and Emmanuel Levinas (1905–1995), writing in the early to mid-twentieth century, were concerned to delineate the personal relation between the individual subject and the other. Buber's famous I–You and I–It relations are depicted in his major work *I and Thou*, which describes the myriad ways to engage with oneself, with others and with the Eternal Thou. In an interview with François Poirié, Levinas tells us that he was very much influenced by *I and Thou*. While for Buber the I–You relation is experienced as full reciprocity between myself and an "other," be it a person, tree or the divine Thou, Levinas emphasizes the asymmetry of the relation, claiming that the feeling that the I *owes* everything to the You, is of paramount importance.

Nowhere are these existentialist themes expressed more explicitly than in the works of Joseph Soloveitchik (1903–1993), influential rabbi, philosopher and teacher who served as a role-model for an entire generation of twentieth-century Jews. In his seminal work "The Lonely Man of Faith," Soloveitchik used the two accounts of creation in Genesis 1 and 2 to introduce the bifurcation between the world of science and that of faith, represented respectively by Adam I and Adam II. Soloveitchik described modern society as one that is technically minded, self-centered, and self-loving, in opposition to the faith individual who lives by a law external to the laboratory. We will explore in Chapter 12 both approaches to the "other," as presented by Buber, Levinas and Soloveitchik.

ROSENZWEIG REDISCOVERS JUDAISM

Franz Rosenzweig (1886–1929) was born into an aristocratic family of highly cultured German Jews. He studied philosophy and history at the University of Leipzig, writing a PhD dissertation on Hegel and the State. At the university, Rosenzweig became caught up in questions of nationalism and similar to Mendelssohn in the eighteenth century, he was forced to face his Judaism seriously for the first time. Two questions arose: with which nationality should he identify – German or Jewish; and second, if religion is true, should he remain a Jew, or convert to Christianity. In 1913, Rosenzweig met Eugen Rosenstock at the university. Rosenstock was a Christian theologian of Jewish descent who introduced Rosenzweig to a whole new way of thinking that emphasized the existential, personal aspect of faith. Rosenstock convinced Rosenzweig that a reconciliation between reason and faith is possible: that one could be an intellectual and still have religious faith based on revelation. Discussions with Rosenstock led to a crisis of faith, culminating in an all-night discussion on July 7, 1913.[3] Unable to counter Rosenstock's attacks on Judaism as a desiccated religion, Rosenzweig realized that he had only one choice, to become a Christian. His decision was based on a philosophical conviction that *the only way to fulfill his Jewish commitment* was through Christianity.

On the traditional account of Rosenzweig's intellectual struggles, he decided he could not convert as a pagan, but as a practicing Jew: he did not want to *reject* Judaism, but to realize its consummation in Christianity. Therefore, he decided he must keep Jewish law up until the last moment. While attending Yom Kippur services as a *preparation for conversion to Christianity*, Rosenzweig underwent an intense religious experience and made the decision not to convert. In a famous letter to his cousin, Rosenzweig explained his reversal as follows: "after prolonged, and I believe thorough, self-examination, I have reversed my decision. It no longer seems necessary to me, and therefore, being what I am, no longer possible. I will remain a Jew."[4]

Rosenstock was understandably upset with his friend's decision, and their conversations took on the status of an extended exchange of letters. Of the many themes expressed in these letters, chosenness is emphasized repeatedly. Rosenstock tried to argue that Judaism is over, that Church has replaced the synagogue: "Israel's time as the people of the Bible has gone by. The Church … is today the Synagogue. The epoch of the eternal Jew comes to an end."[5] In response, Rosenzweig emphasized the uniqueness chosenness of the Jewish people. In comparison to the chosen relation of the Jew to God, he claims, the Christian relation to God is "particularly and extremely pitiful, poverty-stricken, and ceremonious." Christians, he argues need an intermediary, a third person, between themselves and God, whereas for the Jew "what need is there for a third person between me and my father in Heaven?"[6] Both shared the same truths (a theme to which we return below), but Rosenzweig portrayed Christianity as wrapped up in "its externals," while Judaism "has only its hard protecting shell, and one can speak of its soul only from within."[7]

After a brief hiatus, Rosenzweig and Rosenstock resumed their correspondence in 1916, and from this exchange of letters, Rosenzweig developed two themes: the notion that humans organize their world view around revelation, which is reflected in the calendar; and the philosophical importance of language in discussing theological issues. Both of these issues are amplified in Rosenzweig's major works *The Star of Redemption* and in the essay "The New Thinking." Rosenzweig's decision not to convert led to a recommitment to Judaism, and he saw his work as an articulation of a new way of thinking about the relationships between God, individuals and the world.

The Star of Redemption is Rosenzweig's most famous work. Written while he was in the trenches on postcards sent to his mother during World War I (August 1918 to February 1919), it combines many of the themes developed in conversation with Rosenstock. Rosenzweig wrote the essay "The New Thinking" four years after the publication of the *Star*. In it he tried to offer a summary of the major themes in the *Star*, but without the technical language. After the war, Rosenzweig helped with Martin Buber to establish a Jewish School (*Judische Lehrhaus*) for Jews who were estranged from their Judaism and wanted to return to their roots. In 1922, paralysis set in (ALS); Rosenzweig slowly lost control of his body in an agonizing decline, and died in 1929. During this latter period, he translated the Bible into German with Buber and concentrated on translating medieval Hebrew poetry.

THE STAR OF REDEMPTION: DEATH AND NOTHINGNESS

The Star of Redemption attempts to examine the dialogue that obtains between humans, God, and the world. It is a difficult work and was received by readers and critics in many different ways. Few of its first readers appeared to have any idea what Rosenzweig was trying to say in it.

His Christian friends read the book and were convinced that he had finally accepted Christianity, while the German-Jewish community on the other hand, touted the *Star* as a nice "Jewish book." It has been presented as a work of existentialism rivalling that of Heidegger; it has been read as a guide leading assimilated Jews back to a traditional Jewish lifestyle; it has even been hailed as a monument of early postmodernism.[8]

But is the *Star* even a book of Jewish philosophy? Rosenzweig himself decried that view, claiming that it "is not a 'Jewish book,' at least in the sense that those buyers, who were so angry with me, think of a Jewish book."[9] He construed it as a "system of philosophy," one that incorporated both Jewish and Christian elements. This "system of philosophy" should not be reduced to that of Hegel however: Rosenzweig clearly wanted to distinguish himself from the systematizing found in Hegelian Idealism. How does Rosenzweig's "system of philosophy" differ from that of Hegel? In a move similar to that of later existentialists, Rosenzweig replaced the Hegelian insistence upon the Absolute with the *individual*. More specifically, Rosenzweig had in mind the task of recognizing individual human beings in their particularity; his project emerged from identifying the unique individuating characteristics of each of us as subjects. In this way, Rosenzweig's system differed markedly from that of Hegel and other German idealists.

Rosenzweig explained his conception of the system in a letter to Rosenstock: "we recognize the problem of system in the Idealists ... but it doesn't control the form of our philosophy as it does theirs; we don't want to be philosophers when we are philosophizing, but human beings, and so we must bring our philosophy into the form of our humanity."[10] In Rosenzweig's system, individuals emerge out of their own nonexistence into a state of being by entering into relations with others. In a deep metaphysical sense, other human beings offer redemption from an individual's state of nothing: "we come to recognize the truth of the interconnectedness of all beings; we come to understand how everything that is must take on systematic form in order to be what it is – and not to be 'nothing'."[11]

The emphasis upon the individual "I" was already reflected in a letter to his cousin Rudolf Ehrenberg in 1917. This letter is known as the "*Urzelle*" and contains in embryo the core ideas developed in the *Star*. In the "*Urzelle*" Rosenzweig contrasted the act of philosophizing done by the Idealists to his own. Once one has engaged in the idealist quest, he realized that "he, who has long been philosophical digested, is still there as an 'I' ... I, a complete common private-subject, I fore- and surname, I dust and ashes. I am still there."[12] We cannot help but be reminded in this context of Descartes's rediscovery of the "ego cogito," of Kierkegaard's individual knight of faith, and subsequently of Heidegger's Dasein, all of which reflect the primacy of the individual over and against the universal, absolute system.

Reflecting the emphasis upon the individual, the *Star* begins on a dramatic note. Quoting Schiller's poem "From death, from the fear of death, there begins all knowledge of the Whole," Rosenzweig offered a rejoinder: "Man is not to throw off the fear of the earthly; he must remain in the fear of death, but he must remain."[13] Rosenzweig starts the *Star* with death: "All knowledge of the All begins in death, in the fear of death."[14] The very possibility of suicide – that I can initiate my own death – reinforces awareness of my "nothing;" the "I" is annihilated, and in its place there remains only an "it." As Heidegger will remind us several years later in *Being and Time*, I am the only one who can experience my death; nobody else can die for me. I own my death in a way that nobody else can.[15]

In short, fear and recognition of one's own death reveal the interconnection of being and nothing. Anticipating

Sartre's famous descriptions of "nothing" in *Being and Nothingness*, Rosenzweig noted that this Nothing is a something: each new Nothing-of-death introduces a new Something. Both Rosenzweig and Heidegger agree that death alone "yields philosophy a glimpse at the nothingness hidden in the fissures of what there is."[16] Death thus represents the nothingness of the "I", the recognition of the separateness of the "I" from the world, from the earth itself. Anticipating both Heidegger and Sartre, Rosenzweig argued that our essence as humans is always in process. Rosenzweig describes the abstract, meta-ethical human being as "nothing;" by this he means that humans are not born with a pre-existent essence. Rosenzweig levelled a scathing critique against Western philosophy's attempt to deny this truism by replacing the individual with an idealist "All." Rosenzweig saw this idealist All shattering into three separate pieces – God, human, world. Of these three pieces we know nothing, and the task of the *Star* is to come to understand the interconnections among these disparate pieces. In this process, then, the acknowledgement of death thus leads to knowledge of ourselves and the world.

According to Rosenzweig, creation, revelation and redemption formed the boundaries of the temporalized process that unite God, humans and world. Already in *Urzelle*, Rosenzweig described the tripartite breaking of the Absolute into three parts. The three points form a triangle: Revelation is a middle point between creation and redemption, "because it occurs at the point, the rigid, deaf, immovable point, the stubborn I, that 'I just am.'"[17] Revelation represents the gift from God to humans, and the love of humans for God and others; it "holds a pivotal place ... since it is God's love that lays down the model for human love and community."[18]

In *Star* Rosenzweig amplifies this taxonomy and envisions a six-pointed star the points of which are

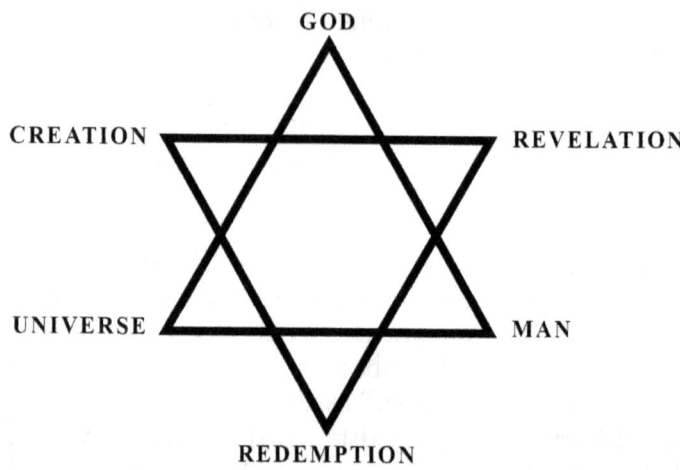

Figure 11.1 Star of redemption.

intertwined (Figure 11.1). On this model, creation refers to when God relates to the world (God gives the world reality); revelation is when God relates to humans (the personal world of God, which is both concrete and historical); and redemption is when humans relate to the world (the "moral" component, translating love for God into love of neighbor). Much of the *Star* is devoted to laying out the intricacies of this complex system.

ROSENZWEIG'S "NEW WAY OF THINKING"

As we have seen, Rosenzweig joined forces with modern thinkers who, along with Kierkegaard, Nietzsche and others, rebelled against German idealism. In the essay "The New Thinking," written in 1925, Rosenzweig emphasized the bankruptcy of idealist philosophy, rooted as it was in rationalism and science. This essay was written for a primarily Jewish readership and focused specifically on the purpose of human existence: what does it mean to exist, to be, and how does my existence relate to my actions?

Rosenzweig proposed his "new thinking" as an alternative to what he saw as a dead-end, ossified Idealist system. We saw above Rosenzweig's reaction against much of the history of philosophy that prioritized essence over existence. Rosenzweig warns us in "New Thinking" that none of the three great basic concepts of philosophy (God, world, humans) can be reduced to one another: each is to be reduced only to itself: "the essence of man and the essence of the world – the essence – are no more within reach than the essence – the essence – of God."[19]

Time itself is a key metaphysical player for Rosenzweig. The new thinking's method, he tells us, "originates out of temporality."[20] The new thinking, as opposed to the old thinking, is preoccupied with time; it teaches "the understanding at the right time." We cannot cognize independently of time: "knowledge is at every moment, bound to this very moment and cannot make [that moment's] past not past, or its future not future."[21] God's actions, as well as our own, must be understood within the context of the flux of time. Rosenzweig contrasted thinking, which is timeless and solitary, with speaking, which is time-bound and rooted in conversation with an "other." In actual conversation I do not know what the "other" will say to me, and so I am rooted in the present moment. To *need time* is having to wait for everything. Unlike the old thinking, which prioritized private thought, the new thinking needs to hear the speech of the other and so must take time seriously.[22] In order to engage with speaking, Rosenzweig claimed that the "I" requires a "you" or "Thou" or "other" as an interlocuter. My own existence is thus intertwined with the other, and ultimately with God.

The *Star* ends famously with an exhortation to abandon the book, put it aside, and resume living. Rosenzweig reiterated this admonition in "New Thinking" as well. What replaces the book is "No-longer-book," namely becoming aware that "this step of the book toward the limit can only be atoned for by – ending the book."[23] And by ending Rosenzweig has in mind stepping out into the world of everyday life. We must all take the time to philosophize, but then we must step away from the domain of philosophy and re-enter lived existence.

JUDAISM AND CHRISTIANITY: A "DOUBLE TRUTH THEORY"

Already at the beginning of his intellectual quest, Rosenzweig was obsessed with the tensions and relationships between Judaism and Christianity. As we saw above in his pre-1913 discussions, Rosenzweig agreed with Rosenstock that the task of the church was to redeem humans through dialogue; Judaism had no meaning in its continued existence and had been replaced by the Church. After his 1913 crisis and return to Judaism, however, Rosenzweig saw the synagogue as complementing the Church: the synagogue serves as a reminder to the world that revelation comes from God, and not from rational faculties.

In the final portion of the *Star*, Rosenzweig laid out a comparison of Judaism and Christianity (Islam is given short shrift). Most famously he suggested that although the two religions are internally incompatible, they are mutually reinforcing; both stand as necessary witnesses to redemption.[24] There are however important differences between the two: as noted in the *Star*, Judaism represents eternal life, while Christianity is the eternal way.[25] By this cryptic phrase, Rosenzweig suggested that while Christianity functions *within history*, Judaism lives outside the historical stream. Its sole task is to exist: by its biological existence, Israel bears witness to God in the world.[26] Whereas Christianity unfolds through history and linear time, Judaism he claims is outside of the flow of history; Jews are *in* time, but time for Judaism is cyclical, not linear, and so on Rosenzweig's reading, Jews exhibit an indifference to lived history: "Because the Jewish people is beyond the contradiction that constitutes the vital drive in the life of the nations ... it knows nothing of war."[27] Rosenstock disagreed with this comparison, however and argued that through Zionism, Judaism has re-entered history.[28] We return in Chapter 14 to Rosenzweig's views on Zionism.

CONCLUSION: HEIDEGGER AND ROSENZWEIG COMPARED

Throughout our discussion, I have noted a number of similarities between Rosenzweig and Heidegger. Many of their ideas overlapped, and even some of their word choices aligned. Scholars have noted that while Rosenzweig and Heidegger remained strangers in life, much of what they wrote bespeaks an intimate commonality of ideas.[29] Rosenzweig himself marked this resemblance in an essay published (posthumously) in 1929, which he drafted as a commentary on the Davos encounter, a famous public debate between Heidegger and the rationalist philosopher Ernst Cassirer who was an assimilated Jew, the student of Hermann Cohen and the intellectual heir to neo-Kantianism. Heidegger and Cassirer each gave lectures on the topic "What is Man?" Rosenzweig appears to have heard of the debate from the philosopher Leo Strauss, and from what he heard and read, he identified himself not with Cassirer, whose approbation of Hermann Cohen he shared, but rather with Heidegger's views. Rosenzweig saw himself and Heidegger as "philosophical partisans" in the development of the "new thinking."[30]

We can delineate several strands of commonality between Rosenzweig and Heidegger. The most important strand reflects their mutual rejection of idealist philosophy with its emphasis upon universalism and absolutism. On the cusp of World War I, and just after, the collapse of the older academic style of philosophy required a new way of thinking, one embraced by both Heidegger and Rosenzweig. Both thinkers emerged during the 1920s to forge a new kind of philosophy.[31] As Rosenzweig wrote in his analysis of the Davos debate, Heidegger advocated in this debate "a philosophical position [that is] precisely our position, that of the new thinking."[32] We have no direct evidence that Rosenzweig actually read Heidegger's *Being and Time*, which was published in 1927. And of course Rosenzweig was unaware of the moral and political implications of Heidegger's thinking that emerged in light of Nazi ideology: he was certainly unaware of the right-wing, anti-Semitic side of Heidegger's thinking. We can only speculate how he might have modified his view of Heidegger in light of World War II. Nonetheless, in 1929, at the very end of his life, Rosenzweig saw in Heidegger a partner in the quest for a "new thinking."

NOTES

1 For further descriptions of existentialist themes, see Aho 2023.
2 See Pollock 2009; see also below.
3 For details see Altmann 1971; Glatzer 1961.
4 Glatzer 1961, 28, 331–334. See also Pollock 2009. In this work, Pollock has argued that while this celebrated tale of Rosenzweig's near-conversion and return to Judaism may well be inspiring and instructive as a myth about modern Jewish identity, there is little evidence to support it.
5 Rosenzweig 1971, 140.
6 Rosenzweig 1971, 113, 131.
7 Rosenzweig 1971, 133.

8 Pollock 2009, 1.
9 Rosenzweig 2000a.
10 Rosenzweig 1971, 167.
11 Pollock 2009, 9.
12 Rosenzweig 2000b, 53.
13 Rosenzweig 1970, 4.
14 Rosenzweig 1970, 3.
15 See Heidegger 1962.
16 Gordon 2005, 174.
17 Rosenzweig 2000b, 63.
18 Rosenzweig 1970, 131.
19 Rosenzweig 2000a, 118.
20 Rosenzweig 2000a, 125.
21 Rosenzweig 2000a, 123.
22 Rosenzweig 2000a, 127.
23 Rosenzweig 2000a, 137.
24 Gordon 2007, 134.
25 Rosenzweig 1970, 328.
26 Rosenzweig 1970, 342.
27 Rosenzweig 1970, 329.
28 Rosenzweig 1971, 140.
29 Gordon 2005, xxiii.
30 Gordon 2005, xxiv, 13.
31 Gordon 2005, 5.
32 Rosenzweig 2000c, 150.

FURTHER READING

Gordon, P.E. (2007). "Franz Rosenzweig and the Philosophy of Jewish Existence," in M.L. Morgan and P.E. Gordon (eds), *The Cambridge Companion to Modern Jewish Philosophy*. Cambridge: Cambridge University Press, 122–146.

Herberg, W. (1956). *The Writings of Martin Buber*. New York: Meridian.

Levinas, E. (1990). *Nine Talmudic Readings*, trans. A. Aronowicz. Bloomington, IN: Indiana University Press.

Morgan, M. L. (2007). *Discovering Levinas*. Cambridge: Cambridge University Press.

Rosenzweig, F. (1971). *Judaism Despite Christianity: The Letters on Christianity and Judaism between Eugen Rosenstock-Huessy and Franz Rosenzweig.* New York: Schocken Press.

Sartre, J.-P. (1995). *Anti-Semite and Jew*, trans. George J. Becker. New York: Schocken Books.

PHILOSOPHY OF DIALOGUE

INTRODUCTION

This chapter continues our exploration of the challenges faced by contemporary Jewish thinkers in response to and incorporation of existentialist themes predominating in continental philosophical circles. As noted in Chapter 11, existentialism arose in the early twentieth century as an attempt to reposition the primacy of the individual into philosophical thought. Franz Rosenzweig emphasized the importance of dialogue as an ethical component of human living. Both Martin Buber (1878–1965) and Emmanuel Levinas (1905–1995), writing in the early to mid-twentieth century, were concerned as well to delineate the personal relation obtaining between the individual subject and the other. Buber's famous I–You and I–It relations are depicted in his major work *I and Thou*, which describes the myriad ways to engage with oneself, with others, and with the eternal You. While for Buber the I–You relation was experienced as full reciprocity between myself and an "other," be it a person, tree or the divine Thou, Levinas emphasized the asymmetry of the relation, claiming that the feeling that the I *owes* everything to the You, is of paramount importance. We will explore below both approaches to the "other," as presented by Buber and Levinas.

Joseph Soloveitchik (1903–1993) continued in many of his works to explore the bifurcation between the world of science and that of faith. Soloveitchik described modern society as one that is technically minded, self-centered, and self-loving, in opposition to the faith individual who lives by a law external to the laboratory. His main work *Lonely Man of Faith* characterized the faith individual in existentialist terms.

BUBER'S I–YOU PHILOSOPHY OF DIALOGUE

Martin Buber exemplifies what can be regarded as a philosophy of dialogue. Buber was born in Vienna and studied at the Universities of Vienna, Leipzig, Zurich and finally Berlin, where he joined the Zionist movement. He then took up the study of Hasidism (Jewish mysticism) and eventually published a number of works related to the Hassidic masters, most notably *The Tales of Rabbi Nachman* and *The Legends of the Baal-Shem*. After World War I, Buber became increasingly involved with the Zionist platform, emphasizing that Zionists should address themselves to the needs of both Jews and Arabs. In 1923 he published his *I and Thou* (*Ich und Du*), a work that has become known as his philosophy of dialogue. As mentioned in Chapter 11, he also worked with Rosenzweig on a translation of the Bible into German. In 1938 Buber moved to Palestine and took up a position at the Hebrew University where, until his death, he fought tirelessly for the establishment of a joint Palestinian/Jewish state.

Buber rejected "systematic philosophy," regarding it as a desiccated mode of thought that destroyed dialogue. He acknowledged that his rejection of the Hegelian system, and its dialogical thought, was indebted to Rosenzweig.

As we shall see below, there are many points of similarity between the two, in particular with their mutual emphasis upon the I as a dialogical I. Throughout his writings, Buber articulated an understanding of human embeddedness in the world that consists of two different modes of being, conceptualized as the basic words I–It and I–You.

> The basic words are not single words but word pairs.
> One basic word is the word pair I–You.
> The other basic word is the word pair I–It ...[1]

In contradistinction to the Cartesian insistence upon the solitary thinking "ego" (popularized in Descartes's phrase "I think therefore I am"), Buber insisted that "the I of man is also twofold. For the I of the basic word I–You is different from that in the basic word I–It."[2] The words I–It and I–You are not literally spoken by a subject: instead, they "establish a mode of existence" between subject and object. In the I–It relation, the engagement always remains on the surface level, as neither the subject nor the object truly participates in the experience – not the subject, because the experience is for her entirely internal, and not the object, because of its passive accessibility. In other words, there is no *reciprocity* in the utterance of the basic word I–It, and it is this lack that differentiates it, in a fundamental way, from the basic word I–You. Whereas the I–It relation structures the world of experience, Buber asserted that the I–You relation structures the world of relation. The word "I–You" is invoked when one is drawn into a relation that transforms the It into a You: the You confronts the I bodily and must be dealt with.

Buber offered a number of examples to elucidate the difference between I–It and I–You. Consider my experience of a tree. I can objectify it as a member of a species, as a member of a universal. But I can also enter into relation with the tree and at that moment the tree ceases to be an It: "the power of exclusiveness has seized me ... what I encounter is neither the soul of a tree nor a dryad, but the tree itself."[3] Is Buber suggesting that the tree is conscious of and responding to the relation? In later works he disavowed that inference, emphasizing the strong relation I have with other objects, both animate and inanimate. Think, for example, of the sort of relationship climate scientists might have toward our environment. The implication here is that *a thing's status as an It is mutable* – if the subject has the appropriate attitude when contemplating the thing, if they speak with their being the word I–You, then the It can be elevated to the status of a You. That dynamic clearly applies to interactions between the subject and other humans, and it is from this specific type of the I–You relation that Buber's ethics emerges.

Speaking the word I–You in a relation with another human being raises them from the realm of experience to the realm of relation, and the confrontation then becomes, to use Buber's term, an "encounter." In the encounter between I, the subject, and You, the object, there is nothing that mediates their relation from the relation itself – it is wholly immediate. It is also the only circumstance in which the present exists: "only as the You becomes present does presence come into being."[4] The I of the basic word I–It has "only a past and no present ... What is essential is lived in the present, objects in the past."[5]

And yet, Buber warned his readers that every You must become an It in our world: "Every You in the world is doomed by its nature to become a thing or at least to enter into thinghood again and again."[6] One cannot live in the pure present: it would consume us if care were not taken that it is overcome quickly and thoroughly. Evoking poetic imagery, Buber suggested that the It is the chrysalis, the You the butterfly. Every individual You "must disappear into the chrysalis of the It in order to grow wings again."[7]

THE ETERNAL YOU

The relation between the I and the eternal You is discussed in the third part of *I and Thou*. Buber maintained that the eternal You is addressed through every I–You encounter. "Extended, the lines of relationships intersect in the eternal You. Every single You is a glimpse of that."[8] Like Rosenzweig, Buber characterized the relation between humans and the Eternal as an active encounter, not as an abstract posit. God can only be experienced in the inter-subjective encounter, not in philosophical theorizing. We cannot experience the Eternal except through our relations with fellow human beings. By saying "You," I catch a glimpse of God. Buber cites love as an example of the I–You relation: "When a man loves a woman so that her life is present in his own, the You of her eyes allows him to gaze into a ray of the eternal You."[9]

In a move suggestive of Kierkegaard, who argued in *Concluding Unscientific Postscript* that the pagan who worships idols was more connected to God than the church-goer who goes through worship mindlessly, Buber suggested that the intensity and direction of relation defines true union with God:

> Whoever pronounces the word God and really means You, addresses, no matter what his delusion the true You of his life ... but whoever abhors the name and fancies that he is godless – when he addresses with his whole devoted being the You of his life that cannot be restricted by any other, he addresses God.[10]

In other words, individuals who solely directs their life toward serving God (think of the mystic communing with

"God"), while neglecting the I–You relation with others, will not achieve that relation with the true God; the eternal You can only be experienced through relation with the human You.

To the extent that Buber's philosophy contains an ethical quality, it is in the import he places on the I–You relation – a rare and transient connection between two discrete entities – and in the implicit imperative that one should attempt to relate to those around them in that genuinely authentic human being. "Without It a human being cannot live. But whoever lives only with that is not human."[11] Reciprocity and relation with others render life heavy with meaning. Meaning "is guaranteed. Nothing, nothing can henceforth be meaningless. The question about the meaning of life has vanished … the meaning we receive can be put to the proof in action only by each person in the uniqueness of his being and in the uniqueness of his life."[12]

THE ECLIPSE OF GOD

After World War II, Buber had to contend with God's apparent abandonment of the Jews during the Holocaust. In *The Eclipse of God*, written in 1952, Buber famously posited that God's face has been eclipsed by the evil deeds perpetrated by humanity. Just as we can only experience the living God through our encounter with others, so too the obstruction of inter-personal relations leads to an eclipse of the Eternal. What do we mean when we speak of an eclipse of God? Buber described this eclipse as something stepping between our existence and that of God. In our (post-Holocaust) age, the I–It relation "gigantically swollen, has usurped, practically uncontested, the mastery and the rule."[13] This I is unable to say You, unable to meet a being essentially, unable to acknowledge any authentic relation. This I "steps in between and shuts off from us the light of heaven."[14] The cause of this eclipse thus resides in human action, and not in God, and it is ultimately up to humanity to repair the rupture between humans and the eternal You. Buber in this work held out hope for repair of the rupture: "The eclipse of the light of God is no extinction; even tomorrow that which has stepped in between may give way."[15]

There are other times in which the attempt at an I–You relation is not reciprocated; at those times, the world itself rises up against the individual. Channeling existentialist tropes that appear in Kierkegaard, Heidegger and Sartre, Buber recognized the anxiety and alienation that can accompany human existence:

> [When a human being] is for once overcome by the horror of alienation and the world fills him with anxiety, he looks up … then he sees that the I is contained in the world, and that there really is no I, and thus the world cannot harm the I, and he calms down; or he sees that the world is contained in the I and there really is no world, and thus the world cannot harm the I, and he calms down…but the moment will come, and it is near, when man, overcome by horror, looks up and in a flash sees both pictures at once. And he is seized by a deeper horror.[16]

There is no escape from alienation other than interaction with the other.

EMMANUEL LEVINAS: INTELLECTUAL BIOGRAPHY

Emmanuel Levinas developed an existentialist picture of human relations that was similar in many ways to that of Buber. Levinas was born in 1906 in Kaunas, Lithuania. He began studying philosophy in 1923 in France where he received training as a phenomenologist from Edmund

Husserl and Martin Heidegger, both of whom greatly influenced his early work. In 1929 he was present at the Davos seminar (referenced in Chapter 11) where Cassirer and Heidegger held their famous debate. In 1940 Levinas was captured by Nazis and imprisoned in a labor camp and his family murdered. After the war, Levinas settled in Paris where he was eventually (in 1961) appointed professor of philosophy at the University of Poitiers, then in 1967 at the University of Nanterre, and finally in 1973 at the Sorbonne. Levinas died on December 25, 1995.

Before the war, most of Levinas's works were devoted to introducing Husserl and Heidegger to a French-speaking audience. Sartre has famously remarked that it was Levinas who introduced him to the works of Heidegger and the phenomenologists. But Levinas found aspects of Heidegger's work troubling and after the war Levinas decried this German tradition. *Totality and Infinity* was published in 1961 and contained extensive attacks upon the entirety of Western philosophy, including in particular the work of Heidegger. Levinas's second major book *Otherwise Than Being* was published in 1974. This book was influenced by both Buber and Rosenzweig, both of whom introduced him to the importance of the "other" as critical to self-reflection.

In addition to these major philosophical works, Levinas contributed numerous Talmudic commentaries, lectures and essays on Judaism. Some of the essays on Judaism were collected in *Difficult Freedom* (1963), *In the Time of the Nations* (1988) and *Talmudic Readings*. Although Levinas did not attempt to harmonize his philosophical and more Jewish writings, recent scholars have paid more attention to the interconnections among all these works. His *Talmudic Readings*, for example, reflect his attempt to approach the Talmud philosophically. Many of the more Jewish works share themes (alterity, responsibility, subjectivity and ethics) similar to his philosophical works. In this chapter we shall focus primarily upon his more philosophical book *Totality and Infinity*, along with several selected essays.

SELF AND OTHER

The term "*Autrui*" (Other) is the key term in all of Levinas's works; it refers to the human Other, which, according to Levinas, is beyond comprehension. The Other is contrasted with both the self, the I that looks out onto the world, and the outside world which he describes as the "*autre*" (other). The term *Autrui* (Other) is reserved for that other human being with whom I have an ethical relation. Levinas introduced his project in *Totality and Infinity* as a defense of subjectivity as "founded in the idea of infinity."[17] As we shall see, the notion of subjectivity incorporates the Other as both independent from and yet in relation to the self. Infinity is the term Levinas used to affirm the relationship between the self and the other, while the term totality expresses the life of the self as separate from the other. This "I" or "same" or "self" is "not a being that always remains the same, but is the being whose existing consists in identifying itself ... throughout all that happens to it."[18] The self desires the other – we are attracted to the world outside of ourselves, what Levinas called "exteriority." The world is what exists outside of the I, but the I finds itself 'at home' in the world: the self "finds in the world a site and a home ... the 'at home' [*chez soi*] is ... a site where I am free."[19] Levinas described the world of the separate self or I as one of "enjoyment" (*jouissance*); the self derives from the intimacy of home and dwelling an ability to recollect and represent. The self for Levinas is totally at home in the world, totally alone.

As noted earlier, Levinas was initially influenced by Husserl and Heidegger, but he soon left them both behind. What Levinas found attractive in Husserl was a razor-focused method of phenomenological reflection, and what he found in Heidegger was a philosophy immersed in the world. In order to ground our knowledge of other minds, Husserl suggested that we can infer the existence of other egos by analogy to our own existence, using what he called empathy. By the time of writing *Time and the Other* in 1947, Levinas had rejected Husserl's views on the self and its relation to the outside world. Both Levinas (and Heidegger) found Husserl's argument unpersuasive. In effect, Husserl assumed that other egos, persons, are *like me*; but isn't that the very thing that is in question? For Levinas, Husserl's assumption that the Other is a reflection of me begs the question.

Finding Husserl's theory of empathy unsatisfactory, Levinas argued that the *apparent* independence of the self is possible only because the existence of the Other defines my awareness of my own existence. In order to account for the existence of the Other, Levinas introduced the term *visage* (face) to express the relationship between self and Other: the Other is simply *there* in a relation that Levinas calls *le face à face* (the face to face). Levinas argued that the Other is constituted by alterity: "The Other is in no way another myself, participating with me in a common existence ... we recognize the other as resembling us, but exterior to us; the relationship with the other is a relationship with a Mystery."[20] By "face" Levinas does not mean the physical face that is seen and experienced; it is a revelation, not perceived as an object of knowledge: "The way in which the Other presents himself ... we here name face. This mode does not consist in figuring as a theme under my gaze ... The face of the Other at each moment destroys and overflows the plastic image it leaves me."[21] The Other's face is the distinctive mark of the human personality – it looks back at the self as both witness and judge. We are only able to say what it is not; reminiscent of Maimonides's negative theology, Levinas noted the many ways in which we *cannot* describe the face. In order to avoid the reduction of the Other to a mere phenomenological object, Levinas carefully described the relationship with the Other as "a relation without relation,"[22] one in which the Other retains its Otherness.

How then can we even discuss the Other without destroying its inherent mystery? What does it even mean to think and speak of the Other as Other? According to Levinas, the relation between the self and Other is ethical and lies at the heart of human relationships. Only by discovering the irreducibility of the Other do I come to understand that I am neither alone nor part of a totality to which all others belong. The relation between self and Other can occur through desire. Desire is seen as "desire for the absolutely Other"[23] and is founded in an erotic relation in which the loved one is caressed but not possessed.

In the face to face, the self confronts its freedom and obligations with respect to the Other. More specifically, the Other confers upon the self its freedom, inasmuch as it is confronted with real choices with respect to my behavior towards the Other. Ethics is the location of a point of otherness, or exteriority, that cannot be reduced to the same. An ethical relation occurs when the self *faces* the other person. This relation is asymmetrical however: it recognizes that the self is obligated to make itself available to the other, without regarding the other as being similarly obliged.

In an interview with François Poirié, Levinas notes that while he was very much influenced by Buber's *I and Thou*, "the principal thing that separates us is what I call the asymmetry of the I-[You] relation."[24] As we have seen previously, the I–You relation for Buber is experienced as reciprocity. Levinas however emphasized the asymmetry of the relation, claiming that "The feeling that the I owes everything to the [You], that its responsibility for the other is gratitude, and that the other has always, and rightfully, a right over me," is of paramount importance.[25] Levinas criticized Buber on the grounds that the dialogical relation does not depend upon the Other's acceptance and recognition of me, but is fundamentally asymmetrical. According to Levinas, the dialogical relation (as opposed to that of Buber) is both non-cognitive and non-reciprocal: what I permit myself to demand of myself is not comparable with what I may demand of the Other. This metaphysical asymmetry reinforces my inability to see myself from the outside, and hence my inability to speak "in the same sense of oneself and of the others."[26] Levinas portrays his own project as a recognition that "ethics arises in the relation to the other and not straightaway by a reference to the universality of a law."[27] He thus rejected Kant's categorical imperative which enjoins us to act as if our actions can be universalized.

EVIL AND THEODICY

In a work entitled *Useless Suffering*, published in 1982, Levinas grappled with trying to understand human suffering within the context of his dialogical analysis. As noted in previous chapters, theodicy has been used throughout history as a way of justifying God's actions in light of the existence of evil in the world: if God is good, why do evil and suffering exist. For Levinas, theodical solutions to evil have been necessary for the teleology of community life, to make sufferings here on earth comprehensible. "It has been, at least up to the trials of the twentieth century, a component of the self-consciousness of European humanity."[28] Levinas sited the Holocaust as the paradigm of gratuitous human suffering "where evil appears in its diabolical horror."[29] What can be said to justify such extreme suffering? The unspeakable amount of evil and suffering of the twentieth century (in particular the Holocaust) reveals "the unjustifiable character of suffering in the other"[30] and undercuts the very notion of theodicy. If God was absent in the extermination camps, "the devil was very obviously present in them."[31]

Levinas offers us a phenomenology of suffering in terms of gratuitous evil.[32] In its own right, suffering is literally useless and cannot be unified under a single objectively valid and meaningful whole. Levinas claimed that while the suffering of the Other is useless and meaningless, our own suffering *for the other* can be useful in that it opens us to the ethical perspective of what Levinas calls the interhuman. More specifically, Levinas distinguished between suffering in the Other, which for the self is unpardonable, and suffering in the self, which takes on a meaning in becoming a suffering for the suffering of someone else. It is this attention to the Other that is "raised to a supreme ethical principle."[33] The justification of my neighbor's pain is "the source of all immorality."[34] Consciousness of this obligation to the Other brings one closer to God and spirituality more than any theodicy ever could. The interhuman lies in a non-indifference of one to another, in a responsibility of one for another, that precedes social contracts and ethical systems. It reflects "the interhuman perspective of my responsibility for the other person, without concern for reciprocity…in the asymmetry of the relation of one to the other."[35] Levinas emphasized in many of his works that only by responding to the evil inflicted upon the Other do I become fully human. And this response was absent in Auschwitz. Chapter 13 deals extensively with the challenges faced by the Holocaust.

SOLOVEITCHIK AND THE FAITH INDIVIDUAL

We end this chapter with R. Joseph Soloveitchik, who served as the spiritual leader of modern Judaism in the latter part of the twentieth century. Born into an illustrious Lithuanian rabbinical family in Pruzhana, he eventually moved with his family to Warsaw in 1920 and entered the Free Polish University in 1924. In 1926 he moved to the University of Berlin where he wrote his PhD thesis on the metaphysics of Hermann Cohen. In 1932 Soloveitchik emigrated with his wife Tonya Lewitt (who also received a PhD) to the United States, where he became a rabbi in Boston, MA, as well as "Rosh Yeshiva" (head of the Yeshiva) at the Elchanan Theological Seminary of Yeshiva University in New York. He became known as the "Rav" of these communities and was renowned for his weekly learning sessions in both cities. Although he gave numerous public lectures and classes, few of these were published during his lifetime. His most famous lecture "The Lonely Man of Faith" was presented to an interfaith audience at a Catholic seminary. His major publication *Halakhic Man* (*Ish ha-Halakhah*) was published in 1983; this was followed with an English translation in 1986 of *The Halakhic Mind*, a work that complemented *Halakhic Man*. A sermon in honor of Israel Independence Day, published in 1961 as "Hark! My beloved is knocking" (*Kol Dodi Dofek*), emphasized a more existentialist approach similar to that found in *The Lonely Man of Faith;* we will discuss this work in more detail in Chapter 14. To this day, thousands of recordings and manuscripts remain unpublished.

Soloveitchik's works, both published and unpublished, exhibit an extra-ordinary attempt to reconcile the religious with the philosophical perspectives, both in his own life, and for his readers and followers. More specifically, Soloveitchik confronted in many of his works the tensions between religion and modernity. A second concern centered around ethical obligations within the framework of *halakhah*. Soloveitchik was concerned with the philosophical problem of "*Ta'amei ha-mitzvot*" (reasons for the commandments) throughout his life. We have already encountered this classic problem in Chapter 8, most notably in the works of Saadiah Gaon, Maimonides, Spinoza and Mendelssohn. For Soloveitchik, the problem took on a different nuance, and focused on the sort of individual who lives in accordance with Jewish law. He believed that it is mistaken to question why the commandments, especially non-rational ones, were mandated; the process of assigning moral justifications or reasons for the commandments threatens to render them subservient to absolute moral principles.[36]

Soloveitchik's works are replete with references to secular philosophers outside the Jewish terrain, ranging from Kant and Nietzsche to Scheler and Kierkegaard. In what follows, we shall see how Soloveitchik portrays the tensions between two ways of life – the secular and the religious – and how these tensions can be resolved.

THE ONTOLOGY OF FAITH

In many of his works, both published and unpublished, Soloveitchik developed distinct personality typologies that are both opposed to one another, and yet dependent upon one another. The ideal individual draws upon the two extremes; the halakhic ideal involves living with the tension of these opposing personalities.[37] Soloveitchik's celebrated distinction between the religious and secular personality is elaborated in both *Halakhic Man* and *The Lonely Man of Faith*.[38]

Let us start with *Halakhic Man*. In this work, Soloveitchik distinguished two personality types: the "cognitive man (*ish ha-daat*)" of science, and the "homo religiosis" *(ish ha-dat)* or religious man of faith. Cognitive man is exemplified by the mathematical physicist, bent upon mastering and subduing the environment, whereas religious man is more attuned to the miraculous powers in nature, to a transcendent reality.[39] But both types are deficient in serious ways. Cognitive man has one goal – to understand the underlying order of the universe: "cognitive man's desire is to uncover the secret of the world and to unravel the problems of existence…he is filled with one exceedingly powerful yearning, which is to search for clarity and understanding, for solutions and resolutions."[40] Cognitive man thus prizes objectivity; much like Kierkegaard's objective scientist in *Fear and Trembling*, and Dostoyevsky's "l'homme de la Nature" in *Notes from Underground*, they share a desire to objectify the natural world around them.[41]

In contrast to cognitive man, who is steeped in a rational objectifying intellectualism, religious man revels in mystery, seeing it everywhere. He seeks a world beyond this one, and aspires to ascend to this higher, eternal reality: "he gazes at that which is obscure without the intent of explaining it and inquires into that which is concealed without the intent of receiving the reward of clear understanding."[42] Religious man is the "God-intoxicated mystic," with no interest in the "physical" world around him. Impervious as he is to the objective reality surrounding him, he loathes the physical world and its demands, yearning for a spiritual life beyond this one. Soloveitchik identified this yearning for a supernal existence with Philo, Plato, Spinoza, Kant, Christian scholasticism, Husserl, Scheler, Hermann Cohen and others: like these and many others in the history of philosophy, religious man seeks transcendence and "yearns for its Creator and rebels against the concrete reality that so entirely surrounds it."[43]

Let us compare this typology to that found in Soloveitchik's later work *The Lonely Man of Faith*. This work starts with his rejection of the Cartesian Ego: "I am lonely because, in my humble, inadequate way, I am a man of faith for whom to be means to believe, and who substituted 'credo' for 'cogito' in the time-honored Cartesian maxim."[44] Soloveitchik used this distinction to highlight the difference between "credo" (belief) and "cogito" (knowledge); the distinction is reflected in two personality types, Adam the first and Adam the second, which correspond roughly to cognitive man and religious man. As we shall see, however, the tensions between the two sets of personalities are resolved differently.

Like cognitive man, Adam the first is paradigmatic of the contemporary individual involved in subduing nature, focused upon scientific advances, asking "How does the cosmos function?"[45] His is a practical, not a metaphysical, concern, and his telos incorporates a utilitarian understanding of the nature of the universe. His motto is success, triumph over the cosmic forces, and he is best exemplified by the mathematical scientist. In contradistinction to Adam the first, Adam the second is both receptive and passive; he studies the world "with the naiveté, awe, and admiration of the child who seeks the unusual and wonderful in every ordinary thing and event," and he forms an "intimate relation with God" rather than an abstract relation based on conceptual understanding.[46] Adam the second realizes that he is existentially alone, alienated from the natural world, "experiencing ontological incompleteness and casualness, because there is no one who exists like the 'I' and because the *modus existentiae* of the 'I' cannot be repeated, imitated, or experienced by others."[47] Adam the second reflects the existential loneliness expressed already by Heidegger, Sartre, Rosenzweig, Buber and Levinas. But unlike religious man depicted in *Halakhic Man*, Adam the second does not reject the physical world; nor does he try to escape this world through mystery and asceticism.

Soloveitchik noted that Adam the first was created simultaneously with Eve, reinforcing the metaphysical fact that Adam the first from his inception lives in society, with the other: "Adam the first is never alone ... Adam the first was not left alone even on the day of creation. He emerged into the world together with Eve and God addressed Himself to both of them as inseparable members of one community."[48] Adam the second, on the other hand, is created without a mate, and must sacrifice a part of himself in order to attain an equal companion.[49] Adam the second must be introduced to Eve by God.

As it did in the works of Rosenzweig, time plays an important role in Soloveitchik's characterization of Adam the first and second. Soloveitchik was very much aware of the differing temporal models recognized and utilized by his two paradigmatic individuals. Adam the second is aware of the tragedy of passing time. He is immersed in the flow of temporal time: he recognizes there was an endless past, is aware of an endless future, and, with a nod to Aristotle's definition of the "now," he recognizes the ephemeral nature of the present instant, which vanishes before it is experienced.[50] Whereas Adam the second experiences both the transcendence and evanescence of the "now," Adam the first is completely unaware of the passage of time. For Adam the first lives in micro-units of clock time, moving with ease from "now" to "now," completely unaware of a "before" or an "after."[51]

Unlike the Aristotelian, for whom the "now" is ephemeral and defies capture, Adam the second finds redemption by means of cyclic time, according to which every temporal experience both reconstructs and recalls the past, while anticipating the future. Within the covenantal community, "each single experience of time is three-dimensional, manifesting itself in memory, actuality, and anticipatory tension."[52] This awareness cuts through linear time and unites generations of practitioners. Unlike Adam the first, Adam the second can thus feel both rooted in the past and related to the future.

CONCLUSION

Buber, Levinas and Soloveitchik were all concerned with delineating the dialogical relation between humans and their neighbors, as well as between humans and God. This dialogue can be appreciated most keenly in Soloveitchik's depiction of the tensions between cognitive man and religious man, on the one hand, and Adam the first and Adam the second on the other. Adam the second and Eve participate in the existential experience of *being*, not merely *working*, together. Soloveitchik argued that the prayer community is what redeems the relationship between Adam the second and Eve. Only when God revealed Himself from the transcendent darkness do Adam and Eve "reveal themselves to each other in sympathy and love on the one hand and in common action on the other."[53] True existential friendship, according to Soloveitchik, can be realized "only within the covenantal community, where in-depth personalities relate themselves to each other ontologically and total commitment to God and fellow man is the order of the day."[54] Soloveitchik ended "The Lonely Man of Faith" by arguing that Adam the first and Adam the second represent "not two different people locked in an external confrontation as an 'I' opposite a 'Thou', but one person who is involved in self-confrontation."[55] In all of us there resides both Adam the first and Adam the second. By rejecting Adam the second, we run the risk of losing sight of the covenantal community altogether; but by rejecting Adam the first, we lose our connection to modernity.

In *Halakhic Man*, however, Soloveitchik offered a more nuanced characterization of the relation between cognitive and religious man. He claimed that the ontological duality of cognitive man and religious man transcends the typology of the two extremes, leaving them behind. For halakhic man, holiness is defined as the implementation of Jewish law. Unlike religious man, halakhic man is devoid of any element of transcendence; it is "this world that sets the stage for the *halakhah*, the setting for halakhic man's life."[56] Soloveitchik rejected the other-worldliness of religious man, claiming that it is unethical. In a stunning rebuke of hyper-religiosity, he claims that religious man "forgets all too frequently the lower realms and becomes ensnared in the sins of ethical inconsistency and hypocrisy":

> [They are] so intoxicated by their dreams of an exalted supernal existence that they have failed to hear ... the sighs of orphans, the groans of the destitute ... There is nothing so physically and spiritually destructive as diverting ones attention from this world.[57]

Halakhic man, in contradistinction to religious man, is rooted in real world, and yet also attuned to God. He is identical "in many respects, to prosaic, cognitive man; on the other hand he is a man of God ... taken as a whole he is uniquely different from both of them."[58] Both halakhic man and the natural scientist approach the world in terms of their a priori systems and both use their systems as comprehensive models of orienting themselves to and comprehending reality.[59] By keeping his attention upon this world, halakhic man brings God into the world.

NOTES

1 Buber 1970, 53.
2 Buber 1970. Some translations use "I–Thou" and "the eternal Thou;" in this chapter I adhere to the word "You" as a translation of the German term "Du."
3 Buber 1970, 58.
4 Buber 1970, 63.
5 Buber 1970, 64.
6 Buber 1970, 69.
7 Buber 1970, 69, 148.
8 Buber 1970, 123.
9 Buber 1970, 154.

10 Buber 1970, 124.
11 Buber 1970, 85.
12 Buber 1970, 159.
13 Buber 1952, 129.
14 Buber 1952, 129.
15 Buber 1952.
16 Buber 1970, 121–122.
17 Levinas 1969, 26.
18 Levinas 1969, 36.
19 Levinas 1969, 37.
20 See Davis 1996, 31.
21 Levinas 1969, 50–51.
22 Levinas 1969, 79–80.
23 Levinas 1969, 34.
24 The interview with Levinas can be found in Robbins 2001, 72.
25 Robbins 2001.
26 Levinas 1969, 53.
27 Levinas 1969.
28 Levinas 1988, 161.
29 Levinas 1988, 162.
30 Levinas 1988.
31 Levinas 1988, 163.
32 Levinas 1988, 157.
33 Levinas 1988, 159.
34 Levinas 1988, 163.
35 Levinas 1988, 165.
36 Zelcer and Zelcer 2021, 73.
37 See Zelcer and Zelcer 2021, 88.
38 I will stick to the term "man" in this presentation, in order not to confuse Soloveitchik's own text. Unless otherwise noted, I do think, however, that "man" is an inclusive rather than "exclusive" term.
39 Soloveitchik 1983, 3–4.
40 Soloveitchik 1983, 5.
41 See Dostoyevsky 1976.
42 Soloveitchik 1983, 7.
43 Soloveitchik 1983, 14.

44 Soloveitchik 1992, 5.
45 Soloveitchik 1992, 13.
46 Soloveitchik 1992, 23.
47 Soloveitchik 1992, 41.
48 Soloveitchik 1992, 27.
49 Soloveitchik 1992, 39.
50 Soloveitchik 1992, 69.
51 Soloveitchik 1992.
52 Soloveitchik 1992, 71.
53 Soloveitchik 1992, 68.
54 Soloveitchik 1992, 69.
55 Soloveitchik 1992, 85.
56 Soloveitchik 1983, 30.
57 Soloveitchik 1983, 41.
58 Soloveitchik 1983, 3.
59 See Kaplan 1987, 151. Kaplan develops in extensive detail what science means for Soloveitchik, and how it differs from medieval and Aristotelian conceptions of science that are grounded in teleology.

FURTHER READING

Herberg, W. 1956. *The Writings of Martin Buber*. New York: Meridian.

Levinas, E. 1990. *Nine Talmudic Readings*, trans. Annette Aronowicz. Bloomington, IN: Indiana University Press.

Morgan, M. L. 2007. *Discovering Levinas*. Cambridge: Cambridge University Press.

Reinier M. 1996. *The Rationale of Halakhic Man: Joseph B. Soloveitchik's Conception of Jewish Thought*. Amsterdam: J.C. Gieben.

Soloveitchik, R.J.B. 1986. *The Halakhic Mind: An Essay on Jewish Tradition and Modern Thought*. New York: The Free Press. (Originally published in Hebrew in 1944.)

RESPONDING TO THE HOLOCAUST

INTRODUCTION: THEODICY REVISITED

Chapter 5 introduced the problem of evil in the context of medieval Jewish philosophy. We examined various attempts at theodicy, namely the process of justifying the ways of God in light of human suffering. Attempts at theodicy continued throughout the centuries, reaching a climax in the twentieth century. We need just list the many catastrophic events that have occurred in the past century or so: the Holocaust, two world wars, the Armenian genocide, the Stalinist gulag, Hiroshima and Nagasaki, Maoist purges, Cambodian killing fields, Bosnia and Rwanda.[1] We can now add the Israel–Hamas war to the list.

Each of these tragedies is horrific in its own sense. For Jewish thinkers, however, the Holocaust raised questions unique to the Jewish people, as reflected in the following queries: where was God in the Holocaust? Was the Holocaust a unique event, a turning point in Jewish history that required a paradigm shift, or was it on a scale with other traumatic events in Jewish history? Does the Holocaust require a transformative response in Judaism, or do the traditional theodical responses suffice?

Traditional theodicy responses to the Holocaust have rested on the belief that inasmuch as all events that occur

DOI: 10.4324/9781003504030-16

are good (reflecting Leibniz's "best of all possible worlds" theodicy), so too must there be a justification for the Holocaust. Various justifications have been given to understand and/or justify the horrific suffering of the Jews in the camps. Reflecting traditional theodicy claims that suffering is punishment for prior actions, justification might lie in arguing that the victims "deserved" in some way the punishment inflicted by God; that Hitler was carrying out God's will; that the Holocaust was a necessary cause for the establishment of the State of Israel; or that the Holocaust was the result of human free will and does not reflect upon God.[2]

But are these theodicies sufficient to account for the unspeakable tragedy of the Holocaust? The novelist Elie Wiesel struggled with trying to find meaning in light of the unspeakable. His widely read and universally acclaimed autobiographical novella *Night* depicted in graphic detail the horrors of the camps, and described in excruciating detail Wiesel's own struggles with maintaining belief in God. The psychologist and Holocaust survivor Victor Frankl struggled as well, and wrote his influential and autobiographical work *Man's Search for Meaning* in an attempt to offer a glimmer of hope to survivors of the camps who felt that life was meaningless; his own family perished in the camps. In part as a response to the camps, Frankl founded the school of logotherapy, which posited that one must create meaning in the events of one's life.

In light of these atrocities, anti-theodicies arose. These anti-theodicies, which refused to justify, explain, or accept the relationship between God and evil, have ranged from emphasizing the incomprehensibility of the event, to castigating God directly.[3] Anti-theodicies emphasize the ultimate historical and theological uniqueness of the Holocaust, a radical event that has ruptured the ability to offer conventional theodicy responses. We cannot help but be reminded of Ivan in Dostoevsky's *The Brothers Karamazov*, who rebels against a world in which children suffer torments. No theodicy can justify the suffering of innocents, he tells his brother Alyosha, who is studying to be a priest:

> From love of humanity, I don't want it. I would rather be left with unavenged suffering. I would rather remain with my unavenged suffering, and unsatisfied indignation, even if I were wrong. Besides, too high a price is asked for harmony; its beyond our means to pay so much to enter on it. And so I hasten to give back my entrance ticket, and if I am an honest man I am bound to give it back as soon as possible.[4]

RICHARD RUBENSTEIN AND THE DEATH OF GOD

Richard Rubenstein's *After Auschwitz* is one of the most extreme examples of anti-theodicy theology. Following in the footsteps of Protestant "Death of God" theologians such as Harvey Cox, Rubenstein denied God's transcendence altogether. Rubenstein started out as a rabbinical student at Hebrew Union College, but after the publication of *After Auschwitz* he was reviled and marginalized by the Jewish community for his radical position. Scholars and rabbis castigated him for following radical Protestant theologians who, echoing Nietzsche's madman who already in the nineteenth century announced the death of God, renounced classical theism. If classical theism postulates God as the supreme omnipotent and perfect Deity, then it is difficult not to attribute the Holocaust to God's own supreme will. Rubenstein is unable to accept this theological position.

Rubenstein stated the issue succinctly: "the problem of God and the death camps is the central problem for Jewish theology in the twentieth century."[5] Indeed, Rubenstein went so far as to call this problem the pre-eminent measure of the adequacy of all contemporary Jewish theologies. In a symposium organized by *Commentary* magazine in 1966, Rubenstein's position was starkly stated as follows:

> God really died at Auschwitz. This does not mean that God is not the beginning and will not be the end. It does mean that nothing in human choice, decision, value, or meaning can any longer have vertical reference to transcendent standards. We are alone in a silent, unfeeling cosmos. ... What then of Judaism? It is the way we Jews share our lives in an unfeeling and silent cosmos. It is the flickering candle we have lighted in the dark to enlighten and to warm us.[6]

What does it mean to live in a time of the death of God? Again, Rubenstein was explicit in his response:

> When I say we live in the time of the death of God, I mean that the thread uniting God and man, heaven and earth, has been broken. ... After Auschwitz, what else can a Jew say about God? To see any purpose in the death camps, the believer must "regard the most demonic, antihuman explosion in all history as a meaningful expression of God's purposes. The idea is simply too obscene for me to accept.[7]

In this passage, Rubenstein clearly and unequivocally rejected the uplifting covenantal relationship between God and humans. No longer can we believe in a providential Deity who oversees human affairs, and stands in relation with human beings. Instead of the Deity of traditional theology, Rubenstein did offer his readers what he calls an "insightful paganism." In an absurd universe, the suffering person represents not a figure of guilt, but rather a victim of tragic happenstance. Combining the language of Jewish mysticism and feminism, Rubenstein envisioned a non-theistic theology, emphasizing the immanence of God. This "God of Holy Nothingness" evokes God's mystery. This God is an amoral power that has a demonic side. In the second edition of *After Auschwitz* Rubenstein expressed his inability to pray in synagogue to this God of Nothingness: "we are struck dumb by words we can no longer honestly utter. All that we can offer is our reverent and attentive silence before the Divine."[8] We cannot help but think of Maimonides's conclusion in chapter 59 of *Guide for the Perplexed* that the only proper response to God is silence.

EMIL FACKENHEIM AND THE 614TH COMMANDMENT

A slightly different response to theodicy is expressed by Emil Fackenheim (1916–2003), who labored throughout his life to articulate an authentic response to the Holocaust in the context of *halakhah*. Born in Germany, he escaped the war and lived and taught for many years in Toronto and Jerusalem. After many years of avoiding the challenge posed by the Holocaust, Fackenheim's first published statement on the Holocaust was at a conference in 1966, and his most systematic and deepest discussion, *To Mend the World,* appeared in 1982. In these early works, Fackenheim argued that no intellectual understanding of Auschwitz is possible. The event has no meaning, and yet a response is required. Philosophical responses being inadequate, Fackenheim suggested a more existential response rooted in human behavior: in particular, Fackenheim argued that Jews must actively devote their lives to negating the Holocaust.

In his 1968 essay "Jewish Faith and the Holocaust" Fackenheim argued that the task of the contemporary

Jewish thinker is to face Auschwitz, and honor the victims within the context of Jewish faith. The "commanding Voice of Auschwitz" commands Jews to remember the Holocaust and live a full Jewish life. Morgan provided a summary of Fackenheim's thinking in this early work as follows:[9]

1. Both Jews and non-Jews, seeking to understand the Holocaust, have avoided the particularity or distinctiveness of the event, but it is distinctive, unprecedented, unique.
2. Auschwitz resists satisfying rational and religious explanations; it has no purpose or meaning.
3. Response is necessary.
4. There are no traditional, acceptable models for such response.
5. Jews after the destruction remained committed to Jewish survival.
6. Such a commitment to Jewish survival can be understood as a response of opposition to Nazi purposes, a "bearing witness" against the "demons of Auschwitz."
7. What accounts for this commitment to Jewish existence as an act of opposition is a "commanding Voice [that] speaks from Auschwitz."
8. This commanding but not redeeming voice is heard by religious Jews but not by secular Jews; the commandment to resist is heard by both.
9. The content of this absolute commandment is: Jews are forbidden to grant posthumous victories to Hitler.
10. This commandment can be elaborated to mean: survive as Jews, remember the victims of Auschwitz, do not despair of humankind and the world, and do not despair of the God of Israel.

Fackenheim clearly saw Auschwitz as unique and incommensurate with other events: it is evil for evil's sake. The

Holocaust requires a response, but what sort of response is adequate in light of such evil? Fackenheim famously proposed a 614th commandment "not to give Hitler posthumous victories" by turning ones back on Jewish belief and practice:

> [Jews] are commanded to survive as Jews, lest the Jewish people perish. They are commanded to remember the victims of Auschwitz, lest their memory perish. They are forbidden to despair of man and his world, and to escape into either cynicism or otherworldliness, less [*sic*] they cooperate in delivering the world over to the forces of Auschwitz. Finally, they are forbidden to despair of the God of Israel, lest Judaism perish.[10]

It is important to note that, unlike Rubenstein, Fackenheim did not give up his belief in a supernatural, transcendent Deity. In this and subsequent works, Fackenheim reminded Jews to survive, and to remember the Holocaust. His edict forbad religious Jews from despairing of God, and prohibits prohibited secular Jews from despairing the world.

Fackenheim's thought represents an attempt to "find a small shard of good upon which to reconfigure Jewish life after Auschwitz."[11] But is this attempt successful? Critics have noted the inherent contradictions in Fackenheim's thought, arguing that the pieces do not cohere. More specifically, how does one remember Auschwitz without introducing despair; and how can one retain belief in the inherent goodness of humanity in light of the atrocities of the Holocaust?

In his 1982 work *To Mend the World* Fackenheim addressed some of these criticisms. Drawing on the works of Jewish mystics, he emphasized the power of *tikkun* or repair. In the mystical/kabbalistic literature of Isaac Luria, divine catastrophe is described as a situation in which God shatters divine vessels, the pieces of which fall to earth, awaiting redemption by human beings. On this model, redemption consists in mending or repairing these broken shards, thus restoring a broken universe to wholeness. In *To Mend the World* Fackenheim tried to imagine the sorts of activities that might call for repairing the rift created by the Holocaust. Remiscent of Camus's Sisyphus who overcomes his struggles with an attitude of revolt, Fackenheim suggested that individual acts of resistance were in fact able to surpass the evil. But has Fackenheim resolved the original question – where was God at Auschwitz? Ultimately Fackenheim has no answer to that pressing question; faith has taken its place.

HANNAH ARENDT AND THE BANALITY OF EVIL

With Hannah Arendt (1906–1975) we turn to yet another facet of post-Holocaust thought. Born in Germany, Arendt studied philosophy and commenced a life-long relationship with her teacher Heidegger. In 1933 she fled to Paris and subsequently to the United States in 1941 where she taught for many years as a political theorist. The author of numerous books, including *The Origins of Totalitarianism, The Human Condition,* and *The Life of the Mind,* she is perhaps best known for her coverage of the Eichmann trial in Jerusalem. Her work *Eichmann in Jerusalem: A report on the Banality of Evil* was published in 1963 and aroused immediate controversy and notoriety. She is equally famous, or perhaps infamous, for her intense relationship with Heidegger, whom she never disavowed, even after he was accused of advancing Nazism.

Already in *The Origins of Totalitarianism*, Arendt was concerned with anti-Semitism and the ways in which it contributed to totalitarianism. Arendt understood totalitarianism to be an entirely new political phenomenon that differed "essentially from other forms of political oppression known to us such as despotism, tyranny and dictatorship"[12] and thus broke with all political and legal tradition. In the third part of the work, Arendt analyzes the conditions and features of what she terms this novel form of government, concluding that several factors made totalitarianism possible. In particular, totalitarianism thrived on collapsed political structures and masses of uprooted people in a world marked by socio-economic transformation, revolution and war. While the leaders of the movements belonged to the "mob," their many supporters were recruited from these rootless and lonely masses through propaganda.[13]

While totalitarian regimes openly claim unlimited power and aim at world domination, their "real secrets" are the concentration and extermination camps. According to Arendt, the camps "serve as laboratories in which the fundamental belief of totalitarianism that everything is possible is being verified."[14] The total terror in the camps is the essence and goal of totalitarian government, because here total domination reaches its abysmal goal, namely to reduce "the infinite plurality" of human beings into one interchangeable "bundle of reactions" and thus eliminate "spontaneity itself."[15] According to Arendt, the real mission of the totalitarian apparatus was to "to make men superfluous." But no totalitarian regime can create a new world order; totalitarianism ultimately leads to nothing but unprecedented destruction. According to Arendt, it even "bears the germ of its own destruction."[16] In her concluding remarks she writes: "The danger of the corpse factories and holes of oblivion is that today, with populations and homelessness everywhere on the increase, masses of people are continuously rendered superfluous as we continue to think of our world in utilitarian terms."[17] Written in the last century, these words still resonate in our own time.

In 1961 the Israeli government put the Nazi war criminal Adolf Eichmann on trial. Eichmann was a German SS member of the Gestapo during the second world war and organized the deportation of Jews from Germany and other countries as part of the Final Solution. His work contributed to the extermination of six million Jews. The prosecution called over 100 witnesses, many of them survivors of the camps. An observer at the trial, Arendt reported her observations to *The New Yorker* and then subsequently in her 1963 book *Eichmann in Jerusalem*. In this work Arendt made several controversial and incendiary claims: that the Jewish institutions were in part responsible for the Holocaust; that the victims themselves did not sufficiently fight against the Nazis, and most notably, that Eichmann represented what she called the bureaucratic "banality of evil."

How did Arendt come to this conclusion? She was struck by the fact that Eichmann himself appeared to be totally normal, not at all sinister, a superficial conformist with no sense of personal responsibility. His motives were totally banal and he regarded his actions to be in total conformity with the Nazi hierarchy and bureaucracy. He thought of himself as an exemplary civil servant, obeying orders and carrying out his role with precision.[18] He was what Arendt called a "thoughtless" agent, incapable of independent judgment. And so the "banality of evil" came to replace Arendt's former emphasis on radical evil; far from being a demonic figure, Eichmann on Arendt's depiction was simply an ordinary, normal agent carrying out orders.

Arendt did not question Eichmann's guilt, and she supported his death sentence by hanging. Nor did she mean to claim (as her critics accused her of arguing) that Eichmann's *actions* were themselves banal. Rather her purpose in the work was to elucidate how ordinary people could be coerced into committing atrocities. The idea that we are all potential Eichmanns, that any one of us might have committed these crimes, was unsettling to a Jewish readership.

FORGIVENESS AS A PHILOSOPHICAL PROBLEM: JANKÉLÉVITCH, DERRIDA AND LEVINAS ON REMEMBERING THE SHOAH

Thus far we have considered philosophical responses to how one might respond to the events of the Holocaust. But what about the perpetrators themselves? To what extent are we able to forgive the perpetrators for their atrocities? Unlike Christianity, which prioritizes forgiveness as a desideratum, Judaism's approach has been more nuanced. Rabbinic texts focused primarily upon God's forgiveness of human behavior; texts broached as well the issues surrounding perpetrators asking forgiveness of their victims. But less attention was paid to the question of the conditions under which victims might expect to forgive perpetrators.[19]

From a philosophical perspective, the very notion of forgiveness, fraught with metaphysical and moral implications, raises many additional questions. Can one reconcile with a perpetrator without also forgiving them, or forgive a person without reconciling? Can parties be reconciled if forgiveness is refused? What is the ultimate goal of forgiveness; is it in fact the re-establishment or resumption of relations ruptured by wrong doing? If that is the case, can forgiveness be granted on behalf of the deceased? The benefits of forgiveness affect wrong doers as well, releasing them from guilt they may (or may not) feel, allowing them to move forward. But is it possible to forgive unrepentant wrong doers? And finally, how does time itself figure into the process of forgiveness? Does forgiveness have a transformative power in reconfiguring the past? Does forgiveness involve changing the past, making the past not to have been? Does forgiveness carry with it forgetting the past; starting anew; a clean slate?

For philosophers Victor Jankélévitch, Levinas and Derrida, the question of forgiveness takes on heightened urgency in light of the Holocaust. In 1963, Levinas and Jankélévitch organized a conference of French speaking Jewish intellectuals on the topic of forgiveness. Derrida responded to some of the themes developed in this conference in his own subsequent work. Against the backdrop of the traditional philosophical and theological responses to forgiveness and repentance, these philosophers struggled to articulate the extent to which the Nazis should be forgiven their atrocities. We will start with Jankélévitch and then turn to critiques of his work by Derrida and Levinas.

JANKÉLÉVITCH ON THE MORALITY OF FORGIVENESS

Born in fin-de-siècle France to Russian-Jewish immigrants, Victor Jankélévitch (1905–1985) attended the prestigious École Normale Supérieure. Graduating at the top of his class in 1926, Jankélévitch seemed positioned for intellectual renown. But in 1939 he was mobilized in the war and injured in 1940. When the Nazis occupied France, his citizenship, along with that of all naturalized French Jews, was revoked. Jankélévitch joined the resistance, writing for an anti-Nazi organization, and organized secret lectures that were circulated underground. After the war, Jankélévitch was appointed to a post at the Sorbonne, where he taught and wrote until his retirement in 1979. In these latter years, Jankélévitch found himself out of step with French philosophers and his works became increasingly marginalized, in part because he refused to engage with the German philosophy (in particular that of Heidegger) so popular in France at the time.

In 1964–1965 the French government initiated public debates over the question of statutory limits with regard to crimes against humanity. Jankélévitch participated in these debates and argued that these crimes are not only irreversible but also irrevocable and thus not subject to statutory limits. His position was subsequently published in two works: "Pardonner?" ("Should we Pardon Them") written in 1971, based on an essay written in 1965, and the longer book *Le Pardon (Forgiveness)* written in 1967.

Rooted in the notion of time, forgiveness for Jankélévitch informs the importance of the passage of time. "Has the time come to forgive, or at least to forget?"[20] he asks. Is there a moment, perhaps when sufficient time has passed and the pain has abated, that forgiveness is appropriate? If so, does forgiveness result in forgetting, in the erasure of the past? Further, are there actions for which forgiveness is never a possibility, despite the passage of time?

In answer, Jankélévitch posed a paradoxical reply – although nothing is impossible for forgiveness, some acts are ontologically inexcusable; but it is those very acts that call for forgiveness. This paradox is expressed in both of his works, but in different contexts. In "Should we Pardon Them" he argued that "forgiveness died in the concentration camps."[21] Jankélévitch emphasized in this essay the lack of remorse on the side of the perpetrators, leaning on the importance of "conditional forgiveness." And of course Jankélévitch reminded us that German Nazis themselves have never asked to be forgiven. "Pardoning died in the death camps."[22] Furthermore, he declaimed, what right have we to forgive the crimes perpetrated upon others? "I do not see why it should be up to us, the survivors, to pardon ... ask the little children to pardon you yourselves."[23]

In *Forgiveness*, however, Jankélévitch provided a more nuanced philosophical account, offering a model of "pure forgiveness" that is rarely attainable. This pure forgiveness was what Jankélévitch called a "limit-experience," an experience that lies at the very limits of human power.

Faced with human evil, humans are confronted with the moral dilemma of a choice between justice and love – to forgive evil in an act of love, or to violently resist it and seek its prosecution in the name of justice. Jankélévitch recognized that the two actions are in tension with one another, but he noted the inevitable nature of the contradiction as follows: "between the absolute of the law of love and the absolute of vicious liberty there is a tear that cannot be entirely sundered. I have not attempted to reconcile the irrationality of evil with the omnipotence of love. Forgiveness is as strong as evil, but evil is as strong as forgiveness."[24]

Jankélévitch reminded us in *Forgiveness* that forgiveness is an act done on behalf of the dead, who cannot forgive on their own. The deed itself, the crimes are irreversible and irrevocable. We cannot change the past, but we can render the future free of the past. "Forgiveness liberates, liquidates, and liquefies the running water that rancor held prisoner."[25] The "as if-ness" of the past thus frees the perpetrator from moral guilt, free to move into a present and future unencumbered by the past. In Jankélévitch's words: "forgiveness decides to consider the event as null and as not having come to pass, even though it did, alas!"[26] While it is impossible to undo the past, in a sense forgiveness does the impossible. Is it logically possible for Auschwitz to have happened and to not have happened? Is this not a logical contradiction? Jankélévitch recognized the conundrum and suggests that "We can *make it as if*, but we cannot *make it that*, we can make it as if that which happened did not happen, but not that what happened did not happen."[27]

Returning to the idea of the miraculous nature of forgiveness, Jankélévitch pointed to the simultaneity of the "having-done" and the "not-having-done": "Forgiveness is simultaneously omnipotent and impotent. It is the very miracle of forgiveness that in a burst of joy annihilates the having-been and the having-done."²⁸ On the one hand, the bloodstains of an action can never be washed away; on the other hand the stains are washed away. By means of this pure forgiveness, the perpetrator becomes innocent; pure forgiveness "effaces all, sweeps away all, and forgets all."²⁹ In this sense forgiveness does in fact carry with it forgetting. Forgiveness is not bound by time, space or external considerations. Ideally, pure forgiveness forgives everyone for everything for all times. It extends "unlimited credit" to the guilty person.

On the other hand, Jankélévitch noted that if we cease to think about the victims, they will be definitively annihilated. Jankélévitch reminds us that the past cannot defend itself as do the present and the future: "The dead depend entirely on our loyalty ... Our celebrations must endlessly save [the past] from nothingness, or at least hold back the nonbeing to which it is destined."³⁰ Jankélévitch agreed that occasionally time can dull our reactions; but in this case, "crimes against humanity are imprescriptible, that is, the penalties against them cannot lapse; time has no hold on them."³¹

DERRIDA'S CRITIQUE OF JANKÉLÉVITCH

Can the apparent contradictions between Jankélévitch's two works be reconciled? Both Derrida and Levinas responded in several publications to Jankélévitch in attempting to resolve the tensions. A French-Algerian philosopher of Jewish descent, Jacques Derrida (1904–1980) is best known as the founder of deconstructionism, a far-ranging theory that influenced philosophy, literary criticism and theory, art, architectural theory and political theory. He was very much influenced by Husserl and Levinas; in 1967 he published three works that introduced the term "deconstruction" and catapulted him to fame.

In 2001, Derrida wrote two essays dealing with forgiveness: a two-part article entitled "On Cosmopolitanism and On Forgiveness" and a second essay "To Forgive: The Unforgivable and the Imprescriptible" which appeared in a volume entitled *Questioning God*. The latter work focuses more closely on Derrida's reading of Jankélévitch, and so I will concentrate on that essay here. As we shall see below, Derrida expanded upon and embraced the paradox implicit in Jankélévitch's analysis. Derrida's own position is that forgiveness is required precisely when an act appears unforgivable; were we able to understand the act, or *claim* that it deserves forgiveness, the act would no longer require forgiveness.

The essay "To Forgive" begins with a general query about forgiveness, noting that it is most often expressed in the Abrahamic religions. Derrida listed several questions associated with forgiveness: Who forgives or who asks whom for forgiveness? Who has the right to forgive? And what does the "who" signify? Does one forgive *someone* for a wrong committed, or does one forgive the act itself?[32] Similar to Levinas (whom we discuss below), Derrida suggested that forgiveness can only be asked "face to face;" it is an act between the perpetuator and the victim who "is alone in being able to hear the request for forgiveness, to grant or refuse it. This solitude of two …"[33]

Derrida then turned to Jankélévitch's own account, and pointed to the deep contradiction embedded in his two works. He started out with Jankélévitch's own admission that his treatment of forgiveness contains both ambiguity and contradiction, reminding us of Jankélévitch's claim that "I have not attempted to reconcile the irrationality of evil with the omnipotence of love. Forgiveness is as strong as evil, but evil is as strong as forgiveness."[34] According to Derrida, Jankélévitch says "no" to forgiveness, alleging that one must not forget, speaking on behalf of the victims who are unable to respond. "Forgiveness is impossible. Forgiveness should not be. One should not forgive."[35]

Derrida, however, emphasized the unconditionality of forgiveness. He restated in both his works the inherent *aporia* or paradox embedded in forgiveness: "forgiveness forgives only the unforgivable. One cannot, or should not, forgive; there is only forgiveness, if there is any, where there is the unforgivable."[36] But unlike Jankélévitch, Derrida embraced the paradox and argued that forgiveness is required at the very moment we discover what cannot be forgiven. Forgiveness, like grace, is bestowed in contradistinction to reason; it is both possible and impossible. In short, for Derrida, forgiveness is "mad, and …must remain a madness of the impossible."[37]

LEVINAS AND JANKÉLÉVITCH ON TIME AND FORGIVENESS

Let us turn finally to Levinas, who shared with Jankélévitch a concern with forgiveness and statues of limitations. In Chapter 12 we noted Levinas's obsession with the Holocaust. Levinas co-organized with Jankélévitch the French conference on the topic of forgiveness. At that colloquium he delivered a Talmudic reading entitled "Toward the Other" (*"Envers autrui"*) that examined a passage from Tractate Yoma of the Talmud, which deals with issues of repentance and forgiveness (*Teshuvah*). In this work, subsequently published in 1963, Levinas focuses on the intertwining of forgiveness and justice, and suggests that Jews are being called upon to renounce the right to vengeance, *insofar as they are Jews*. Using a prooftext from 2 Samuel that highlights the wrongs perpetrated upon the tribe of Gideonites by King Saul, Levinas emphasized that King David was right to respond the Gideonites and redress the injustice. For Levinas, this account emphasizes that the Other must come first, even if it results in one's own self-destruction; one cannot force forgiveness or retaliatory justice.[38]

A similar emphasis on forgiveness and time can be found in Levinas's *Time and Infinity*. In the final pages of the work, Levinas turned to the issue of forgiveness against what he calls Jankélévitch's "paradox of the pardon of fault."[39] Levinas considered forgiveness to be "the very work of time."[40] The paradox of pardon lies in the inversion of the natural order, what Levinas called the reversibility of time. Pardon permits the perpetrator "to be as though that instant had not past on, to be as though he had not committed himself."[41] According to Levinas, Jankélévitch has not accounted for the importance of temporal flow in dealing with the other. For Levinas, forgiveness opens up the possibility of a future rid of the burdens of the past; the guilty one can now experience a new past and future. It is the dynamic relation between forgiver and forgiven that resets the ontological status between past and future. "I begin again from the eyes of the other who forgives me."[42] Thus the gift of time can only come from the other. For Levinas, freedom is received in the welcome of the other.

In summary, while for Jankélévitch the act of forgiveness is paramount, Levinas focused on the reception of the other to being forgiven. Jankélévitch and Levinas both emphasized the rupture of the instant. Within the discontinuity of time, Jankélévitch emphasizes the importance of renewal, a "wholly new spring," a new beginning.[43] But this new future cannot be severed from the past; The past is still past, but reinterpreted. For Levinas on the other hand, the paradox of forgiveness "lies in its retroaction," in the reversibility of time itself.[44] Forgiveness thus alters the past. Forgiveness is rooted in the very mystery of time.

"The newness of springtime arrives already heavy with all the springtimes past."[45]

CONCLUSION

Does the Holocaust represent a unique instance of evil, or does it represent just one of many instances of humanity's inhumanity? Jewish philosophers have struggled with this issue and provided a variety of responses. Rubenstein offered compelling reasons to question belief in the traditional God, whereas Fackenheim argued that forgetting or forgiving the Holocaust, or denying God, amounts to offering a victory to the Nazis. Arendt provided a compelling account of the origins of totalitarianism and suggested we might all, like Eichmann, be guilty of horrible crimes. Finally, Jankelevitch, Derrida and Levinas struggled with the limits, if any, of forgiveness; are these limits comprehensible? Are there crimes that are simply unforgivable? We continue to struggle with these issues to this day.

NOTES

1. Braiterman 1998, 3.
2. Martin Buber and others invoked the notion of "*Hester panim*" (God's hiding the face) in an attempt to explain the existence of evil; that God has withdrawn from history in order to make room for human freedom.
3. Braiterman 1998, 4.
4. Dostoyevsky 1976, 226.
5. Rubenstein 1966, 223.
6. Rubenstein 1966, 223, quoted in Morgan 2001.
7. Rubenstein 1966, 224–225, quoted in Morgan 2001.
8. Braiterman 1998, 100.
9. See Morgan 2001, 157; Fackenheim 1968, 26–32.
10. See Morgan 2001, 162; Fackenheim 1968, 32.
11. Braiterman 1998, 136.
12. Arendt 1976, 460.

13 Arendt 1976, 326.
14 Arendt 1976, 436, 437.
15 Arendt 1976, 438.
16 Arendt 1976, 436.
17 Arendt 1976, 443.
18 Arendt 1963, 15–16.
19 We return to this issue below when we turn to Levinas's discussion of forgiveness.
20 Jankélévitch 1996, 553.
21 Jankélévitch 1996, 567.
22 Jankélévitch 1996, 567.
23 Jankélévitch 1996, 569.
24 Jankélévitch 1996, 553.
25 Jankélévitch 2005, 151.
26 Jankélévitch 2005, 98.
27 Jankélévitch 2005, 48.
28 Jankélévitch 2005, 164.
29 Jankélévitch 2005, 145.
30 Jankélévitch 1996, 571.
31 Jankélévitch 1996, 557.
32 Derrida 2001b, 24.
33 Derrida 2001b, 25.
34 Derrida 2001b, 26 quoting Jankélévitch 1996, 553.
35 Derrida 2001b, 27.
36 Derrida 2001a, 32–33; Derrida 2001b, 30.
37 Derrida 2001a, 39.
38 See Hollander 2012, 150. For an extended discussion of this prooftext and Levinas's use of it, see Katz 2014, 178–189.
39 Levinas 1969, 283.
40 Levinas 1969, 284.
41 Levinas 1969, 283.
42 Looney 2015, 275; Levinas 1969, 284.
43 Jankélévitch 2005, 150.
44 Levinas 1969, 284.
45 Levinas 1969; Looney 2015, 277.

FURTHER READING

Arendt, H. 2003. *Responsibility and Judgment*, ed. Jerome Kohn. New York: Schocken.

Fackenheim, E., 1996. *Jewish Philosophers and Jewish Philosophy*, ed. Michael L. Morgan. Bloomington, IN: Indiana University Press.

Frankl, V.E. 2006. *Man's Search for Meaning,* trans. Ilse Lasch. Boston, MA: Beacon Press.

Lang, B., 2007. "Evil Suffering and the Holocaust," in *The Cambridge Companion to Modern Jewish Philosophy*, ed. Michael L. Morgan and Peter Eli Gordon. Cambridge: Cambridge University Press, 277–299.

Levinas, E. 1990. *Nine Talmudic Readings*, trans. Annette Aronowicz. Bloomington, IN: Indiana University Press.

Wiesel, E. 1960. *Night.* New York: Bantam Books.

CONTEMPORARY ISSUES
Zionism and Gender Equality

INTRODUCTION

Jewish philosophy has continued to flourish in the twenty-first century. Responding to recent developments in the sphere of analytic philosophy of religion, Jewish philosophers such as Jerome Gellman, Samuel Lebens, Aaron Segal and Dani Rabinowitz have expanded the conversation to include the analytic philosophy of Judaism. The *Academy for Jewish Philosophy*, a forum for Jewish philosophers to deal with major issues of Jewish faith in the context of contemporary philosophy, was established in the late 1980s. More recently, the volume *Jewish Philosophy in an Analytic Age* has drawn upon contemporary developments in analytic philosophy in order to (quoting the editors) inform our understanding of traditional Jewish philosophers and showcase what Jewish philosophy might look like in an analytic age. This volume is dedicated to the proposition that analytic philosophy, applied to the Jewish tradition, can offer new clarity about "what it is ... that Jews actually stand for, and why it often matters to them so much."[1] The volume applies contemporary analytic methodology to standard topics in Jewish philosophy, ranging from philosophical theology, ethics, to classical rabbinic thought.

This final chapter focuses upon two recent developments in Jewish philosophy, namely Zionism and the role of women in Judaism. While working on this book, war has been waged in Israel and Gaza, and has spread to Lebanon, Syria and Iran. Contemporary Jews cannot help but obsess over the relations between Zionism, anti-Semitism and Palestinian rights. The longing to return to Zion dates back to the earliest years of the Jewish diaspora. By the late nineteenth century, the term Zionism began to be used to refer to the particular movement whose goal was creation of a Jewish state in what Zionists saw as the historical land of Israel. This chapter traces both Zionist and anti-Zionist factions within Jewish thought.

Jewish feminist thought emerged in the early 1970s as an attempt to protest the subordination of women within *halakhah*. This subordination was reflected in their exclusion from the minyan, exemption from study, separation of women from men in traditional synagogue services, and women's inability to function as witnesses in a court of law or to initiate divorce proceedings. To what extent can women be reintegrated into the fabric of Jewish life and law? We examine the roots and results of Jewish feminists in combating the gender inequities in Jewish law.

JUDAISM AND NATIONALISM

Nationalism as a political movement in Western Europe made its appearance roughly in response to the Napoleonic wars and struggles for national liberation. But nationalism was not a major issue for Jews at that time. In fact, most Jews in the early to mid-nineteenth century avoided discussion of Jewish nationalism, not wanting to hinder the rise of Jewish emancipation. As we saw in Chapters 9 and 10, there was a tendency to promote the emancipation of Jews in Europe by emphasizing their allegiance to the European nations. On the other hand, particularly in

Eastern Europe, the land of the Bible – Zion – was a powerful trope. But the rise of anti-Semitism in France, Germany and Russia in the late nineteenth century undermined the aspirations of the Haskalah. In response to pogroms and anti-Semitic attacks, secular Jews began to conceive of a Jewish homeland as the only answer to this situation. Following pogroms in Russia in 1881, a group of eastern European intellectuals formed the group "*Hibbat Tsiyyon*" (lovers of Zion) and started to direct emigration of Jews from Russia to Palestine.

As with other forms of nationalism, Jewish nationalists sought to revive a national language, develop the resources of the land, remove Jews from the diaspora and bring them to Zion, and achieve sovereignty for the new national state. It is important to note that the longing to return to the homeland, to Zion, dates back to the destruction of the first Temple (586 BCE) and is articulated in numerous prayers and psalms. The phrase "Next Year in Jerusalem" occupies a central place, for example, in the Passover liturgy. By the late nineteenth century, the term Zionism began to be used to refer to the particular movement whose goal was creation of a Jewish state in what Zionists saw as the historical land of Israel. Theodore Herzl (1860–1904) the founder of modern political Zionism, convened the first Zionist Congress in Basel, Switzerland in 1897. One of the Congress's aims was to create a home for the Jewish people in Palestine. Most of Herzl's followers were secular and westernized, and the first Zionist emigrations to Palestine were made up of primarily young secular Russian Jews fleeing the pogroms.

It is important to note that not all Zionists hoped for a Jewish state in Palestine. At one point, Herzl himself pursued the idea of purchasing land in Uganda for a Jewish state. American Zionists such as Louis Brandeis (1856–1941) and Horace Kallen (1882–1974) maintained that a full Jewish life could be lived outside of a Jewish State, and the founder of Reconstructionist Judaism, Mordecai Kaplan (1881–1983) emphasized the idea that Jewishness consisted in a total way of life or civilization that could flourish both in the Jewish state and in the diaspora.

There were other forms of Zionism and anti-Zionism as well. Observant Jews developed a form of theological Zionism that emphasized the God-inspired, messianic aspects of the new Jewish state. Yitzhak Yaakov Reines (1839–1915), for example, coined the phrase *merkaz ruhani* (spiritual center), and founded the Mizrahi religious Zionist movement that emphasized spirituality alongside physical labor. However anti-Zionism has remained a strong strain throughout Jewish history. Some Jews (Moses Mendelssohn included) felt that it was unpatriotic, and maybe even treasonous to hold double loyalties. Others took seriously the mission to be a "light unto the nations" and argued that doing so can only be accomplished in the diaspora. As we shall see below, Hermann Cohen felt that Zionism represented a retreat from the Jewish mission of spreading the ideas of monotheism to the nations. In the United States, the Reform Movement rejected Zionism in its original platform statement in 1885, disavowing any aspirations for a Jewish homeland. By 1948, however, in part as a result of the Holocaust, the Reform movement began to support the new Jewish state of Israel. Finally, we must mention the position of Joel Teitelbaum (1887–1979), the Satmar Rabbi, who argued in a number of works that the sin of Zionism was what brought on the Holocaust; in effect he maintained that the Zionists were complicit in the Holocaust, hoping to use the slaughter of Jews as justification for their goals of statehood.[2]

PHILOSOPHICAL REFLECTIONS ON JEWISH NATIONALISM

What did the philosophers covered in this volume have to say about nationalism and creation of a Jewish state?

Spinoza played an important role in stressing the distinctness of the Jews, and offered a secular historical interpretation of what he saw as the ongoing continuation of Jewish life (see Chapters 7 and 8). In his *Theological-Political Treatise*, Spinoza suggested that it was gentile hatred of Jews that consolidated Jewish distinctiveness; he argued that this hatred helped preserve their separate existence throughout the centuries. Spinoza saw no reason to re-enact the Jewish state, and felt that Jewish distinctiveness was sufficient to guarantee their existence. Interestingly, this view was reintroduced by Sartre in his *"Anti-Semite and Jew"* (see Chapter 11).

We mentioned (in Chapter 9) the views of Mendelssohn, whose concern was with Jewish emancipation and the entry of Jews into European society. Mendelssohn saw talk of a Jewish state as antithetical to his goals. In the nineteenth century, Nachman Krochmal (see Chapter 10) elaborated in his *Guide of the Perplexed of our Times* a philosophy of history that highlighted the spiritual perfection of the Jewish people; he was one of the few thinkers who espoused a nationalistic stance. Later Zionist thinkers used Krochmal's depiction of the Jewish people and history in their own nationalist tracts.

By the early twentieth century, when the dream of a Jewish state was becoming more vivid, some philosophers denounced Zionist aspirations as misguided. Hermann Cohen rejected the notion of the importance of Jewish statehood. Cohen was committed to an anti-Zionist position (see Chapter 10); he accused Zionists of replacing belief in a transcendent Deity with a Spinozistic pantheism that reduced the role played by religion. For Cohen, Judaism was primarily a religion standing outside of any physical place, and he argued that action rather than place or nationhood defined what it meant to be a Jew. Committed to the importance of participating in the state (in his case, Germany), Cohen argued that the only way to preserve Judaism was to root it in the non-Jewish state.[3] In 1915 he published a pamphlet in which he argued for the legitimacy of a Jewish minority as an essential component of the German national identity. He followed this with an article in which he castigated German Jews that were devoting their efforts to the creation of a Jewish national state.

In contradistinction to Cohen, Martin Buber supported a form of cultural Zionism that defended the role of Jews in Palestine. As we saw in Chapter 12, Buber immigrated to Palestine in 1938, living there for the rest of his life. In 1916 Buber wrote a reply to Hermann Cohen's anti-Zionist criticism entitled *Homeland*, arguing that Cohen was oblivious to the importance of a nation-state. Buber argued that Palestine was to be a home not just for Jews, but for all of humanity, arguing that the new homeland was "to be made independent of the preoccupations of nations ... and of 'external politics' ... so that it might marshal all forces toward the inner elaboration and thereby the fulfillment of Judaism."[4]

As we saw in Chapter 11, Franz Rosenzweig, like Hermann Cohen, rejected the historization of Jews, arguing that they existed outside of worldly history, and thus were not subject to notions of a homeland or other temporal markers. In the final portion of the *Star*, Rosenzweig claimed that while Christianity functions *within history*, Judaism lives outside the historical stream – its sole task is to exist; by its very existence, Israel bears witness to God in the world.[5] While Christianity unfolds through history and time, Judaism, he claimed, exists outside of the flow of history. It would be interesting indeed to speculate what Rosenzweig, writing twenty years before the establishment of the State of Israel, would have thought of Israel's reinsertion into history and subsequent history of constant warfare.

Joseph Soloveitchik's attitudes toward Zionism were complex and underwent interesting developments. In contradistinction to his grandfather Hayyim Soloveitchik who was fiercely anti-Zionist on halakhic grounds, Soloveitchik himself sought to make room for a modern Jewish state within the framework of *halakhah*. Early on, he was influenced by anti-Zionism, but by 1939 he publicly declared his support for Zionism. After the war, Soloveitchik embraced both secular and religious Zionism, arguing fervently that Jews must work together to establish the new homeland. His 1956 work *Kol Dodi Dofek* (*My Beloved Knocks*) laid out his support for religious Zionism in passionate terms. Starting with the classic problem of evil, Soloveitchik moved from Job's travails to the evil encountered in the Holocaust. Soloveitchik argued that God is knocking on our door, beckoning us back to the homeland. Using what he called the wondrous events surrounding the establishment of the State of Israel, Soloveitchik urged religious Jews to support the state; having abnegated our duty to save Jews during the Holocaust, now is our time to support Israel: "We all sinned by our silence in the face of the murder of millions … In the crisis that the land of Israel is [at present] passing through, Providence is again testing us."[6] Dov Schwartz notes that *Kol Dodi Dofek* has made its way into the religious and Zionist yeshivot: "this work has become the unofficial manifesto of the next generation of religious-Zionism."[7]

Needless to say, controversy over Zionism and Zionist goals has not abated. Take for example two recent works: *The Necessity of Exile* by Shaul Magid and *The No State Solution: A Jewish Manifesto* by Daniel Boyarin.[8] Boyarin offers an alternative to what he calls the Zionization of contemporary Judaism, while Magid suggests that living in diaspora or "exile" provides an important antidote to what he calls liberal Zionism. Both writers hearken back to the diasporic vision espoused by the Reconstructionist movement in Judaism founded by Mordecai Kaplan, which emphasized the Americanization of a modern Judaism divorced from the Jewish state. Magid acknowledges the land of Israel as the homeland of both the Jewish and Palestinian people, but he does not believe that Zionism can accommodate and protect the rights of both peoples. "By distinguishing the nation-state from Zionism ... we can begin to cultivate a new collective ideology that, if enacted, could serve Israel as a more liberal and more democratic place."[9] This counter-Zionist stance, especially in light of recent events, is aspirational at best.

JUDAISM AND FEMINISM

The second issue confronting contemporary Jews is the role of women in the Jewish canon. As a movement, Jewish feminist thought emerged in the early 1970s as an attempt to protest the subordination of women within the Jewish tradition. These original feminist works agreed on the marginalization of women in Judaism, as reflected in their exclusion from the minyan, exemption from study, separation of women from men in traditional synagogue services, and women's inability to function as witnesses in a court of law or to initiate divorce proceedings.[10] In a number of works, feminist Jewish theologian Judith Plaskow (1947–present) argued that these exclusionary examples were symptoms of the radical Otherness of women residing in the central categories of Jewish thought. Feminists have noted that since virtually all the sources for Jewish theology and *halakhah* were composed by and for men, women's concerns have been rendered invisible. Plaskow, among others, has thus called for a reconceptualization of every aspect of the Jewish religious experience. It is important to note, however, that while the majority of these inequities remain within Orthodox

Judaism, non-Orthodox movements have resolved a number of touch-points. We can point, for example, to the ordination of women rabbis and cantors in both the Reform and Conservative movements, as well as the elimination of biases against women functioning as witnesses in rabbinical courts of law.

The interactions between feminism, philosophy, and Judaism have undergone serious development in recent decades. Many feminists have argued that Western philosophy has systematically excluded women. More specifically, what Western male philosophers have presented as "essentially human" is in fact rooted in the male experience and does not reflect women's experiences; that because the (male) ideals of reason were formed completely without female input, the Western philosophical tradition is thus biased; and that many philosophical works, written by men, contain numerous misogynist statements. In a similar vein, feminist theologians have maintained that western religious traditions have systematically excluded women's voices; that religious institutions have been predominantly male-oriented and reflect male concerns and priorities; and that many canonical religious texts, written almost exclusively by men, contain misogynist statements. As an example, in the volume entitled *Jewish Philosophy in an Analytic Age*, Tzvi Novick notes in his contribution that of the sixteen contributors to the volume, only two are women, and their titles are the only ones to include the words "moral" or "morality," reinforcing the trope that women are primarily concerned with inter-personal relations rather than "hard-core" issues in metaphysics or epistemology.[11]

That feminist philosophers and theologians have risen to the challenges raised by an androcentric philosophical and theological canon has been well documented. So too, Jewish feminists, influenced by their peers, have begun to level significant attacks against what they see as a

Judaism entrenched in patriarchal institutionalism. This patriarchy is perhaps best expressed by Judith Plaskow in her seminal work *Standing Again at Sinai*:

> Underlying specific halakhot ... is an assumption of women's Otherness far more basic than the laws in which it finds expression ... men – and not women with them – define Jewish humanity. Men are the actors in religious and communal life because they are the normative Jews. Women are "other" than the norm; we are less than fully human. This Otherness of women as a presupposition of Jewish law is its most central formulation.[12]

Nonetheless, while scholars of religion, Talmudists, and Jewish cultural historians have explored feminist concerns in the corpus of Jewish law, Jewish philosophers have been conspicuously absent from this endeavor. With some exceptions, Jewish philosophers (both male and female) have for the most part not taken up the challenges posed by their non-Jewish feminist peers. On the one hand, many female philosophers agree that the revealed misogyny of Western philosophy and theology cannot simply be dismissed as accidental; on the other hand, they are determined to pursue philosophy, the one discipline that purports to value critical thinking and rational discourse. This tension is heightened for Jewish feminists, as underscored by Plaskow's exclamation, "I am not a Jew in the synagogue and a feminist in the world. I am a Jewish feminist and a feminist Jew in every moment of my life."[13]

Some of the most exciting and innovating recent work in feminist thought has occurred in Christian feminist theology. Feminist theologians have taken the reconstruction of gender paradigms into the theological realm, questioning patterns of theology that justify male dominance and female subordination, such as exclusive male language for God, the view that males are more like God than females, that only males can represent God as leaders in Church and society, or that women are created by God to be subordinate to males. Jewish feminists have followed suit, questioning the rituals and patterns of exclusion that have been so endemic in rabbinic Judaism. Most Jewish feminist scholars have agreed that *halakhah* is a document written by men for men, one in which women are conceived as "other." As Plaskow has so strikingly reminded us, women were conspicuously absent from the moment of revelation at Sinai: "At the central moment of Jewish history, women are invisible … the Otherness of women finds its way into the very center of Jewish experience."[14]

Temporal parameters are often used to marginalize women from Jewish practices. Nowhere is the exclusion of women manifested more clearly than in the rabbinic discussion of women's exemption from positive time-bound ritual commandments, a discussion in which Maimonides the legalist played an important role. In the following rabbinic mishnah, women's and men's obligations are compared with respect to ritual observance:

> And all positive *mitzvot* that are time-bound, men are obligated but women are exempt. And all positive *mitzvot* that are not time-bound, the same holds for men and for women, they are [both] obligated. And all negative *mitzvot*, whether or not time-bound, the same holds for men and for women, they are obligated.[15]

Only in the area of positive time-bound commandments are women exempt from obligation. Examples of positive time-bound commandments are given by the rabbis: "What is an example of a positive time-bound commandment? *Succah*, *lulav*, *shofar*, *tzitzit*, and *tefillin*."[16]

In articulating these particular examples, the rabbis were presumably exempting women from observances that were to be performed at a particular time of day. But the rabbis do not explain why it is that women are exempt from these positive time-bound commandments. Talmud scholar Judith Hauptmann examines some of the reasons commonly given for this exemption, e.g. that performance of these commandments might interfere with women's domestic responsibilities, and she finds these apologetic reasons inadequate. Her own suggestion is that these exemptions reflect the fact that a woman is owned by another and therefore "cannot be independently obligated to perform them [positive time-bound rituals]."[17] Pointing out that the phrase "positive time-bound" is mentioned only in connection with women, Hauptmann argues further that the very taxonomy existed only to distinguish between a women's ritual obligations and her exemptions; therefore the essence of the distinction must reside in the meaning of the phrase itself, namely in that these are the "key mitzvot of marking Jewish time."[18] By exempting women from those very ritual acts that mark Jewish time, women are cut off, as it were, from the temporal patterns that define a religious community. If the positive time-bound commandments represent the key commandments involved in marking time, and if the Children of Israel are commanded to sanctify time, then clearly women are excluded from this enterprise. Activities such as reciting a particular prayer *(Shema)* three times a day and putting on phylacteries are central public duties that mark the passage of time. By exempting women from these duties, time itself has been utilized to erode the relation between women and the Deity.[19]

Many feminists have tried to suggest that the Torah must contain the basis within itself for eliminating the subservience of women by invoking "justice" as an absolute criterion. Arguing from the perspective of Jewish orthodoxy, Tamar Ross has recently suggested that *halakhah* contains within itself the wherewithal to counteract the centuries of patriarchy. In a daring work, she starts with Yeshayahu Leibowitz's statement that "the question of Women and Judaism is more crucial than all the political problems of the state."[20] Ross claims that this question goes far beyond practical considerations, and addresses "moral sensibilities that are pivotal to human experience, touching upon religious attitudes and principles that define our total vision of ourselves, the nature of human sexuality, the family, and society at large."[21] Recognizing that feminist concerns tear at the heart of Judaism, Ross argues that "Jewish tradition itself provides ways and means of dealing with the challenges" by reinterpreting *halakhah* creatively.[22] She and other Jewish feminist theologians and philosophers have devoted themselves to pushing the bounds of *halakhah* in order to reinstate women into the fabric of Jewish life.

NOTES

1 Lebens, Rabinowitz and Segal 2019, 3–4.
2 I am indebted to Zelcer and Zelcer 2021 for this brief overview of Zionism. Of course this is a large topic, and many works address the rise of Zionism as a political movement.
3 See Katz 2014, 69.
4 Quoted in Barash 2018, 58.
5 Rosenzweig 1970, 342.
6 Soloveitchik 2006, 78.
7 Schwartz 2006, 72.
8 Boyarin 2023; Magid 2023.
9 Magid 2023, 18.
10 Plaskow 1997, 885.
11 Novick 2019, 327; the underlying bias here is that women are more concerned with ethical matters and not so much with theoretical issues.
12 Plaskow 1997, 63.

13 Plaskow 1997, xi.
14 See Plaskow 1990, 25.
15 *Mishnah Kiddushin* 1:7b, quoted in Hauptmann 1998, 224.
16 *Kiddushin* 1:10, quoted in Hauptmann 1998, 224.
17 Hauptmann 1998, 226.
18 Hauptmann1998, 227.
19 See Millen 2004.
20 Ross 2021, xiii.
21 Ross 2021, xv.
22 Ross 2021, xvii.

FURTHER READING

Avineri, S. (2017). *Making of Modern Zionism: Intellectual Origins of the Jewish State*. New York: Basic Books.

Biale, R. (1984). *Women and Jewish Law: An Exploration of Women's Issues in Halakhic Sources*. New York: Schocken.

Fricker, M. and Hornsby J. eds, (2000). *The Cambridge Companion to Feminism in Philosophy*. Cambridge: Cambridge University Press.

Halkin, A. S. (ed.). (1961). *Zion in Jewish Literature*. New York: Herzl Press.

Hertzberg, A. (ed.). (1997). *The Zionist Idea: A Historical Analysis and Reader*. Philadelphia, PA: Jewish Publication Society.

Heschel, S. and Imhoff, S. (2025). *The Woman Question in Jewish Studies*. Princeton, NJ: Princeton University Press.

Laqueur, W. (1972). *A History of Zionism*. New York: Holt, Rinehart and Winston.

Lebens, S, Rabinowitz, D. and Segal, A. (eds). (2019). *Jewish Philosophy in an Analytic Age*. Oxford: Oxford University Press.

Ross, T. (2021). *Expanding the Place of Torah: Orthodoxy and Feminism*. Waltham, MA: Brandeis University Press.

Tirosh-Rothschild, H. (ed.). (2004). *Women and Gender in Jewish Philosophy*. Bloomington, IN: Indiana University Press.

CONCLUDING POSTSCRIPT

This volume has provided an overview of major themes and thinkers in Jewish philosophy. The book started with a question: what is Jewish philosophy, and how does it interact with other philosophical schools. I suggested that Jewish philosophy represents a mode of analytic reflection about classic philosophical problems, against the backdrop of Jewish texts. Starting with the Jewish Bible, and progressing through the centuries, I have introduced a narrative that emphasizes the enduring tension between faith and reason. Faith of course is rooted in Judaic beliefs and texts, while reason incorporates the philosophical schools dominant at the time. I have tried to emphasize that Jewish philosophy has never existed in a vacuum, but has in every age engaged in fruitful interaction with the external world, be it the world of Aristotle, of early Christianity and Islam, of modern science, or the challenges confronted by the twentieth and twenty-first centuries. In each of these eras, we have seen Jewish philosophers grapple creatively with the ideas and influences of their contemporaries.

We started our journey in Part I with Philo, the first philosopher to attempt a synthesis of Greek thought with Torah. We then examined the early Jewish philosophers, including Saadiah Gaon who was influenced by the Islamic Kalam thinkers, and the Jewish Neoplatonists Isaac Israeli, Solomon ibn Gabirol, Bahya ibn Paquda and Judah Halevi, who introduced Neoplatonist themes into their works. The high point of medieval Jewish philosophy, from the twelfth to fourteenth centuries focused upon the works of Maimonides, Gersonides and Hasdai Crescas, with particular emphasis upon major philosophical themes arising in medieval Aristotelian thought. We thus looked at issues connected to divine science; creation; divine omniscience and evil; and moral theory.

Part II turned to the modern period, spanning the fifteenth century to the present era. We started with fifteenth-century Jewish philosophers, and then discussed Baruch Spinoza, Moses Mendelssohn, Solomon Maimon, Nahman Krochmal and Hermann Cohen. Each of these philosophers incorporated influences from the secular Enlightenment world, ranging from the works of Descartes, Hegel and Kant. We highlighted the incorporation of these secular themes into modern Jewish philosophy. Major twentieth-century themes focused upon the works of Franz Rosenzweig, Martin Buber, Emmanuel Levinas, Joseph Soloveitchik, Emile Fackenheim, Vladimir Jankélévitch and Hannah Arendt. These philosophers were highly integrated into modern philosophy and incorporated many of the reigning existentialist themes into their works. Not surprisingly, the Holocaust has played an important role in their thought, as Jewish philosophers have attempted to make sense of the twentieth-century carnage.

This engagement with contemporary events has continued into our own time, as Jewish philosophers actively engage with the philosophical world around them. In Chapter 14 we mentioned recent works grappling with the role Zionism has played in Judaism, with some authors advocating a rejection of classical Zionism. We mentioned as well attempts among contemporary Jewish feminists to carve a more meaningful role for women in religious Judaism. Other more recent developments have included the engagement of Jewish philosophers with the Anglo-American analytic tradition now dominant in philosophy. The recent volume *Jewish Philosophy in an Analytic Age* has introduced new dimensions to Jewish philosophy.

Jewish philosophy will continue to flourish in the twenty-first century as many of the themes, questions and problems outlined in this work continue to animate Jewish philosophers. Hopefully this volume has contributed to your ability to recognize the major themes and influences upon this rich and enduring tradition.

GLOSSARY

A posteriori A proposition known to be true based on empirical sense perception.

A priori A proposition known to be true without empirical investigation (e.g. all bachelors are unmarried).

Active intellect The final intellect in the chain of intellects that emanates from God. The active intellect governs the sublunar world and provides human beings with knowledge.

Anthropomorphism Attributing to God human form and characteristics.

Anti-semitism Hatred directed at Jews simply because they are Jews.

Apophatic theology Also known as negative theology, the claim that God can only be known through a process of negating the qualities that do not apply to God.

Ash'arites The more fundamentalist school of Islamic Kalâm theologians (see *Kalâm*).

Atomism The theory according to which the universe is made up of indivisible atoms that God creates, destroys and recreates at each instant.

Autrui In Levinas, a term that refers to other human beings with whom I have an ethical relation.

Cogito The act of thinking, or being conscious.

Compatibilism The view that human actions can be both free and determined.

Corporeal A substance that has a material nature.

Correlation In Cohen, a principle that describes the relation between God and human beings.

Cosmological argument Argument for God's existence based on the need for a first cause to explain the existence of the universe.

Cosmology The study of the structure of the universe.

Creation *ex nihilo* Creation of the universe by God out of absolutely nothing.

Determinism The view that every event is determined, including human actions. Theological determinism is the view that human actions are determined by God's knowledge of them.

Dialectic In Aristotle, refers to logical forms of argument; in Hegel dialectic describes the movement from an affirmation (thesis) to a contrary (antithesis), until a synthesis is achieved.

Empiricism The view that sense experience provides knowledge of the external world.

Enlightenment An intellectual period (seventeenth to eighteenth centuries) affected by changes in science, political thought and philosophy.

Epistemology The philosophical study of knowledge.

Eudaimonia A term used by Aristotle to denote human happiness, characterized as a type of human psychic flourishing.

Existentialism A school of philosophy associated with Sartre, Heidegger, Camus and others, that emphasized the irreducibility of the human being.

Geist According to Hegel, the ultimate reality humans can come to know.

Halakhah Jewish Law.

Haskalah Jewish Enlightenment period (eighteenth to nineteenth century) that encouraged Jews to take their place in Western society while not relinquishing their Judaism.

Herem Excommunication from the Jewish community.
Imitatio dei The imitation of God's actions.
Incompatibilism The view that human freedom is incompatible with determinism.
Incorporeal A substance that has no physical or material nature.
Judeo-Arabic Arabic language written using Hebrew letters.
Kabbalah A mystical tradition within Judaism.
Kalâm Islamic school of theology.
Karaism Anti-Rabbinic movement advocating a return to fundamentalist readings of the Bible.
Marburg School A school of neo-Kantian philosophy founded by Hermann Cohen.
Midrash Referring to rabbinic interpretation, in particular works of biblical exegesis.
Mishnah The first written compilation of the oral law.
Mitzvah Commandments.
Mutakallimûn Practitioner of the Kalâm school (see *Kalâm*)
Mutazilites The more rationalistic school of Kalâm thinkers (see *Kalâm*).
Natural Law The notion that certain laws are universally applicable, and accessible by reason.
Neoplatonism A school of philosophy associated with Plotinus, emphasizing an ontology based on emanation (downward causation) from the One/God to the world.
Noahide Commandments The set of commandments given to Noah in the Bible that are considered to be applicable to all human beings.
Noumena In Kant's system, the underlying reality that exists beyond the world of appearances.
Ontology The study of being, or existence.
Pan-entheism The view that God and nature are identical.

Phenomena In Kant's system, refers to how reality appears to us, as opposed to how it really is.

Platonic forms In Plato, the Forms represent abstract ideas that are more real than their physical exemplars.

Practical syllogism A form of argument used for moral reasoning.

Providence The theological view that God cares and provides for human beings.

Quran The central authoritative Scripture of Islam.

Sapere aude Kant's challenge to his readers, to use one's own understanding in the pursuit of knowledge.

Shoah The term means calamity but refers in particular to the Holocaust in World War II.

Skepticism In philosophy, a view that questions whether humans can demonstrate the existence of an external world.

Ta'amei ha-mitzvot The reasons for the commandments.

Talmud Compilation of the oral law, based on discussions around the Mishnah.

Teleological argument Argument for God's existence based on the contention that the universe displays design or purpose, which can only be imputed to a creator.

Theodicy Defense of God in the face of the existence of evil.

Torah The five books of Moses in Scripture: Genesis, Exodus, Leviticus, Numbers and Deuteronomy

Zionism A form of nationalism encouraging the formation and support of a Jewish state.

BIBLIOGRAPHY

Abraham ibn Daud. (1986). *The Exalted Faith*, ed. G. Weiss, trans. N. Samuelson. London: Associated University Presses.

Aho, K. (2023). "Existentialism." In E.N. Zalta and U. Nodelman (eds), *The Stanford Encyclopedia of Philosophy*. Summer 2023 Edition.

Albo, J. (1946). *Sefer 'Iqqarim (Book of Principles)*, trans I. Husik. Philadelphia, PA: Jewish Publication Society.

Altmann, A. (1971). "Franz Rosenzweig and Eugen Rosenstock: An Introduction to Their Letters on Judaism and Christianity." In F. Rosenzweig, *Judaism Despite Christianity: The Letters on Christianity and Judaism between Eugen Rosenstock-Huessy and Franz Rosenzweig*. New York: Schocken Press.

Altmann, A. (1973). *Moses Mendelssohn: A Biographical Study*. Tuscaloosa, AL: University of Alabama Press.

Altmann, A. (2007). Abridged translation of *Sefer Ha-Kuzari*, in H. Lewy, A. Altmann and I. Heinemann (eds), *Three Jewish Philosophers*. New York: Atheneum.

Altmann, A. (2021). "Hermann Cohen's Concept of Correlation (1962)." In R.S. Schine, and S. Moyn (eds), *Hermann Cohen: Writings on Neo-Kantianism and Jewish Philosophy*. 1st ed. Waltham, MA: Brandeis University Press, 242–262.

Altmann, A. and Stern, S.M. (1958). *Isaac Israeli: A Neoplatonic Philosopher of the Early Tenth Century*. Oxford: Clarendon Press.

Arendt, H. (1963). *Eichmann in Jerusalem: A Report on the Banality of Evil*. New York: Penguin.

Arendt, H. (1976). *The Origins of Totalitarianism*. New York: Schocken Books.

Arendt, H. (2003). *Responsibility and Judgment*, ed. J. Kohn. New York: Schocken.

Aristotle. (1984). *The Collected Work of Aristotle*, ed. J. Barnes. Princeton, NJ: Princeton University Press.

Avineri, S. (2017). *The Making of Modern Ziionism: Intellectual Origins of the Jewish State*. New York: Basic Books.

Baer, F.Y. (1966). *A History of the Jews in Christian Spain*, vol 1. Philadelphia, PA: Jewish Publication Society.

Baḥya ibn Pakuda. (2004). *The Book of Direction to the Duties of the Heart*, trans. M. Mansoor. Oxford: The Littman Library of Jewish Civilization.

Barash, J.A. (2018). "Politics and Theology: The Debate on Zionism between Hermann Cohen and Martin Buber." In P. Mendes-Flohr (ed.), *Dialogue as a Trans-disciplinary Concept: Martin Buber's Philosophy of Dialogue and its Contemporary Reception*. Berlin: De Gruyter, 49–60.

Batnitzky, L. (2004). "Dependency and Vulnerability: Jewish and Feminist Existentialist Constructions of the Human." In H. Tirosh-Samuelson (ed.), *Women and Gender in Jewish Philosophy*. Bloomington, IN: Indiana University Press.

Beiser, F.C. (2018). *Hermann Cohen: An Intellectual Biography*. Oxford: Oxford University Press.

Bennett, J. (1984). *A Study of Spinoza's Ethics*. Indianapolis, IN: Hackett Press.

Bergman, S.H., and Amir, Y. (2007). "Cohen, Hermann." In M. Berenbaum and F. Skolnik (eds), *Encyclopaedia Judaica*. 2nd edn., vol. 5. New York: Macmillan Reference USA, 18–20.

Bergman, S.H. and Meir, E. (2007). "Buber, Martin." In M. Berenbaum and F. Skolnik (eds), *Encyclopaedia Judaica*. 2nd edn., vol. 4. New York: Macmillan Reference USA, 231–236.

Bernstein, R.R. (2002). "Evil and the Temptation of Theodicy." In S. Critchley and R. Bernasconi (eds), *The Cambridge Companion to Levinas*. Cambridge: Cambridge University Press, 252–267.

Biale, D. (2005). "Zionism." In Jones, L. (ed.), *Encyclopedia of Religion*, 2nd ed., vol. 14. New York: Macmillan Reference USA, 9976–9983.

Boyarin, D. (2023). *The No-State Solution: A Jewish Manifesto.* New Haven: Yale University Press.

Braiterman, Z. (1998). *(God) After Auschwitz: Tradition and Change in Post-Holocaust Jewish Thought.* Princeton, NJ: Princeton University Press.

Bristow, W. (2023). "Enlightenment." In E.N. Zalta and U. Nodelman (eds), *The Stanford Encyclopedia of Philosophy.* Summer 2023 Edition.

Buber, M. (1952). *Eclipse of God.* New York: Harper and Rowe.

Buber, M. (1970). *I and Thou,* trans. W. Kaufmann. New York: Scribner.

Caputo, J.D. (2001). "Introduction: God Forgive." In J.D. Caputo, M. Scanlon and M. Dolley (eds), *Questioning God.* Bloomington, IN: Indiana University Press, 1–18.

Cohen, H. (1971). *Reason and Hope: Selections from the Jewish Writings of Hermann Cohen,* trans. E. Jospe. New York: W.W. Norton.

Cohen, H. (1993). *Reason and Hope: Selections from the Jewish Writings of Hermann Cohen,* ed. and trans. E. Jospe, Cincinnati, OH: Hebrew Union College Press.

Cohen, H. (1995). *Religion of Reason Out of the Sources of Judaism,* trans. and with an introduction by S. Kaplan, 2nd ed. Atlanta, GA: Scholars Press.

Cohen, R.A. (ed.). (1986). *Face to Face* with *Levinas.* Albany, NY: State University of New York Press.

Crescas, H. (1929). '*Or Adonai* [selections], in H.A. Wolfson, *Crescas' Critique of Aristotle.* Cambridge, MA: Harvard University Press.

Crescas, H. (2018). *Light of the Lord,* trans. and intro by R. Weiss. Oxford: Oxford University Press.

Davidson, H.A. (1987) *Proofs for Eternity, Creation, and the Existence of God in Medieval Islamic and Jewish Philosophy.* Oxford: Oxford University Press.

Davidson, H.A. (2005). *Moses Maimonides: The Man and his Works.* Oxford: Oxford University Press.

Davis, C. (1996). *Levinas: An Introduction.* Notre Dame, IN: University of Notre Dame Press.

Delmedigo, J. (1864). *Sefer Elim.* Odessa.

Derrida, J. (2001a). *On Cosmopolitanism and Forgiveness*. London: Routledge.

Derrida, J. (2001b). "To Forgive: The Unforgivable and the Imprescriptible." In J.D. Caputo, M. Scanlon and M. Dolley (eds), *Questioning God*. Bloomington, IN: Indiana University Press, 21–51.

Dostoyevsky, F. (1976). *The Brothers Karamazov*, trans. C. Garnett. New York: W.W. Norton.

Draper, J.W. (1874). *History of the Conflict between Religion and Science*. New York: D. Appleton and Company.

Drews, W. (2004). "Medieval Controversies about Maimonidean Teachings." In G.K. Hasselhoff (ed.), *Dicit Rabbi Moyses. Studien zum Bild von Moses Maimonides im lateinischen Western vom 13. bis zum 15. Jahrhundert*. Würzburg: Königshausen und Neumann, 113–135.

Ebreo, L. (1937). *The Philosophy of Love (Dialoghi d'Amore)*, trans. F. Friedenberg-Seeley and J.H. Barnes. London: Soncino Press.

Edgar, S. (2021). "Hermann Cohen." In E.N. Zalta and U. Nodelman (eds), *The Stanford Encyclopedia of Philosophy*. Winter 2021 Edition.

Eisenstein, I. (1966). *Varieties of Jewish Belief*. New York: Reconstructionist Press.

Fackenheim, E. (1968). "Jewish Faith and the Holocaust: A Fragment." *Commentary* 46: 30–47. Reprinted in E. Fackenheim, *The Jewish Return into History*. New York: Schocken Books, 25–42.

Fackenheim, E. (1982). *To Mend the World: Foundations of Future Jewish Thought*. New York: Schocken Books.

Fackenheim, E. (1996). *Jewish Philosophers and Jewish Philosophy*, ed. Michael L. Morgan. Bloomington, IN: Indiana University Press.

Feldman, S. (1980). "The Theory of Eternal Creation in Hasdai Crecas and Some of His Predecessors." *Viator*, 11: 289–320.

Feldman, S. (2003). *Philosophy in a Time of Crisis: Don Isaac Abravanel: Defender of the Faith*. London: Routledge.

Fontaine, T.A.M. (1990). *In Defense of Judaism: Abraham ibn Daud*. Assen, Netherlands: Van Gorcum Press.

Frank, D. and Leaman, O. (eds). (1997). *Routledge History of World Philosophies Vol II: History of Jewish Philosophy*. London: Routledge.

Frankl, V.E. (2006). *Man's Search for Meaning,* trans. Ilse Lasch. Boston, MA: Beacon Press.

Franks, P.W. (2007). "Jewish Philosophy after Kant: The Legacy of Salomon Maimon." In M.L. Morgan and P.E. Gordon (eds), *The Cambridge Companion to Modern Jewish Philosophy.* Cambridge: Cambridge University Press.

Franks, P.W. and Morgan, M.L. (ed. and trans.). (2000). *Franz Rosenzweig: Philosophical and Theological Writings.* Indianapolis, IN: Hackett Press.

Freudenthal, G. (ed.). (2011). *Science in Medieval Jewish Cultures* Cambridge: Cambridge University Press.

Funkenstein, A. (1986). *Theology and the Scientific Imagination from the Middle Ages to the Seventeenth Century.* Princeton, NJ: Princeton University Press.

Gersonides. (1946). *The Commentary of* Levi *ben Gerson on the Book of Job,* trans. A.L. Lassen. New York: Bloch.

Gersonides. (1984). *The Wars of the Lord,* volume 1, trans. S. Feldman. Philadelphia, PA: Jewish Publication Society of America.

Gersonides. (1987). *The Wars of the Lord,* volume 2, trans. S. Feldman. Philadelphia, PA: Jewish Publication Society of America.

Gersonides. (1998). *Commentary on Song of Songs. Levi ben Gershom (Gersonides),* trans. M. Kellner. New Haven: Yale University Press

Gersonides. (1999). *The Wars of the Lord,* volume 3, trans. S. Feldman. Philadelphia, PA: Jewish Publication Society of America.

Glasner, R. (2015), *Gersonides: A Portrait of a Fourteenth-Century Philosopher-Scientist.* Oxford: Oxford University Press.

Glatzer, N.N. (1961). *Franz Rosenzweig: His Life and Thought.* New York: Schocken Books.

Gordon, P.E. (2005) *Between Rosenzweig and Heidegger: Between Judaism and German Philosophy.* Berkeley, CA: University of California Press.

Gordon, P.E. (2007). "Franz Rosenzweig and the Philosophy of Jewish Existence." In M.L. Morgan and P.E. Gordon (eds), The Cambridge Companion to Modern Jewish Philosophy. Cambridge: Cambridge University Press, 122–146.

Gottlieb, M. (ed.). (2011). *Moses Mendelssohn: Writings on Judaism, Christianity & The Bible.* Waltham, MA: Brandeis University Press.

Grant, E. (1982). "The effect of the Condemnation of 1277." In A. Kenny, N. Kretzmann and J. Pinborg (eds), *The Cambridge*

History of Later Medieval Philosophy. Cambridge: Cambridge University Press, 537–540.

Grant, E. (1994). *Planets, Stars and Orbs: The Medieval Cosmos 1200–1687*. Cambridge: Cambridge University Press.

Grant, E. (1997). *Physical Science in the Middle Ages*. Cambridge: Cambridge University Press.

Guttmann, J. (1964). *Philosophies of Judaism*, trans. D. Silverman. New York: Holt, Rinehart and Winston.

Halevi, J. (1947). *Kuzari: The Book of Proof and Argument*, trans. I. Heinemann. Oxford: East and West Library.

Harris, J.M. (1991). *Nachman Krochmal: Guiding the Perplexed of the Modern Age*. New York: New York University Press.

Harvey, S. (2000). *The Medieval Hebrew Encyclopedias of Science and Philosophy*. Dordrecht: Kluwer Academic Publishers.

Hauptmann, J. (1998). *Rereading the Rabbis: A Women's Voice*. Boulder, CO: Westview Press.

Hayes, C. (2015). *What's Divine about Divine Law? Early Perspectives*. Princeton, NJ: Princeton University Press.

Hegel, G.W.F. (1977). *Phenomenology of Spirit*, trans. A.V. Miller. Oxford: Oxford University Press.

Heidegger, M. (1962). *Being and Time*, trans. John Macquarrie and Edward Robinson. New York: Harper Press.

Heschel, S. (1987). "Feminism." In A.A. Cohen and Mendes P.-Flohr (eds), *Contemporary Jewish Religious Thought: Original Essays on Critical Concepts, Movements, and Beliefs*. New York: Scribner, 255.

Hillel ben Samuel of Verona. (1981). *Sefer Tagmulei ha-Nefesh le-Hillel ben Shmu'el mi-Verona*, ed. J. Sermoneta. Jerusalem: Magnes Press.

Hollander, D. (2012). "Contested Forgiveness: Jankelevitch, Levinas and Derrida at the Colloque des Intellectuals Juifs." In E. Weber (ed.), *Living Together: Jacques Derrida's Communities of Violence and Peach*. New York: Fordham University Press.

Hyman, P. (1995). *Gender and Assimilation in Modern Jewish History: The Roles and Presentations of Women*. Seattle, WA: University of Washington Press.

Ivry, A. (2016). *Maimonides' 'Guide of the Perplexed': A Philosophical Guide*. Chicago, IL: University of Chicago Press.

Jankélévitch, V. (1996). "Should We Pardon Them?" trans A. Hobart. *Critical Theory* 22(3) (Spring): 552–572.

Jankélévitch, V. (2005). Forgiveness, trans. A. Kelley. Chicago, IL: University of Chicago Press.

Jauernig, A. (2021). *The World According to Kant: Appearances and Things in Themselves in Critical Idealism*. Oxford: Oxford University Press.

Jospe, R. (1988). *Torah and Sophia: The Life and Thought of Shem Tov ibn Falaquera*. Cincinnati, OH: Hebrew Union College Press.

Jospe, R. (2009). *Jewish Philosophy in the Middle Ages*. Boston, MA: Academic Studies Press.

Kajon, I. (2006). *Contemporary Jewish Philosophy: An Introduction*. New York: Routledge.

Kant, I. (1963). *Critique of Pure Reason*, trans. N.K. Smith. New York: Palgrave Macmillan.

Kaplan, A. (1997). *Sefer Yetzirah: The Book of Creation*. York Beach, ME: Samuel Weiser.

Kaplan, L. (1987). "Rabbi Joseph B. Soloveitchik's Philosophy of Halakha." *The Jewish Law Annual* 7: 139–197.

Katz, C.E. (2004). "From Eros to Modernity: Love, Death, and 'the Feminine' in the Philosophy of Emmanuel Levinas." In H. Tirosh-Samuelson (ed.), *Women and Gender in Jewish Philosophy*. Bloomington, IN: Indiana University Press.

Katz, C.E. (2014). *An Introduction to Modern Jewish Philosophy*. London: I.B. Taurus.

Kaye, L. (2018). *Time in the Babylonian Talmud: Natural and Imagined Times in Jewish Law and Narrative*, Cambridge: Cambridge University Press.

Klein-Braslavy, S. (1986). *Maimonides' Interpretation of the Adam Stories in Genesis*. [Hebrew]. Jerusalem: Rubin Mass.

Kraemer, J.L. (2008), *Maimonides: The Life and World of one of Civilization's Greatest Minds*. New York: Doubleday Press.

Kreisel, H. (2001). *Prophecy: The History of an Idea in Medieval Jewish Philosophy*. Dordrecht: Kluwer Academic Publishers.

Krochmal, N. (1961). *The Guide of the Perplexed of the Time*, ed. S. Rawidowicz. Waltham, MA: Ararat Press.

Lamm, N. (1990). *Torah Umaddah: The Encounter of Religious Learning and Worldly Knowledge in the Jewish Tradition*. Maggid Books, Koren Publ.

Lang, B. (2007). "Evil Suffering and the Holocaust." In M.L. Morgan and P.E. Gordon (eds), *The Cambridge Companion to Modern Jewish Philosophy*. Cambridge: Cambridge University Press, 277–299.

Langermann, Y.T. (1993). "Some Astrological Themes in the Thought of Abraham ibn Ezra." In I. Twersky and J.M. Harris (eds), *Rabbi Abraham ibn Ezra: Studies in the Writings of a Twelfth-Century Jewish Polymath*. Cambridge, MA: Harvard University Press, 28–85.

Langermann, Y.T. (2008). "My Truest Perplexities." *Aleph*, 8: 301–317.

Lebens, S., Rabinowitz, D. and Segal, A. (eds). (2019). *Jewish Philosophy in an Analytic Age*. Oxford: Oxford University Press.

Lerner, R. and Mahdi, M. (eds). (1963). *Medieval Political Philosophy*. New York: Free Press.

Levinas, E. (1947). *Time and the Other*, trans. R.A. Cohen. Pittsburgh, PA: Duquesne University Press.

Levinas, E. (1969). *Totality and Infinity: An Essay on Exteriority*, trans. A. Lingis. Pittsburgh, PA: Duquesne University Press.

Levinas, E. (1969). *Totality and Infinity: An Essay on Exteriority*, trans. A. Lingis. Pittsburgh, PA: Duquesne University Press.

Levinas, E. (1988). "Useless Suffering." Trans. R. A. Cohen. In R. Bernasconi and E. Woods (eds), *The Provocation of Levinas*. London: Routledge, 156–167.

Levinas, E. (1990). *Difficult Freedom: Essays on Judaism*, trans. S. Hand. London: Athlone Press.

Levy, Z. (1997). "Zionism." In D.H. Frank and O. Leaman (eds), in *Routledge History of World Philosophies Vol II: History of Jewish Philosophy*. London: Routledge, 776–788.

Levy, Z. 1987. "Sur quelques influences juives dans le développement philosophique du jeune Spinoza." *Revue des Sciences Philosophiques et Théologiques*. 71: 67–75.

Lichtenstein, A. (1975). "Does Jewish Tradition Recognize an Ethic Independent of Halakha?" In M. Fox (ed.), *Modern Jewish Ethics: Theory and Practice*. Columbus, OH: Ohio State University Press, 62–88.

Lloyd, G.E.R. (1976). [1973]. "Views on Time in Greek Thought." In *Cultures and Time*. Paris: UNESCO Press, 117–149.

Loewe, R. (1989). *Ibn Gabirol*. London: Peter Halban.
Looney, A. (2015). *Vladimir Jankélévitch: The Time of Forgiveness*. New York: Fordham University Press.
Magid, S. (2023). *The Necessity of Exile*. New York: Ayin Press.
Maimonides, M. (1962). *Mishneh Torah: Book of Knowledge*, trans. M. Hyamson. Jerusalem: Boys Town Publishers.
Maimonides, M. (1963). *Guide of the Perplexed*, 2 vols., trans. S. Pines. Chicago, IL: University of Chicago Press.
Maimonides, M. (1972a). "Commentary on the Mishnah. Introduction to Helek: Sanhendrin, Chapter Ten." In I. Twersky (ed.), *A Maimonides Reader*. New York: Behrman House, 387–400.
Maimonides, M. (1972b). "Kings and Wars." In I. Twersky (ed.), *A Maimonides Reader*. New York: Behrman House, 215–227.
Maimonides, M. (1975a). "*Eight Chapters* [introduction to commentary on *Mishnah Avot*]." In R.L. Weiss and C. Butterworth (eds and trans.), *Ethical Writings of Maimonides*. New York: Dover, 60–104.
Maimonides, M. (1975b). "Laws Concerning Character Traits." In *Ethical Writings of Maimonides*. New York: Dover, 27–58.
Maimonides, M. (1985). "Epistle to Yemen." In A. Halkin and D. Hartmann (eds and trans.) *Crisis and Leadership: Epistles of Maimonides*. Philadelphia, PA: Jewish Publication Society, 91–131.
Maimonides, M. (1985). "Essay on Resurrection." In A. Halkin and D. Hartmann (eds and trans.) *Crisis and Leadership: Epistles of Maimonides*. Philadelphia, PA: Jewish Publication Society, 209–233.
Maimonides, M. (1985). *Crisis and Leadership: Epistles of Maimonides*, ed. and trans. A. Halkin and D. Hartmann. Philadelphia, PA: Jewish Publication Society.
Maimonides, M. (2002). *Guide of the Perplexed*. 2 vols, trans. M. Schwartz. Ramat Aviv: Tel Aviv University Press.
Manekin, C.H. (1997a). "Hebrew Philosophy in the Fourteenth and Fifteenth Centuries: An Overview." In D.H. Frank and O. Leaman (eds), *History of Jewish Philosophy*. New York: Routledge, 350–378.
Manekin, C.H. (1997b). "When the Jews Learned Logic from the Pope: Three Medieval Hebrew Translations of the Tractatus of Peter of Spain." *Science in Context* 10(3): 406.

Manekin, C.H. (1999). "Scholastic Logic and the Jews." *Bulletin de Philosophie Medievale* 41: 123–147.

McKirahan, R. (ed and trans.). (2010). *Philosophy Before Socrates*. Indianapolis, IN: Hackett Press.

Meir, E. (2007). "Levinas, Emmanuel." In M. Berenbaum and F. Skolnik (ed.), *Encyclopaedia Judaica*. 2nd edn., vol. 12. New York: Macmillan Reference USA, 715–717.

Melamed, Y.Y. and Socher, A.P. (2018). *The Autobiography of Solomon Maimon: The Complete Translation*, trans. P. Reitter. Princeton, NJ: Princeton University Press.

Mendelssohn, M. (1983). *Jerusalem or on Religious Power and Judaism*, trans. A. Arkush, intro and commentary A. Altmann. Hanover, NH: University Press of New England.

Millen, R.L. (2004). *Women, Birth, and Death in Jewish Law and Practice*. Hanover, NH: University Press of New England, 2004.

Morgan, M.L. (2001). *Beyond Auschwitz: Post Holocaust Jewish Thought in America*. New York: Oxford University Press.

Morgan, M.L. and Gordon, P.E. (2007). *The Cambridge Companion to Modern Jewish Philosophy*. Cambridge: Cambridge University Press.

Nadler, S. (1999). *Spinoza: A Life*. Cambridge: Cambridge University Press.

Nadler, S. (2001). *Spinoza's Heresy: Immortality and the Jewish Mind*. Oxford: Oxford University Press.

Nadler, S. (2009). "Theodicy and Providence." In S. Nadler and T.M. Rudavsky (eds), *The Cambridge History of Jewish Philosophy: From Antiquity through the Seventeenth Century*. Cambridge: Cambridge University Press, 619–658.

Nadler, S. (2011). *A Book Forged in Hell: Spinoza's Scandalous Treatise and the Birth of the Secular Age*. Princeton, NJ: Princeton University Press.

Nadler, S., and Rudavsky, T.M. (eds). (2009). *The Cambridge History of Jewish Philosophy: From Antiquity through the Seventeenth Century*. Cambridge: Cambridge University Press.

Neusner, J. (1991) [1972]. *There We Sat Down: Talmudic Judaism in the Making*. Nashville, TN: Abingdon Press.

Novick, T. (2019). "Jewish Philosophy and Analytic Philosophy of Judaism." In S. Lebens, D. Rabinowitz and A. Segal (eds),

Jewish *Philosophy in an Analytic Age*. Oxford: Oxford University Press, 326–335.

Ochs, C.R. (1997). *Women and Spirituality*. London: Rowman and Littlefield.

Ozick, C. (1983). "Notes toward Finding the Right Question." In S. Heschel (ed.), *On Being a Jewish Feminist: A Reader*. New York: Schocken, 120–151.

Pessin, S. (2013). *ibn Gabirol's Theology of Desire: Matter and Method in Jewish Medieval Neoplatonism*. Cambridge: Cambridge University Press.

Philo. (1960). *On the Eternity of the World (De Aeternitate Mundi)*, vol 9, trans. F.H. Colson and G.H. Whitaker. The Loeb Classical Library. Cambridge, MA: Harvard University Press.

Philo. (2001). *On the Creation of the Cosmos According to Moses*, trans. and commentary D.T. Runia. Leiden: E.J. Brill.

Pines, S. (1963). "Translator's Introduction: The Philosophic Sources of *The Guide of the Perplexed*." In S. Pines (ed.), *The Guide of the* Perplexed. Chicago, IL: University of Chicago Press, lvii–cxxxiv.

Pines, S. (1977). "Scholasticism After Thomas Aquinas and the Philosophy of Hasdai Crescas and his Predecessors." *Studies in the History of Jewish* Philosophy: *The Transmission of Texts and Ideas*. Jerusalem: Bialik Institute, 277–305.

Plaskow, J. (1990). *Standing Again at Sinai: Judaism from a Feminist Perspective*. New York: Harper Collins.

Plaskow, J. (1997). "Jewish Feminist Thought." In *Routledge History of World Philosophies Vol II: History of Jewish Philosophy*, 885–894.

Plato. (1971). *The Collected Dialogues of Plato*, ed. E. Hamilton and H. Cairns. Princeton, NJ: Princeton University Press.

Plotinus. (1966). *The Enneads*, trans. and notes H.A. Armstrong. Cambridge, MA: Harvard University Press, The Loeb Classical Library.

Pollegar, I. (1984). *Ezer ha-Dat*, ed. J. Levinger. Tel Aviv: Tel Aviv University Press.

Pollock, B. (2009). *Frank Rosenzweig and the Systematic Task of Philosophy*. Berkeley, CA: University of California Press.

Poma, A. (2007). "Hermann Cohen: Judaism and Critical Idealism." In M.L. Morgan and P.E. Gordon (eds), *The Cambridge Companion to Modern Jewish Philosophy*. Cambridge: Cambridge University Press, 80–101.

Ptolemy. (1940). *Tetrabiblos*, ed. and trans F.E. Robbins. Cambridge, MA: Harvard University Press.

Ptolemy. (1984). *Almagest*, trans and annotated G.J. Toomer. London: Duckworth.

Quinn, T.S. (2021). *Apiqoros: The Last Essays of Salomon Maimon*. Cincinnati, OH: Hebrew Union College Press.

Radzik, L. and Murphy, C. (2023). "Reconciliation." In E.N. Zalta and U. Nodelman (eds), *The Stanford Encyclopedia of Philosophy*. Fall 2023 Edition.

Ravitzky, A. (1996a). *History and Faith: Studies in Jewish Philosophy*. Amsterdam: J.C. Gieben.

Ravitzky, A. (1996b). "The Secrets of Maimonides: Between the Thirteenth and the Twentieth Centuries." In Ravitzky, A. *History and Faith: Studies in Jewish Philosophy*. Amsterdam: J.C. Gieben, 246–303.

Redding, P. (2020). "Georg Wilhelm Friedrich Hegel." In E.N. Zalta and U. Nodelman (eds), *The Stanford Encyclopedia of Philosophy*. Summer 2023 Edition.

Robbins, J. (ed.). (2001). *Is It Righteous to Be?* Interviews *with Emmanuel Levinas*. Stanford, CA: Stanford University Press.

Rosenstock, B. (2010). *Philosophy and the Jewish Question: Mendelssohn, Rosenzweig, and Beyond*. New York: Fordham University Press.

Rosenzweig, F. (1970). [1930]. *The Star of Redemption*, trans. W.W. Hallo. Notre Dame, IN: University of Notre Dame Press.

Rosenzweig, F. (1971). *Judaism Despite Christianity: The Letters on Christianity and* Judaism *between Eugen Rosenstock-Huessy and Franz Rosenzweig*. New York: Schocken Press.

Rosenzweig, F. (2000a). "The New Thinking." In P.W. Franks and M.L. Morgan (ed. and trans), *Franz Rosenzweig: Philosophical and Theological Writings*. Indianapolis, IN: Hackett Press, 109–139.

Rosenzweig, F. (2000b). "Urzelle to the Star of Redemption." In P.W. Franks and M.L. Morgan (ed. and trans), *Franz Rosenzweig: Philosophical and Theological Writings*. Indianapolis, IN: Hackett Press, 48–72.

Rosenzweig, F. (2000c). "Transposed Fronts." In P.W. Franks and M.L. Morgan (ed. and trans), *Franz Rosenzweig: Philosophical and Theological Writings*. Indianapolis, IN: Hackett Press.

Rosenzweig, F. (2021). "Introduction to the Jewish Writings of Hermann Cohen." In R.S. Schine and S. Moyn (eds), *Hermann Cohen: Writings on Neo-Kantianism and Jewish Philosophy*. 1st ed. Waltham, MA: Brandeis University Press, 184–241.

Ross, T. (2021). *Expanding the Palace of Torah: Orthodoxy and Feminism*. Waltham, MA: Brandeis University Press.

Rothkoff, A. and Schwartz, D. (2007). "Soloveitchik, Joseph Baer." In M. Berenbaum and F. Skolnik (eds), *Encyclopaedia Judaica*. 2nd edn., vol. 18. New York: Macmillan Reference USA, 777–780.

Rubenstein, R.L. (1966). *After Auschwitz: Radical Theology and Contemporary Judaism*. 1st edn. Indianapolis, IN: Bobbs-Merrill. Reprinted in R.L. Rubenstein, *After Auschwitz: History, Theology, and Contemporary Judaism*. 2d ed. Baltimore, MD: Johns Hopkins University Press.

Rudavsky, T.M. (1997). "Medieval Jewish Neoplatonism." In D.H. Frank and O. Leaman (eds), *History of Jewish Philosophy*. London: Routledge, 149–187.

Rudavsky, T.M. (2000). *Time Matters: Time, Creation and Cosmology in Medieval Jewish Philosophy*. Albany: State University of New York Press.

Rudavsky, T.M. (2004). "Judaism and Feminism: Reflections on Metaphysics and Epistemology." In H. Tirosh-Samuelson (ed.), *Judaism, Philosophy and Feminism*. Bloomington, IN: Indiana University Press.

Rudavsky, T.M. (2009). "Time, Space and Infinity." In S. Nadler and T.M. Rudavsky (eds), *The Cambridge History of Jewish Philosophy: From Antiquity through the Seventeenth Century*. Cambridge: Cambridge University Press, 388–433.

Rudavsky, T.M. (2010). *Maimonides*. London: Wiley-Blackwell.

Rudavsky, T.M. (2018). *Jewish Philosophy in the Middle Ages: Science, Rationalism, and Religion*. Oxford: Oxford University Press.

Ruderman, D. (1995). *Jewish Thought and Scientific Discovery in Early Modern Europe*. New Haven: Yale University Press.

Rynhold, D. and Harris, M.J. (2018). *Nietzsche, Soloveitchik, and Contemporary Jewish Philosophy*. Cambridge: Cambridge University Press.

Saadiah Gaon. (1948). *The Book of Beliefs and Opinions*, trans. S. Rosenblatt. New Haven: Yale University Press.

Saadiah Gaon. (1988). *The Book of Theodicy: Translation and Commentary on the Book of Job*, trans. L. Goodman. New Haven: Yale University Press.

Samuelson, N.M. (2003). *Jewish Philosophy: A historical Introduction*. London; New York: Continuum International Publishing Group.

Sartre, J.-P. (1995). *Anti-Semite and Jew*, trans. G.J. Becker. New York: Schocken Books

Sartre, J.-P. (1984). *Being and Nothingness*. Trans. H. Barnes. New York: Washington Sq. Press.

Sartre, J.-P. (1989). "Existentialism is a Humanism." In W. Kaufman (ed.), *Existentialism from Dostoyevsky to Sartre*, Meridian Publ.

Scheindlin, R. (1986). *Wine Women and Death:* Medieval *Hebrew Poems on the Good Life*. Oxford: Oxford University Press.

Schine, R.S. and Moyn, S. (eds). (2021). *Hermann Cohen: Writings on Neo-Kantianism and Jewish Philosophy*. Waltham, MA: Brandeis University Press.

Scholem, G. (1995). *Major Trends in Jewish Mysticism*. New York: Schocken.

Schwartz, D. (2006). "*Kol dodi dofek*: A religious-Zionist alternative." *Tradition* 39(3): 59–72.

Schweid, E. (2011). *A History of Modern Jewish Religious Philosophy: Volume 1: The Period of the Enlightenment*, trans. L. Levin. Leiden: Brill.

Seeskin, K. (1995). "How to Read *Religion of Reason*." In H. Cohen (ed.), *Religion of Reason Out of the Sources of Judaism*. 2nd edn., trans and with an introduction by S. Kaplan. Atlanta, Georgia: Scholars Press, 21–42.

Sela, S. (2003). *Abraham ibn Ezra and the Rise of Medieval Hebrew Science*. Leiden: Brill.

Sells, M.A. (1994). *Mystical* Languages *of Unsaying*. Chicago, IL: University of Chicago Press.

Sirat, C. (1990). *A History of Jewish Philosophy in the Middle Ages*. Cambridge: Cambridge University Press.

Socher, A.P. (2006). *The Radical Enlightenment of Solomon Maimon*. Stanford, CA: Stanford University Press.

Solomon ibn Gabirol. (1901). *Tikkun Middot ha-Nefesh (The Improvement of Moral Qualities)*, trans. S.S. Wise. New York: Columbia University Press.

Solomon ibn Gabirol. (1925). *Solomon ibn Gabirol's Choice of Pearls*, trans. A. Cohen. New York: Bloch Publishing Company.

Solomon ibn Gabirol. (1961). *The Kingly Crown*, trans. B. Lewis. London: Valentine, Mitchell.

Solomon ibn Gabirol. (1964). *Sefer meqor hayyim [me-et] Shelomo ben Gabirol*, trans. Y. Blovstein, in Sifroni, A. (ed.), *Otsar Ha-Mahshavah shel ha-Yahadut*. Israel: Mahberot le-sifrut.

Solomon ibn Gabirol. (1987). *The Fountain of Life (Fons Vitae)*, trans. A.B. Jacob. Washington, DC: Sabian Publishing Society.

Soloveitchik, J.B. (1983). *Halakhic Man*, trans by Lawrence Kaplan. Philadelphia, PA: Jewish Publication Society.

Soloveitchik, J.B. (1992). "The Lonely Man of Faith." In J.B. Soloveitchik, *The Lonely Man of Faith*. New York: Doubleday Press. (Originally published in 1965 as an article in *Tradition* 7(2): 5–67.)

Soloveitchik, J.B. (2006). *Kol Dodi Dofek: Listen My Beloved Knocks*, ed. J.R. Woolf, trans. D.Z. Gordon. New York: Yeshivah University Press.

Sorabji, R. (1980). *Necessity, Cause and Blame: Perspectives in Aristotle's Theory*. Ithaca, NY: Cornell University Press.

Sorabji, R. (1983). *Time, Creation and the Continuum*. Ithaca, NY: Cornell University Press.

Sorkin, D. (2019). *Jewish Emancipation: A History Across Five Centuries*. Princeton, NJ: Princeton University Press.

Spinoza, B. (1985). *Ethics*. in *The Collected Works of Spinoza*, trans. E. Curley. Princeton, NJ: Princeton University Press.

Spinoza, B. (1995). *The Letters*, trans. S. Shirley. Indianapolis, IN: Hackett Publishing.

Spinoza, B. (2001). *Theological-Political Treatise*. 2nd edn, trans. S. Shirley. Indianapolis, IN: Hackett Publishing. [TPT]

Steinsaltz A. (1976). *The Essential Talmud*. New York: Basic Books.

Strauss, L. (1995). "Introduction." Trans. S. Kaplan. In H. Cohen, *Religion of Reason: Out of the Sources of Judaism*, 2nd ed. Atlanta, GA: Scholars Press, i–vi.

Thielke, P. and Melamed, Y. (2004). "Salomon Maimon." In E.N. Zalta and U. Nodelman (eds), *The Stanford Encyclopedia of Philosophy*.

Tirosh-Rothschild, H. (1991). *Between Worlds: The Life and Thought of Rabbi David ben Judah Messer Leon*. Albany, NY: SUNY Press.

Tirosh-Rothschild, H. (1997). "Jewish Philosophy on the Eve of Modernity." In D.H. Frank and O. Leaman (eds), *Routledge History of World Philosophies Vol II: History of Jewish Philosophy*. London: Routledge, 499–576.

Tirosh-Samuelson, H. (2003). *Happiness in Premodern Judaism: Virtue, Knowledge, and Well Being*. Cincinnati, OH: Hebrew Union College.

Tirosh-Samuelson, H. (ed.). (2004). *Judaism, Philosophy and Feminism*. Bloomington, Indiana: Indiana University Press.

Twersky, I. (1972). *A Maimonides Reader*. New York: Behrman House.

Urbach, E.E. (1975). *The Sages: Their Concepts and Beliefs*, trans. I. Abrahams. Jerusalem: The Hebrew University Magnes Press.

Wiesel, E. (1960). *Night*. New York: Bantam Books.

Wolfson, H.A. (1929). *Crescas' Critique of Aristotle*. Cambridge, MA: Harvard University Press.

Wolfson, H.A. (1962). *Philo: Foundations of Religious Philosophy in Judaism, Christianity and Islam* (2 vols). Cambridge, MA: Harvard University Press.

Zelcer, H. and Zelcer, M. (2021). *The Philosophy of Joseph B. Soloveitchik*. London: Routledge.

INDEX

Note: Page numbers followed by "n" denote endnotes.

Abner of Burgos 121
Abraham bar Ḥiyya 118
Abraham ibn Daud 6, 43, 47–48, 63, 88–89
Abraham ibn Ezra 118, 166
Abravanel, Isaac 120, 123
Abravanel, Judah 123–24, 126
Absolute: Krochmal and absolute spirit and truth 168; and Rosenzweig 193–94
Academy for Jewish Philosophy 1, 244
Academy for the Scientific Study of Judaism 170
Active Intellect 74–75, 104, 106, 107, 161
Adam I/II 10–11, 188, 217–18, 219
Aesthetics of Pure Feeling (Cohen) 169
Aeternitate Mundi (Eternity of the Universe) [Philo] 27
After Auschwitz (Rubenstein) 225–27
Aims of the Philosophers (Maqāsid al-falasifah) [al-Ghazâlî] 44
Akiba (Rabbi) 85

Albo, Joseph 6, 57–58, 93, 133, 136–37
Alexander of Aphrodisias 93n5
Almagest (Ptolemy) 20
Anan ben David 46
anti-materialism: and Neoplatonism 31; Plato 19
Anti-Semite and Jew (Sartre) 185–86, 248
anti-Semitism 198, 230, 246
antithesis 165
anxiety: and Buber 207; and existentialism 185, 187
apophatic theology 66, 77
Aquinas *see* Thomas Aquinas
Arabic: Judeo-Arabic 51; and Solomon ibn Gabirol 34; transmission of Greek philosophy through 5, 32–33, 43, 118
Arendt, Hannah 11, 230–32
Aristotle and Aristotelianism: and Baḥya ibn Paquda 39, 42, 100; and cause and effect 73; and change 44, 69; and cosmology 7, 20, 26, 124–26; and creation 70–71, 134; and Crescas 6, 57,

69, 71–72; doctrine of the mean 99, 100, 102–3; and encyclopedists 118–19; and ethics and morality 96–97, 99, 100; and Gersonides 6, 55, 56, 69, 71, 77; and al-Ghazâlî 45; and Halevi 39–42; and happiness 7, 96–97; and imagination 104–5; influence of 5–8, 19, 30, 43, 46–47; and intellectual perfection 97, 106; and Italian Renaissance 123; and Kabbalah 148; and Maimonides 6, 69, 77; and matter and form 47, 69, 134; and miracles 74; overview of 5–8; and providence 81–82; and reality 7, 19; and Saadiah Gaon 6; and sciences 19, 47; and soul 36; and space 71–72; and time 27, 69, 77, 218; translation of works into Arabic 5, 32–33, 43; and virtue 96, 99, 100, 102, 103
Ash'arites 43–44
astrology 20, 107, 122
astronomy: and Delmedigo 124–25; and Gersonides 55; and Maimonides 51; and Ptolemy 20; and Renaissance 8, 124–25; *see also* cosmology
atheism 152, 166, 187
atomism 44–45
"Autrui" see Other
Avencebrol *see* Solomon ibn Gabirol
Averroës: and encyclopedists 118–19; and Gersonides 55; and Greek philosophy 33; and Maimonides 50; and Narboni 121; translations by Delmedigo 122, 123

Avicebrol/Avicebron *see* Solomon ibn Gabirol
Avicenna 33, 50, 105, 119

Babylonian Talmud 24
Bacullus Jacobi (Jacob's staff) 55
Baḥya ibn Paquda 5, 38–39, 42, 63–65, 100–101
ibn Bâjja 50
Bayle, Pierre 127
Behinat ha-Dat (The Examination of Religion) [Delmedigo] 123
Being and Nothingness (Sartre) 185
Being and Time (Heidegger) 185, 192–93, 198
Beit al-Ḥikmah ("The House of Wisdom") 32
Beliefs and Opinions see The Book of Beliefs and Opinions (Saadiah Gaon)
Bible: authorship of and Spinoza 130, 141–43; and Gersonides commentaries 55, 56; influential books in Jewish philosophy 21–23; and Karaism 46; lack of theodicy in 21; and Mishnah 24
Bildung 154
Blijenbergh, Willem van 127
body: bodily perfection 110; and Descartes 128; of God 60; and hylomorphism 36; and Neoplatonism 31; and Plato 19; and prophets 106; and Solomon ibn Gabirol 36; and Spinoza 129
Bonnet, Charles 151
The Book of Beliefs and Opinions (Saadiah Gaon) 46, 61, 73, 80–81, 137–39
Book of Creation *see Sefer Yetzirah (Book of Creation)*

Book of Definitions (Isaac Israeli) 33
Book of Knowledge see *Mishneh Torah* (Maimonides)
Book of Light (Sefer Bahir) 148
Book of Principles (Albo) 58, 136–37
The Book of Splendor see *Zohar (The Book of Splendor)*
Book of Substances (Isaac Israeli) 33
The Book of the Light of the Lord see *Light of the Lord* (Crescas)
The Book of Theodicy (Saadiah Gaon) 81
The Book of the Refutation of the Principles of the Christians (Sefer bittul Iqqarei ha-Nozrim) [Crescas] 57
Boyarin, Daniel 250–51
Brahe, Tycho 125
Brandeis, Louis 246
The Brothers Karamazov (Dostoevsky) 225
Buber, Martin: biography 202; and dialogue 10, 187, 201–7; and evil 241n2; and existentialism 187, 201–7; and Levinas 208, 211, 212; and Other 10, 187, 201–7; and Rosenzweig 190, 202–3; and Zionism 202, 249

Cassirer, Ernst 197, 208
categorical imperative 174
change: and Aristotle 44, 69; and atomism 44–45; in Heraclitus and Parmenides 18; and Plato 18, 68
character: and Aristotle 97–98; and Maimonides 101–3
Character Traits (Hilkhot Deot) [Maimonides] 102
chosenness 189

Christianity: and Albo 57–58; and Crescas 57; and disputation 119–20; early Jewish-Christian engagement 117, 119–22; excommunication in 151; and forgiveness 233; and Hegel 165, 168; and hylomorphism 38; and Kabbalah 149; and Kant 156–57; and Maimonides, bans on 53–54; and Neoplatonism 32; and patriarchy 253–54; and Philo 28; and Rosenzweig 10, 187–89, 191, 196; and Solomon ibn Gabirol 38; and time 196–97, 249
cognitive man *vs.* "homo religious" 215–16, 217, 219–20
Cohen, Hermann 9, 156, 169–81, 197, 247–49
commandments: and Crescas 108–9; ethical nature of 98, 154; generalities *vs.* particulars in 140–41; and happiness 108–9; and Maimonides 52, 133, 139–41; and Mendelssohn 134, 153–54; and natural law 136–37, 179; and non-Jews 179; rationality of 133, 137–41; and revelation 138–39, 145; and Saadiah Gaon 133, 137–39; "614th commandment" 11, 229; and Soloveitchik 214–15
Commentary on Job (Gersonides) 83, 84
The Commentary on the Mishnah (Maimonides) 50
compatibilism and free will 84–88
Concept of Religion within the System of Philosophy (Cohen) 169, 174

Concluding Unscientific Postscript (Kierkegaard) 205
conventional law in Albo 136–37
conversion to Christianity: and Abravanel family 123; and Mendelssohn 149, 151, 161; and Pollegar 121; and Rosenzweig 187–89, 191, 196; and violence 121
Copernican Revolution 147–48, 172
Copernicus 8, 125, 126, 147
correlation in Cohen 170, 177, 178
cosmology: and arguments for existence of God 63–65; and Aristotle 7, 20, 26, 124–26; and Isaac Israeli 33; and Kabbalah 148; and Maimonides 51; and Philo 26, 27; and Ptolemy 20; and Schelling 149; and science 2–3, 124–26, 147; and Solomon ibn Gabirol 38
covenant: and Rubenstein 226; and Soloveitchik 218, 219
Cranz, August Friedrich 151
created Glory (Shekhinah) 104
creation: and Aristotle 70–71, 134; in classical Jewish philosophy 68–72; and Cohen 177; and Crescas 71–72, 77; and existence of God 61, 62, 64–65; *ex nihilo* 33, 69–72; and Gersonides 55, 71, 72; Isaac Israeli 33; and Kalâm school 44–45; and Maimonides 51, 69–70, 77; and miracles 74; in overview 7; and Philo 25–27; and Plato 68–69, 134; and Rosenzweig 193–94; in *Zohar* 23
Crescas, Hasdai: and Albo 58, 93; and Aristotle 6, 57, 69, 71–72; biography 56–57; and creation 71–72, 77; and determinism/free will 57, 91–92; and disputation 120; and Gersonides 54–55, 72, 91; and happiness 108–9, 113; influence of 43; and Maimonides 67, 68; and miracles 73; and negative predication 68; and space 71–72
Critique of Pure Reason (Kant) 147–48, 156, 159–60

Daroca debates 57–58
Dasein 185, 192
Davos debate 197, 208
De Anima (Aristotle) 104–5
death and the dead: death of God 187, 226–27; and existentialism 185, 187, 192–93; and Heidegger 192–93; and Maimonides 52, 53; and predetermination in Ecclesiastes 22–23; and resurrection 52, 53; and Rosenzweig 192–93
Decisive Treatise (Averroës) 123
De Fato (On Providence) [Alexander of Aphrodisias] 93n5
Deleuze, Gille 128
Delmedigo, Elijah 122–23
Delmedigo, Joseph Solomon 124–26
Democritus 44
Derrida, Jacques 233–34, 237–39
Descartes, René 126, 128, 192, 203
Descartes's Principles of Philosophy (Descartes) 128
desire and Levinas 210–11
despair: and existentialism 185, 187; and Holocaust 228, 229

determinism 57, 91–92, 107, 121–22
dialectic, Hegelian 164–65, 166
Dialoghi d'amore (Dialogues of Love) [Abravanel] 123–24
dialogue: and Buber 10, 187, 201–7; and Levinas 10, 187, 201, 209–13; and Rosenzweig 195, 201; and Soloveitchik 10–11, 215–19; *see also* Other
Dialogues of Love (Dialoghi d'amore) [Abravanel] 123–24
dietary laws 46, 103, 138–39
Difficult Freedom (Levinas) 208
divine: divine authorship and Spinoza 130, 141–43; law and natural law 136–37; union with in Solomon ibn Gabirol 36–37; *see also* God
divine legislation 153
divine predication 66–68
divine providence *see* providence
Divine Throne *(Kisse ha-Kavod)* 37
divine will: and chains of causation 86; and Kalâm school 44–45; and Solomon ibn Gabirol 37, 38
divorce 12, 245, 251
doctrine of the mean 99, 100, 102–3
Dohm, Wilhelm von 151
Dostoevsky, Fyodor 184–85, 225
Draper, John William 12n3
dualism: and Aristotle 47; and Descartes 128; and Spinoza 128, 129
Duties of the Heart see *Guide to the Duties of the Heart* (Bahya ibn Paquda)

Ecclesiastes 21–23, 56
The Eclipse of God (Buber) 206

ego: and Descartes 128, 192, 203; and Hegel 164; and Husserl 210; and Soloveitchik 216
Eichmann, Adolf 11, 231–32
Eichmann in Jerusalem (Arendt) 11, 230, 232
Eight Chapters (Shemona Perakim) [Maimonides] 50, 101–3
Einstein, Albert 128
emanations 20–21, 30–31, 33, 168
emancipation of Jews/Haskalah: and Cohen 170; emancipation era 148–50; and Krochmal 9, 165–68; and Mendelssohn 8–9, 150, 161; and nationalism 245
Emden, Jacob 155
'Emunah Ramah (Abraham ibn Daud) 88–89
encyclopedists 117–19
Enneads (Plotinus) 20–21
Epicurus 44
Essay on Transcendental Philosophy (Maimon) 160
Esther, Book of 56
eternity: and Crescas 72, 77; and Philo 26, 27; of world in Aristotle 7, 69, 70, 134
Eternity of the Universe (Aeternitate Mundi) [Philo] 27
The Ethics (Spinoza) 8, 127, 129
ethics and morality: and Aristotle 96–97, 99, 100; and Bahya ibn Paquda 38–39, 100–101; in classical Jewish philosophy 99–103; and Cohen 170, 172–73, 174–76, 179; and commandments 98, 154; and compatibilism 85, 88; and duties 100–101; and forgiveness 234–37; and free will 85, 88; and habit 97; intellectual *vs.* moral perfection 109–12; intention *vs.* action 101; and

Kant 170, 174; and Levinas 211, 212; and Maimon 159; and Maimonides 50, 51, 101–3; and natural law 133, 154–56; and Neoplatonism 96; and nihilism 185; and Noahide Laws 133, 136, 154–55, 179; practical morality 96–99; and prophets 104; and Saadiah Gaon 46; and Solomon ibn Gabirol 99–100; and Spinoza 142–45, 182n18; and women's interest in moral aspects of Jewish philosophy 252
Ethics of Pure Will (Cohen) 169, 174
Ethics of the Fathers see *Eight Chapters (Shemona Perakim)* [Maimonides]
Euclid 128–29
eudaimonia see happiness
Euthyphro (Plato) 140
Eve 217–18, 219
evil: and Arendt 11, 232; and Buber 241n2; and Fackenheim 228–29; and Gersonides 84; and Holocaust 11, 228–29; and Levinas 212–13; in overview 7; *see also* theodicy
The Exalted Faith (Ha-Emunahha-Ramah) [Abraham ibn Daud] 47–48
The Examination of Religion (Behinat ha-Dat) [Delmedigo] 123
excommunication 127, 151
existentialism: in arts and literature 186; and Buber 187, 201–7; and Levinas 187, 201, 207–13; overview of 9–11, 184–88; rise of 181, 184, 201; and Rosenzweig 185–98; and Soloveitchik 187–88, 202, 213–20; *see also* Heidegger, Martin; Sartre, Jean-Paul
"Existentialism is a Humanism" (Sartre) 186
experience: and evil 84; and fideism 64; and *propter quia* arguments 63
Exposition of Science (Midrash ha-Ḥokhmah) [Judah ha-Cohen] 118
Ezer ha-Dat (The Support of the Faith) [Pollegar] 122
ibn Ezra *see* Abraham ibn Ezra

Fackenheim, Emil 11, 227–30
faith: articles of in Maimonides 50; bad faith 186; *vs.* Jewish philosophy 2
Falaquera, Shem Tov ben Joseph *see* Shem Tov ben Joseph Falaquera
al-Fârâbî 33, 50, 105
felicity *see* happiness
fellowship and Cohen 178–79
feminist Jewish philosophy 11–12, 245, 251–56
fideism 63–64
Fons Vitae see *Mekor Hayyim (Fountain of Life)* [Solomon ibn Gabirol]
forgiveness 11, 174, 176, 178, 233–40
Forgiveness see *Le Pardon* (Jankélévitch)
form: and Aristotle 47, 69, 134; and Crescas 72; and hylomorphism 36, 38, 47; and Isaac Israeli 33; Plato's theory of forms 18–19; and Solomon ibn Gabirol 35–38
Fountain of Life (Mekor Hayyim) [Solomon ibn Gabirol] 34–38

freedom/free will: and compatibilism 84–88; and Crescas 57, 91–92; and ibn Daud 88–89; and determinism 57, 91–92, 107, 121–22; and Gersonides 88, 90; and Halevi 85–87; and incompatibilism 85, 88–90; and Levinas 211; and Maimonides 85, 87–88; and omniscience 84–89; and predetermination in Ecclesiastes 22–23; and Saadiah Gaon 85–87
Fusûl Mûsâ (Medical Aphorisms) [Maimonides] 51
future and omniscience 89, 91–93

ibn Gabirol *see* Solomon ibn Gabirol
Galen 51
Galileo Galilei 76, 125, 126
Ganz, David 124
Gaon of Baghdad 53
Geist 164, 168
Genesis 21, 26–27, 56, 134
Germanism and Judaism: in Cohen 169–70, 172–73; in Rosenzweig 188
"Germanism and Judaism" (Cohen) 173
Gersonides: and Aristotelianism 6, 55, 56, 69, 71, 77; biography 54–55; and creation 55, 71, 72; and Crescas 54–55, 72, 91; critiques of 56; and disputation 120; and evil 84; and existence and nature of God 63, 67–68; and happiness 97, 112; and incompatibilism and free will 88, 90; influence of 43, 54; and intellect 74–75, 107, 109, 111–12; and logic 55, 56; and Maimonides 67; and miracles 73–76; and omniscience 89–92; and perfection 109, 111–12; and prophecy 55, 107–8; and providence 55, 83–84; and reason 6, 54, 135; on Scripture 55, 56, 83–84, 112, 135; and suffering 83–84; and time 55, 71, 77
al-Ghazâlî, Muhammed 40, 44, 45, 73, 121
God: and Abraham ibn Daud 63; and Albo 58; anthropomorphic concept of 52, 60, 61, 66, 177; and Aristotle 47; and Bahya ibn Paquda 63–65; body of 60; and Buber 205–7, 241n2; and Cohen 176–78; and Crescas 67, 68; death of 187, 226–27; and divine predication 66–68; and Eternal Thou 10; existence of 61–65, 158, 167; and fideism 63–64; and Gersonides 63, 67–68; and Halevi 63–64; and Hegel 166–68; incorporeality of 61–62, 66; Judaism without 226; and Kalâm school 44–45; and Krochmal 166–68; love/fear of God and happiness 109; and Maimonides 51, 52, 61–62, 65–67; and negative predication 66–68, 77; and Neoplatonism 21, 32; and One in Kabbalah 148; and One in Neoplatonism 30–31; pan-entheism 129–30; and Philo 26; and predetermination in Ecclesiastes 22–23; prophecy as communication with 104; and Rosenzweig 193–94; and Saadiah Gaon 61, 63, 64; and Spinoza 129–30; uniqueness of 62, 176, 177; and unity 61–62;

and Wolff 158; *see also* omnipotence; omniscience; theodicy

Greek philosophy: development of 17–21; and encyclopedists 118; influence on Bible 21–23; in overview of book 4–5; transmission of through Arabic 5, 32–33, 43, 118; *see also* Aristotle and Aristotelianism; Neoplatonism; Philo of Alexander; Plato

Guide of the Perplexed of Our Times (Krochmal) 166–68, 248

Guide of the Perplexed (Maimonides): and compatibilism and free will 87–88; and creation 69–70; and existence and nature of God 51, 65–67; influence of 6; knowledge and virtue 102; and Maimon 157, 158, 160, 161; and miracles 74, 75; Narboni on 121; and obfuscation of scripture 134–35; and perfection 110, 111; and prophecy 105–107; and rationality of commandments 139; and suffering 81–83; writing of 49, 51–52

Guide to the Duties of the Heart (Baḥya ibn Paquda) 5, 38–39, 64–65, 100–101

G'vurot Hashem (Delmedigo) 125–26

habit 97, 102, 103

Ha-Emunahha-Ramah (The Exalted Faith) (Abraham ibn Daud) 47–48

halakhah: and ethics 98; and Maimon 159; and Maimonides 49; and Mendelssohn 145, 153–56, 161; and Soloveitchik 214–15, 219–20; and Spinoza 145, 161; subordination of women in 12, 245, 251, 253–56; and Zionism 250

Halakhic Man (Soloveitchik) 214–16, 219–20

The Halakhic Mind (Soloveitchik) 214

Halevi, Judah: and Aristotelianism 39–42; and atomism 45; biography 5, 39; and existence of God 63–64; and freedom/ free will 85–87; influence of 39; and Jewish spirit 168; and perfection 104; and prophets 104; and truth 39–41

happiness: and Aristotle 7, 96–97; and Cohen 173; and commandments 108–9; and Crescas 108–9, 113; and Gersonides 97, 112; and Kant 173; and law 108–9; and Maimonides 51, 97; and reason 96–97; and virtue 96

"Hark! My beloved is knocking" see *Kol Dodi Dofek* (Soloveitchik)

Hasidism 202

Haskalah period *see* emancipation of Jews/Haskalah

Hauptmann, Judith 255

Hebrew: encyclopedists 117–19; letters and Judeo-Arabic 51; letters and Kabbalah 23; Maimonides use of colloquial 50; and transmission of Greek philosophy through Arabic 5, 33–35, 43, 118; and understanding of Scripture in Spinoza 143

Hegel, Georg Wilhelm Friedrich 164–65, 168, 184, 191
Hegelian dialectic 164–65
Heidegger, Martin: and Arendt 230; and *Dasein* 185, 192; and Davos debate 197, 208; and death 192–93; and Levinas 208–10; Nazism and anti-Semitism of 198, 230; Rosenzweig comparison 197–98; and Sartre 185–86
Heine, Heinrich 127
Heraclitus 17–18
herem see excommunication
Herzl, Theodore 246
Hilkhot Deot (Character Traits) [Maimonides] 102
Hillel of Verona 119
The Hill of the Guide (Maimon) 160
Holocaust: and Arendt 11, 230–32; and Buber 206–7; and evil 11, 228–29; and Fackenheim 227–30; and forgiveness 11, 233–40; and Levinas 212–13, 239; in overview 9, 11; and Rubenstein 225–27; and Soloveitchik 250; and theodicy 11, 82, 206–7, 212–13, 223–27; and Zionism 247
"homo religious" *vs.* cognitive man 215–16, 217, 219–20
The Human Condition (Arendt) 230
Husserl, Edmund 185, 207–8, 209–10, 237
hylomorphism 36, 38, 47

I and Thou (Buber) 10, 187, 202, 205–6, 211–12
idealism: and Cohen 9, 171–72, 173, 176–78; and Hegel 164–65; and Heidegger 198; and Kant 9, 171–72, 173; and Krochmal 9, 165–68; and Plato 18–19; and Rosenzweig 191, 193–95, 198
idolatry 166–67
I-It relations 10, 187, 201–7
imagination 102, 104–5, 106
imitatio Dei 111
immortality 55, 127
incompatibilism and free will 85, 88–90
individual and existentialism 185, 186, 191–94
infinite 55, 209
"The Inner Relations of Kant's Philosophy to Judaism" (Cohen) 172
intellect: Active Intellect 74–75, 104, 106, 107, 161; and Crescas 108; and Gersonides 74–75, 107, 109, 111–12; and imagination 105; intellectual perfection ideal 82–84, 97–100, 109–12, 162n18; and Isaac Israeli 33; and Neoplatonism 31; and Solomon ibn Gabirol 37–38; universal intellect 31, 37–38
In the Time of the Nations (Levinas) 208
Isaac Israeli 5, 33
Ish ha-Halakhah see *Halakhic Man* (Soloveitchik)
Islamic philosophy: influence on Jewish philosophy 3; and Neoplatonism 32; and prophecy 105; and transmission of Greek philosophy through Arabic 5, 32–33, 43, 118; *see also* Kalâm school
I-You relations 10, 187, 201–7, 211–12

Jacobi, Friedrich Heinrich 151
Jacob's staff 55
Jankélévitch, Victor 11, 233–40
Jerusalem (Mendelssohn) 9, 151–53, 155, 156, 159
"Jewish Faith and the Holocaust" (Fackenheim) 227–28
Jewish people: Jewishness and Sartre 185–86; "Jewish question" 169–70, 185–86; Krochmal and national spirit of 166, 168
Jewish philosophy: Ashkenazi and Sephardi learning tensions 53; defined 1–2; *vs.* faith 2; growth of discipline 244; Jewish philosophers as theologians 3–4, 24; overview of 4–12; rabbinical philosophers, overview of 21–24; secular learning *vs.* religious knowledge as central conflict 2–4
Jewish Philosophy in an Analytic Age (Lebens, et al.) 244, 252
"Jewish question" 169–70, 185–86
Job, Book of 21, 56, 80–84
Joseph ben Judah ibn Shimon 51
Joshua, Book of 144
Judah ha-Cohen 118
Judah ibn Tibbon 34, 38, 46
Judaism: Baḥya ibn Paquda on superiority of 5; and chosenness 189; Cohen's defense of 169–70, 172–73; critique by Kant 156–57; and Daroca debates 57–58; dismissal of in Hegel 165, 168; and forgiveness 233; and Germanism 169–70, 172–73, 188; without God in Rubenstein 226; Jewish spirit and Halevi 168; and patriarchy 253; rationality of 159; Reconstructionist movement 251; Rosenzweig's rediscovery of 10, 188–90; and time 196–97, 249

justice: and feminist Jewish philosophy 255–56; and forgiveness 239

Kabbalah 23, 38, 123, 148, 149, 166
Kalâm school: and Baḥya ibn Paquda 38, 39, 42; described 43–46; and Halevi 39, 40, 42; influence of 6; and Maimonides 50; and miracles 73; occasionalist model 44–45, 73
Kant, Immanuel: and Cohen 9, 169–72; and Copernican Revolution 147–48, 172; and idealism 9, 171–72, 173; influence of 147–48, 156; and Maimon 9, 149, 157–58, 159–60; Marburg School and neo-Kantianism 9, 169–72, 180; and Mendelssohn 150, 156–57; and reason 147–48, 170, 172, 173
Kant's Foundation of Ethics (Cohen) 169, 174
Kant's Foundations of Aesthetics (Cohen) 169
Kant's Theory of Experience (Cohen) 169
Kaplan, Mordecai 247, 251
Karaism 45–46, 137
ibn Kaspi, Joseph 119, 122, 130
Kepler, Johannes 125
Keter Malkhut (Throne of Glory) [Solomon ibn Gabirol] 36–37

Kierkegaard, Soren 184–85, 192, 205
Kisse ha-Kavod (Divine Throne) 37
Kitâb al-Amânât wa-al-I'tiqadât see *The Book of Beliefs and Opinions* (Saadiah Gaon)
Kitâb al-Radd wa'l-Dalîl fi'l-Din al-dhalîl see *The Kuzari* (Halevi)
knowledge: *vs.* belief in Soloveitchik 216–17; and Cohen 172; and Copernican Revolution 147–48, 172; epistemology and Kant 147–48; epistemology and Saadiah Gaon 137–38; *vs.* existence of things 87–88; and Gersonides 107; and Hegel 164; and imagination 104–5; secular learning *vs.* religious knowledge as central conflict 2–4; and virtue in Maimonides 102
Kol Dodi Dofek (Soloveitchik) 214, 250
Krochmal, Nachman 9, 165–68, 248
The Kuzari (Halevi) 5, 39–41, 45, 63–64, 104

Lavater, Johann Caspar 151, 154–55
"Lavater Affair" 151
law: and Albo 136–37; and Bahya ibn Paquda 5, 39, 100; and commandments 133, 136–37, 179; conventional law 136–37; and Crescas 56–57, 108–9; divine law 136–37; and doctrine of the mean 103; and happiness 108–9; and Karaism 45–46; and Maimon 159; and Maimonides 50, 53, 139–40; and Mendelssohn 9, 145, 152–57, 161; and Mishnah 24; and revelation 145; and Saadiah Gaon 45–46; and state 152–53, 159; women as witnesses in 12, 245, 251, 252; *see also* dietary laws; *halakhah;* natural law; Noahide Laws
The Legends of the Baal-Shem (Buber) 202
Leibniz, Wilhelm von 54, 128
Leibowitz, Yeshayahu 256
Leone Ebreo *see* Abravanel, Judah
Le Pardon (Jankélévitch) 11, 235–36
Lessing, Gotthold Ephraim 8–9, 150, 152
Levi ben Gershom *see* Gersonides
Levinas, Emmanuel: biography 207–9; and Derrida 237; and dialogue 10, 187, 201, 209–13; and existentialism 187, 201, 207–13; and forgiveness 233–34, 239–40; and Other 10, 187, 201–2, 208–13, 239–40
Lichtenstein, Aharon 155–56
The Life of the Mind (Arendt) 230
Light of the Lord (Crescas) 6, 57, 72, 91
logic: and Aristotle 47, 56; and disputation 120; and Gersonides 55, 56; influence on early modern Jewish philosophy 120; and medical training 120; and Saadiah Gaon 138
Logic of Pure Knowledge (Cohen) 169
loneliness and Soloveitchik 216–18
"The Lonely Man of Faith" (Soloveitchik) 10–11, 188, 202, 214–16

love: and Cohen 170, 178; and Crescas 109
Luria, Isaac "Ha-Ari" 149, 229

Ma'amar ha-'ibbur (Maimonides) 48
Magid, Shaul 250–51
Maimon, Solomon 9, 149, 157–62
Maimonides, Moses (Moses ben Maimon): and Albo 58; and Aristotelianism 6, 69, 77; and astrology 122; bans on 53–54; biography 48–49; and character 101–3; and Cohen 173; and commandments 52, 133, 139–41; compatibilism and free will 85, 87–88; controversies 52–54; and creation 51, 69–70, 77; and Crescas 67, 68; and ethics and morality 50, 51, 101–3; and Gersonides 67; and *halakhah* 49; and happiness 51, 97; influence of 4, 6, 43, 48–50, 52; and law 50, 53, 139–40; and Maimon 157, 158, 160, 161; and Mendelssohn 154, 155; and miracles 53, 73–76; and Narboni 121; nature and existence of God 51, 52, 61–62, 65–67; negative predication 66–68; and obfuscation 2, 134–35; in overview 2, 4, 6; and perfection 109–11; as physician 49, 51; and Plato 70; and prophecy 51, 53, 105–7; and providence 51, 81–83; and ritual 254; and Spinoza 126; and suffering/Job 81–83; and theodicy 51, 81–83; and time 77; and virtue 101–3, 111

Manasseh ben Israel 125
Man's Search for Meaning (Frankl) 224
Maqāsid al-falasifah (Aims of the Philosophers) [al-Ghazâlî] 44
Marburg School and neo-Kantianism 9, 169–72, 180
material perfection 110
mathematics 55, 128–29, 182n18
matter: and Aristotle 47, 69, 134; and atomism 44; and Crescas 72; and Gersonides 71; hierarchy of 36; and hylomorphism 36, 38, 47; Isaac Israeli 33; and Kalâm school 44; and Solomon ibn Gabirol 35–38; and Spinoza 129
mean, doctrine of the 99, 100, 102–3
Medical Aphorisms (Fusûl Mûsâ) [Maimonides] 51
medicine: logic and medical training 120; and Maimonides 49, 51
Meditations on First Philosophy (Descartes) 128
Megalle 'amuqqot (Jacob's staff) 55
Mekor Hayyim (Fountain of Life) [Solomon ibn Gabirol] 34–38
Melakhim 133
Mendelssohn, Moses: biography 150–52; and commandments 134, 153–54; and conversion to Christianity 149, 151, 161; and emancipation of Jews 8–9, 150, 161; influence of 149; and Kant 150, 156–57; and law 9, 145, 152–57, 161; and Maimon 9, 149, 157–59; and Maimonides 154, 155; major works 150–52; and rationalism

9, 134, 151, 153; and Zionism 247, 248
merkaz ruhani 247
Messer Leon, Judah ben Jehiel 120
metaphysics: and Aristotle 19, 47, 57, 58, 71, 123, 147; and Cohen 171–72, 176; and Crescas 71; and Delmedigo 123, 125; and forgiveness 233; and gender 252; and Gersonides 109; and Kant 171–72; and Krochmal 167; and Levinas 212; and Maimon 158–59, 161; and Maimonides 62, 109; and Neoplatonism 21, 32; and Rosenzweig 195; and Soloveitchik 217–18; and Spinoza 142
Midrash ha-Ḥokhmah (Exposition of Science) [Judah ha-Cohen] 118
Mif'alot Elohim (Wonders of God) [Abravanel] 123
Milhamot ha-Shem see *Wars of the Lord* (Gersonides)
Minhat Kena'ot (Offering of Jealousy) [Abner of Burgos] 121
minyan, exclusion of women from 12, 245, 251
miracles 7, 72–76, 142, 144
Mishnah 24, 50
Mishneh Torah (Maimonides) 4, 48, 50, 53, 62
modernity and Soloveitchik 10–11, 214, 219
monism: and Neoplatonism 20, 30–31; and Spinoza 128–29
Moreh Nevukhei ha-Zeman see *Guide of the Perplexed of Our Times* (Krochmal)
Moses (Biblical character) 26, 98–99, 106–7, 130, 143
Moses ben Joshua (Narboni) 121

Moses ben Maimon see Maimonides, Moses (Moses ben Maimon)
Moses ben Nahman see Nahmanides (Moses ben Nahman)
Moses ben Shemtob de Leon 149
Moses Isserles (Rema) 124
motion and Aristotle 69
Mutakallimûn 43–46
Mu'tazilites 43–44
My Beloved Knocks see *Kol Dodi Dofek* (Soloveitchik)
mysticism: and Buber 202; early works in 23; and Enlightenment 148–49; and Hasidism 202; and Krochmal 166–67; see also Kabbalah

Nahmanides (Moses ben Nahman) 53
Narboni (Moses ben Joshua, Ramban) 121
nationalism 245–46; see also Zionism
natural law: and Cohen 174, 179; and commandments 136–37, 179; debates over 136–39, 145; and ethics and morality 133, 154–56; and Mendelssohn 152–57, 161; and rights 152–53; and Thomas Aquinas 146n5
The Necessity of Exile (Magid) 250–51
negative predication 66–68, 77
Nehmad ve-Na'im (Ganz) 124
Neoplatonism: and Baḥya ibn Paquda 5, 100; critiques of 40; and emanations 20–21, 30–31, 33, 168; and ethics and morality 96; influence of

20–21, 30, 32; and Isaac Israeli 5, 33; and Kabbalah 148; and Krochmal 166, 168; overview of 5, 20–21, 30–31; and reality 30–31; and soul 31, 33, 36, 37; *see also* Halevi, Judah
"The New Thinking" (Rosenzweig) 190, 194–96
Newton, Isaac 8, 128, 147
Nicomachean Ethics (Aristotle) 7, 96, 97, 103
Nietzsche, Friedrich 128, 184–85
Night (Wiesel) 224
Noahide Laws 133, 136, 154–55, 179; *see also* natural law
The No State Solution (Boyarin) 250–51
nothingness: and creation *ex nihilo* 33, 69–72; and Kabbalah 23; and Rosenzweig 191–93
numbers: numbers *(sefirot)* and Kabbalah 23; and Philo 28

occasionalist model 44–45, 73
Offering of Jealousy (Minhat Kena'ot) [Abner of Burgos] 121
omnipotence: and creation *ex nihilo* 72; and Crescas 72; and Kalâm school 44–45; and Saadiah Gaon 61
omniscience: and Abraham ibn Daud 89; and Albo 93; debates and polemics 7, 121–22; and determinism 91–92; and free will 84–89; and future 89, 91–93; and Gersonides 89–92; and Saadiah Gaon 61
"On Cosmopolitanism and On Forgiveness" (Derrida) 237–39
One: and Kabbalah 148; and Neoplatonism 30–31
On Providence (De Fato) [Alexander of Aphrodisias] 93n5

On the Creation of the Cosmos According to Moses (Philo) 26
On the Improvement of the Moral Qualities see *Tikkun Middot ha-Nefesh (On the Improvement of the Moral Qualities)* [Solomon ibn Gabirol]
The Opinions of the Philosophers (Shem Tov ben Joseph Falaquera) 118–19
The Origins of Totalitarianism (Arendt) 230–31
Other: and Buber 10, 187, 201–7; and forgiveness 239–40; and Husserl 210; and Levinas 10, 187, 201–2, 208–13, 239–40; and Rosenzweig 195; and Sartre 186; and Soloveitchik 188; and suffering 213; women as 251, 253, 254; *see also* dialogue
Otherwise Than Being (Levinas) 208

Palestinian Talmud 24
pan-entheism 129–30
Pantheism Controversy 150–51
ibn Paquda *see* Baḥya ibn Paquda
"Pardonner?" (Jankélévitch) 235
Parmenides 17, 18
patriarchy 253–54
Pereq Heleq 50
perfection: and Aristotle 97; bodily 110; and Gersonides 109, 111–12; of God 111; and God's love 109; and happiness 97, 100; intellect and human perfection 83, 84, 97–100, 109–12, 162n18; and Maimon 159; and Maimonides 109–11; material 110; and negative predication 67; and Neoplatonism 30, 32; and prophets 98–99, 103–9, 112; and providence 82, 84; rational 110

Phaedo (Plato) 150
Phaedon (Mendelssohn) 150
phenomenology 185
Phenomenology of Spirit (Hegel) 164
Philo of Alexander 2, 4–5, 24–28, 69
philosopher/kings 104, 105, 107
Pico della Mirandola, Giovanni 122, 123
Pirqe Avot see *Eight Chapters (Shemona Perakim)* [Maimonides]
Plaskow, Judith 251, 253, 254
Plato: and change 18, 68; and creation 68–69, 134; and idealism 18–19; influence of 18–19, 30; and Kant 156; and Maimonides 70; and Mendelssohn 150; and Philo 26; and philosopher/king 104, 107; and reality 18–19; theory of forms 18–19; and time 68–69
Plotinus 20–21, 30–33
Pollegar, Isaac 121, 122
possibility, genuine 89–90
postmodernism 191
predetermination 22–23
predication, negative 66–68, 77
Proclus 20, 30
prophecy: as communication from God 104; and Gersonides 55, 107–8; and Islamic philosophy 105; and Maimonides 51, 53, 105–7
prophets: and body 106; and Cohen 179–80; and Gersonides 112; and Halevi 104; and Islamic philosophy 105; as moral leaders 104; obligations of 107; and perfection 98–99, 103–9, 112; and Saadiah Gaon 104; and Spinoza 142, 144; and suffering 179–80; and truth 144

propter quia arguments 62–65
propter quid arguments 62–63
pros hen equivocals 68
Proverbs 21, 97
providence: and Aristotle 81–82; and free will 84–88; and Gersonides 55, 83–84; and Maimonides 51, 81–83; and miracles 75; in overview 7; and perfection 82, 84
Ptolemy 20
punishment: and Albo 58; and Crescas 108; and Maimonides 85; and Saadiah Gaon 80–81; and suffering 81, 224

Al-Qâdî al-Fâdil al-Baysani 48–49
quaestio method 120
Questioning God (Derrida) 238

rabbis: and Karaism 45–46, 137; overview of rabbinical philosophers 21–24; and rational reasons for commandments 133
RaMBaM *see* Maimonides, Moses (Moses ben Maimon)
RaMbaN (Moses ben Joshua/Narboni) 121
rationalism: and Cohen 179; and commandments 133–34, 137–41; and conversion 121; and Gersonides 54; of Judaism in Maimon 159; and Maimonides 102, 139–40; and Mendelssohn 9, 134, 151, 153; and prophecy 106; rational perfection 110; rejection of in existentialism 184–85; and religion of reason 175; and revelation 138; and Saadiah Gaon 46, 133, 137–39; and Solomon ibn Gabirol 100; and tradition 138

reality: and Aristotle 7, 19; and Cohen 176; and Ecclesiastes 22–23; and Hegel 164, 166; and Heraclitus 18; and idealism 18–19; and Kant 148, 171–72; and Krochmal 166; and Neoplatonism 30–31; and Parmenides 18; and Plato 18–19; and Spinoza 129, 143

reason: and Aristotle 47; and Cohen 170, 172, 173, 175–76; and commandments 138, 139; and double-belief theory 25; and Gersonides 6, 54, 135; and happiness 96–97; and Hegel 164; and Kant 147–48, 170, 172, 173; and Maimonides 139; and Philo 25; practical *vs.* theoretical reason 173; and *propter quid* arguments 62–63; religion as originating from 175; and Saadiah Gaon 46, 61, 138; separation from religion in Spinoza 142

Reason and Hope (Cohen) 170

reciprocity and Buber 203–4, 206

redemption: and Cohen 174, 178; and repair 229–30; and Rosenzweig 192–94, 196; and Soloveitchik 218

Reines, Yitzhak Yaakov 247

relationships: and Buber 10, 187, 201–7, 211–12; and Cohen 176–78; and Levinas 210–12; *see also* dialogue

religion: origins in reason 175; religious denial 166; role of in Cohen 174–75, 179; secular learning *vs.* religious knowledge as central conflict 2–4; *see also* atheism; Christianity; Judaism

religion of reason 175

Religion of Reason Out of the Sources of Judaism (Cohen) 170, 174–76, 177, 179

Religion within the Limits of Reason Alone (Kant) 156

Rema (Moses Isserles) 124

Renaissance: influence on Jewish philosophy 122–24; and rise of modern science 124–26, 147

repair *(tikkun)* 229–30

Republic (Plato) 104

resurrection 52, 53

Retributions of the Soul (Thomas Aquinas) 119

revelation: and Albo 58; and commandments 138–39, 145; and double-belief theory 25; and law 145; and Philo 25; and rationalism 138; and Rosenzweig 190, 193–94; and Saadiah Gaon 138–39

reward: and Albo 58; and Crescas 108; and Job 80, 81; and Maimonides 82, 85

rights and natural law 152–53

ritual 9, 46, 138, 154, 254–55

Rosenstock, Eugen 188–90, 197

Rosenzweig, Franz: biography 188–89; and Buber 190, 202–3; and Christianity 10, 187–89, 191, 196; and Cohen 180–81; and correlation 178; and dialogue 195, 201; and existentialism 185–98; and Heidegger comparison 197–98; and Judaism, rediscovery of 10, 188–90; and Levinas 208; and Other 195; and Zionism 197, 249

Ross, Tamar 256

Rubenstein, Richard 225–27, 229

ibn Rushd *see* Averroës
Ruth, Book of 56

Saadiah Gaon: biography 45–46; and Cohen 173; and existence and nature of God 61, 63, 64; and free will 85–87; influence of 6; and miracles 73; and prophets 104; and rationality of commandments 46, 133, 137–39; and suffering and theodicy 80–81; as theologian as well as philosopher 3
salvation: and Job 83; and Mendelssohn 153, 154; and Neoplatonists 31
Samuel ibn Tibbon 49, 51–52
Sanhedrin 50, 133
Sartre, Jean-Paul 185–86, 208, 248
Schelling, Friedrich Wilhelm Joseph 149
Scholem, Gershom 23
Schwartz, Dov 250
science: and Aristotle 19, 47; and cosmology 2–3, 124–26, 147; and encyclopedists 117–19; and Kant 147–48, 172; and prophets in Islamic philosophy 105; rise of modern 8, 124–26, 147; and Spinoza 126–30
Scripture: commentaries on 24; Gersonides on 55, 56, 83–84, 112, 135; literal *vs.* figurative interpretation 134–35; natural law, debates over 136–39; and obfuscation 134–35; rationality of 133–34, 137–41; and Spinoza 130, 134, 141–45
secular learning: and emancipation of Jews 150, 161; and ethical life 97; and modern conflict in Krochmal 167; and nihilism 185; *vs.* religious knowledge as central tension in Jewish philosophy 2–4; and Soloveitchik 215–20; and Spinoza 2–3, 141–42; tensions between Ashkenazi and Sephardi learning 53
Sefer Bahir (Book of Light) 148
Sefer bittul Iqqarei ha-Nozrim (The Book of the Refutation of the Principles of the Christians) [Crescas] 57
Sefer Elim (Delmedigo) 125–26
Sefer ha-Emunot ve-ha-De'ot see *The Book of Beliefs and Opinions* (Saadiah Gaon)
Sefer ha-heqeshha-yashar (Book of the Correct Syllogism) [Gersonides] 56
Sefer ha-Ikkarim see *Book of Principles* (Albo)
Sefer ha-Kabbalah (Abraham ibn Daud) 47
Sefer ha-Zohar (The Book of Splendor) see *Zohar (The Book of Splendor)*
Sefer Or Adonai see *Light of the Lord* (Crescas)
Sefer Torat Ḥovot ha-Levvavot see *Guide to the Duties of the Heart* (Baḥya ibn Paquda)
Sefer Yetzirah (Book of Creation) 23, 148
sefirot (numbers) and Kabbalah 23
sensation 105, 137–38
Shekhinah (created Glory) 104
Shemona Perakim see *Eight Chapters (Shemona Perakim)* [Maimonides]
Shem Tov ben Joseph Falaquera 35, 118–19

sin: and Cohen 175–76, 177; and Crescas 57
ibn-Sina *see* Avicenna
"614th commandment" 11, 229
skeptical theism 66
skepticism: and Kant 171; of Maimonides and creation of world 70; skeptical theism 66
Solomon ben Abraham 53
Solomon ibn Gabirol 5, 34–38, 99–100
Soloveitchik, Hayyim 250
Soloveitchik, Joseph 10–11, 187–88, 202, 213–20, 250
Song of Songs 21, 56, 112
soul: and Aristotle 36; and Crescas 109; and hylomorphism 36; and Isaac Israeli 33; and Kant 156, 172; and Maimonides 102, 140; and Plato 19, 150; and Solomon ibn Gabirol 36–37, 100; universal soul 31
space 44, 71–72, 176
Spinoza, Baruch (Benedict): biography 126; and books by other philosophers 124–26; and divine authorship 130, 141–43; and ethics and moral truth 142–45, 182n18; excommunication of 127; and Gersonides 54; and *halakhah* 145, 161; and immortality 127; influence of 8, 117, 126; and Mendelssohn 150; and miracles 76, 142, 144; and nature of God 129–30; and prophets 130, 142, 144; reactions to 127–28; and science 126–30; and Scripture 130, 134, 141–45; and teleology 167; tension between secular learning and religious knowledge 2–3, 141–42; and Zionism 248
Spirit and Krochmal 166, 168
Standing Again at Sinai (Plaskow) 253
The Star of Redemption (Rosenzweig) 10, 187, 190–92, 195–97, 249
state: and law 152–53, 159; loyalty to and Judaism 169–70; separation of church and state 152
Strauss, Leo 197
study, exclusion of women from 12, 245, 251
subjectivity: and Aristotle 47; and other in Levinas 209
suffering: and Arendt 230–32; and Cohen 174, 179–80; and Fackenheim 227–30; and Gersonides 83–84; and Holocaust and anti-theodicy 11, 82, 206–7, 212–13, 223–27; and Job 80–84; and Maimonides 81–83; and the Other 213; and prophets 179–80; and punishment 81, 224; and Saadiah Gaon 80–81; *see also* theodicy
Sufism 38
The Support of the Faith (Ezer ha-Dat) [Pollegar] 122
syllogism, practical 47, 99
synthesis: and Cohen 172–73; Hegelian dialectic 165; and Maimon 160–61

The Tales of Rabbi Nachman (Buber) 202
Talmud, Babylonian and Palestinian 24

Talmudic Readings (Levinas) 208
teleology 63, 65, 167, 212
telos: and Aristotle 96, 97, 99; and Krochmal 168; and love/fear of God 109; and Maimon 161; and Soloveitchik 217
Tetrabiblos (Ptolemy) 20
theodicy: and Arendt 230–32; and Fackenheim 11, 227–30; and Gersonides 84; and Holocaust 11, 82, 206–7, 212–13, 223–27; lack of in Bible 21; and Levinas 212–13; and Maimonides 51, 81–83; and Rubenstein 225–27; and Saadiah Gaon 80–81; *see also* suffering
Theological-Political Treatise (Spinoza) 8, 127, 141–45, 248
theology: apophatic theology 66, 77; negative theology 77; theologians as philosophers 3–4, 24
Theology of Aristotle 20–21
theory of forms 18–19
thesis in Hegelian dialectic 164–65
Thomas Aquinas 52, 119–20, 146n5
Thou: and Buber 10, 187; and Cohen 175–76, 179; and Rosenzweig 195
Throne of Glory (Keter Malkhut) [Solomon ibn Gabirol] 36–37
ibn Tibbon, Judah 34, 38, 46
ibn Tibbon, Samuel 49, 51–52
tikkun (repair) 229–30
Tikkun Middot ha-Nefesh (On the Improvement of the Moral Qualities) [Solomon ibn Gabirol] 34, 99–100
Timaeus (Plato) 68

time: and Adam I/II in Soloveitchik 218; and Aristotle 27, 69, 77, 218; and Cohen 176; and Crescas 72; and forgiveness 233, 235, 240; future and omniscience 89, 91–93; and Gersonides 55, 71, 77; and Judaism *vs.* Christianity 196–97, 249; and Kalâm school 44; and Maimonides 77; and Philo 26–27; and Plato 68–69; primordial time 69; and Rosenzweig 195; and women and temporally-bound observances 254–55; *see also* eternity
Time and Infinity (Levinas) 240
"To Forgive" (Derrida) 237–39
To Lessing's Friends (Mendelssohn) 152
To Mend the World (Fackenheim) 227, 229–30
totalitarianism 230–31
Totality and Infinity (Levinas) 208, 209
"Toward the Other" (Levinas) 239
Tractatus (Spinoza) 141–42
tradition and Saadiah Gaon 138–39
transcendence: in Cohen 176, 177; and Soloveitchik 216; and suffering 83
transubstantiation 57
"Treatise on Evidence in the Metaphysical Sciences" (Mendelssohn) 150
Treatise on Free Will (Narboni) 121
Treatise on the Art of Logic (Maimonides) 48
Treitschke, Heinrich von 169, 180
truth: and Halevi 39–40, 41; and Hegel 164–65; and Krochmal

168; and Maimon 159, 161; and Mendelssohn 153; and Philo 25; and prophets 144; and Spinoza 142–45

union: and Krochmal 168; and Neoplatonism 30, 31; and Solomon ibn Gabirol 36–37
uniqueness of God: and Cohen 176, 177; and Maimonides 62; and negative theology 77
unity of God 61–62
universal form and matter 35–38
universal intellect 31, 37–38
universal soul 31
unmoved mover of the universe 47
"Urzelle" (Rosenzweig) 192–93
Useless Suffering (Levinas) 212–13

vacuum 71–72
virtue: and Aristotle 96, 99, 100, 102, 103; and habit 102, 103; and happiness 96; and Maimonides 101–3, 111
visage 210–11

Wars of the Lord (Gersonides) 6, 54, 55, 71, 83, 90, 107, 135
Wiesel, Elie 224
will: and Cohen 174; complete 122; divine 37, 38, 44–45, 86
William of Ockham 94n34
wisdom: and Kabbalah 23; and Maimonides 102, 105; as *telos* 97

Wisdom of ben Sira 22
Wisdom of Solomon 22
Wolff, Christian 157, 158
women: feminist Jewish philosophy 11–12, 245, 251–56; and misogyny of Western philosophy 253; as Other 251, 253, 254; role in Reform and Conservative movements 252
Wonders of God (Mif'alot Elohim) [Abravanel] 123
world, nature of: as eternal 7, 69, 70, 134; and Kant 171–72; *see also* creation

ben Yehoshua, Shlomo *see* Maimon, Solomon

Zionism: anti-Zionism 12, 247–51; and Buber 202, 249; and Cohen 173, 181, 247–49; forms of 246–47; and Gaza Crisis 245; historical roots of 246; and Holocaust 247; and Krochmal 168, 248; and Mendelssohn 247, 248; in overview 11–12; and Rosenstock 197; and Rosenzweig 197, 249; and Sartre 248; and Soloveitchik 250; and Spinoza 248; as term 11–12, 245
Zohar (The Book of Splendor) 23, 28, 148, 149

For Product Safety Concerns and Information please contact our EU representative GPSR@taylorandfrancis.com
Taylor & Francis Verlag GmbH, Kaufingerstraße 24, 80331 München, Germany

www.ingramcontent.com/pod-product-compliance
Lightning Source LLC
Chambersburg PA
CBHW050853160426
43194CB00011B/2143